SAIL PLAN, SPRITSAIL BARGE

KEY

A. TOPMAST STAYSAIL
A₁. STAYS'L SET UP TO STEMHEAD
B. JIB
C. FORESAIL

D. MAINSAIL
E. TOPSAIL
F. MIZZEN
G. BALLOON FORESAIL
OR SPINNAKER

A₁ & G. INDICATED THUS ——·——
SPINNAKER BOOM THUS ≔═══

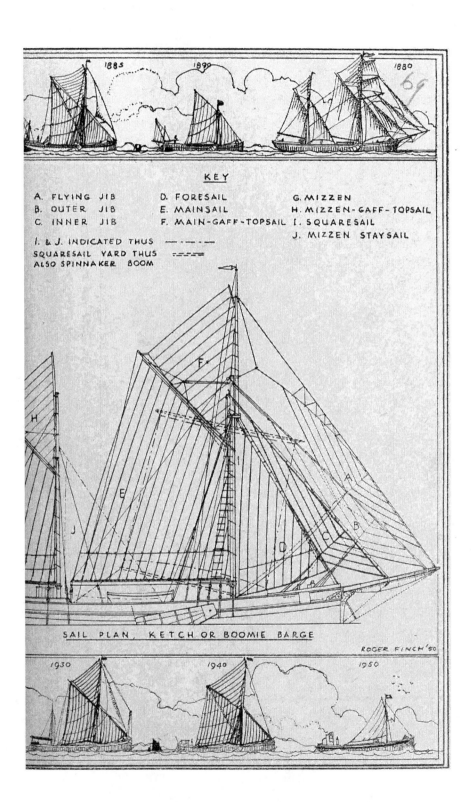

KEY

A. FLYING JIB   D. FORESAIL   G. MIZZEN
B. OUTER JIB   E. MAINSAIL   H. MIZZEN-GAFF-TOPSAIL
C. INNER JIB   F. MAIN-GAFF-TOPSAIL   I. SQUARESAIL
                                     J. MIZZEN STAYSAIL

I. & J. INDICATED THUS   —·—·—
SQUARESAIL YARD THUS   ═·═·═
ALSO SPINNAKER BOOM

SAIL PLAN, KETCH OR BOOMIE BARGE

ROGER FINCH '50

DOWN TOPS'L

Ex Libris

Robert Baldwin Fordyce Barr

By the same Author

LAST STRONGHOLD OF SAIL

*The Story of the Essex Sailing-smacks,
Coasters, and Barges*

With 31 plates in half-tone and
endpaper maps.
Demy 8vo. 200 pages. *Third
impression.*

Captain Josh at the wheel of *Ardwina*, last Ipswich-built barge, while his eighteen-year-old son and mate, Peter, keeps a look-out for buoys

Down Tops'l

THE STORY
OF THE
EAST COAST SAILING-BARGES

by

HERVEY BENHAM

with additional material by

ROGER FINCH *and* PHILIP KERSHAW

George G. Harrap & Co. Ltd
London Sydney Toronto Bombay

ACKNOWLEDGMENTS

THIS book is really a co-operative effort. Soon after I had embarked on it I found that Roger Finch, of Ipswich, and Philip Kershaw, of Thorpe Bay, editor of *Spritsail*, were both keeping notes for a similar purpose. With a generosity not always encountered among rival researchers, both offered to make common cause. Practically all the matter relating to Southend, and in particular the story of the barge-racing there, is Kershaw's. Roger Finch, in addition to illustrating these pages, has contributed the Ipswich story, and also provided first-hand details of the ballast work from the P.L.A. dredger, for he is one of the few amateurs who has participated in this exacting occupation.

All three of us have a host of other collaborators to thank. Sailormen up and down the coast have willingly contributed their memories and experiences, and we hope those not individually mentioned here will not think us either forgetful or unappreciative. In particular, Fred Cooper, of the *Persevere*, has made himself responsible for the story of Wakering and the 'pitch-piners,' and his brother, George Cooper, of *The Miller*, has added a fund of anecdote. Jerry Mann, of the *George Smeed* and *Varuna*, was a prime instigator of the whole project, and Bob Roberts, of the *Greenhithe*, has put us right with coasting details.

At Norwich we have been helped by Roy Clark, the man behind the Norfolk Wherry Trust, which has so triumphantly put the sailing-wherry *Albion* back on the Broads—an example which may yet have to be followed to preserve a sprittie on the London River. At Orford and Aldeburgh George Brinkley and Jerry Wood have ransacked their memories; at Woodbridge Ted Marsh has recalled the days when the Deben was more than a yachtsman's pleasance. Among Ipswich men, Edward Haste, Bob Ruffles, and N. Goodman, of the 'boomie' *Britannia*, have been particularly invaluable, F. O. Whitmore (whose earliest memory is seeing the launch of the *Dunkerque* fifty-six years ago, when he was four) has added many

a story, and R. P. Orvis has made us free of his time and his shipyard. Herbert Cann, of Harwich, has lent his pictures and his
memories; at Mistley Jim Stone has suffered all inquiries gladly,
and Marcus Horlock, in addition to helping with the story of his
family firm, organized a never-to-be-forgotten party of ancient
mariners. Joshua Francis, of Colchester, has submitted to inter-
minable importunities with his customary good humour, and that
fine old-timer the late "Chick" Cripps welcomed me time after
time aboard his house-boat at Francis's yard. Fred Taylor has lent
me photos, and cheerfully sacrificed a morning's production at his
Maldon sail-loft so that with Bill Raven we might sit round his
stove and yarn, and George Hales has lent himself to the same
chapter.

Jim Frost, of Tollesbury, has made my meetings with him at the
Queen's Head as pleasant as they were profitable, and Jack Spitty,
of Goldhanger Chequers, and H. Bell have conjured up the palmy
days of Parker's Bradwell-men. Old times in Southwold have been
recalled by E. W. Stannard, who serves in steam ships now, but still
pines for the days when he was a lad in the *Lord Hartington*, mate of
the *Harwich*, or skipper of the *Eva Annie*. Frank Shuttlewood has
not only taken a lot of trouble to recall the accounts of the Roach;
his enthusiasm has also encouraged me to persevere in my task.
Then at Battlesbridge C. E. Goymer and E. Saunders made me welcome, while at Grays Frank Mummery immediately took charge of
my mission, and E. J. Goldsmith was good enough to read and
correct the manuscript of the whole book.

Southend Antiquarian Society has assisted in reconstructing the
story of the Vandervords, and the National Maritime Museum has
loaned illustrations as well as furnishing facts. The owners of many
photos, including that pioneer of barge enthusiasts Arthur Bennett,
have been trustful with their treasures, and the owners of the old
paintings used—mostly by R. Chappell—have kindly allowed me
to photograph them for reproduction here. Last but not least,
D J. L. Groom, of Woodbridge, has been most generous with
material on the subject of ketch barges, on which he is an authority,
while R. E. Banyard has allowed the inclusion of verses from *The
Last of England's Sail*, a little privately printed booklet which has
more poetry in its dozen pages than many a more pretentious
volume contains in a hundred.

Many of the photographs were taken by the writers or their

friends. Acknowledgment is made to the following: Central Office of Information, *Ardwina* (frontispiece and plate facing p. 161); *Essex County Standard*, plate facing p. 49 (Jim Stone); Fox Photos, plates facing pp. 96 (Woolwich buoys) and 144 (*Veronica*); Mirror Features, plates facing pp. 17 (*Reliance* and *Adieu*) and 96 (*Raybel, Lady Jean*, and *Tollesbury*); Mustograph Agency, plates facing pp. 49 and 113 (*Marjorie*); National Maritime Museum, plates facing pp. 15 (*Unity*) and 17 (swimmie); and Nautical Photo Agency, plates facing pp. 16 (*Phœnician*) and 144 (*Queen* and *Reminder*).

Among those who have loaned photographs we have to thank Mr Arthur Bennett for plate facing p. 129, Mr Fred Taylor, of Maldon, for plate facing p. 16 (*New Hope*), Mr Herbert Cann, of Harwich, for plate facing p. 97 (*Marjorie* and *Kimberley*) and plate facing p. 145 (*Sara*), and the landlords of the Goldhanger Chequers and Tollesbury Queen's Head, together with many private owners, for the paintings and photographs of the ketch barges. The former have been photographed for reproduction by the *Essex County Standard*.

H. B.

Thornfleet,
Fingringhoe
1949

CONTENTS

ILLUSTRATIONS

IN TEXT

INTRODUCTION

We've wallowed in the Wallet,
    awash with sodden deals,
And slipped from Southend jetty,
    the sou'easter at our heels.
Stern winter had his will of us
    on black December days,
Our kedge is on the Buxey
    and our jib is off the Naze.
                  R. E. Banyard

IT is no longer necessary to apologize for writing a book about barges. Indeed, after being neglected, despised, or taken for granted for a century and a half, the sailing-barge has in the last decade become the darling of the yachtsman, the maritime archæologist, and even the deep-sea ship-lover. Her acolytes have banded themselves together in the Thames Barge Sailing Club, publishing its own journal, and sailing their own barge for the joy of it.

The reason for this sudden devotion is, of course, that the sailing-barge is, if not dying out, at least thinning out. Whether her end is in fact at hand is discussed in this book; however that may prove, there is occasion for thankfulness that the interest has been taken in her while she is yet alive. She is the last survivor among British sailing merchantmen, and if only the fascination of the schooners and ketches and brigs which preceded her, and of the carracks and crayers and balingers which preceded them, had been realized and recounted while they were still on the water, what a story of sea-change it would all have made!

The sailing-barge's beauty to the eye, and her value as representing a noble way of life, have always been clear to those of perception. As long ago as 1899 Arnold Bennett, who lived at Thorpe-le-Soken, near the Walton Backwaters, and loved to see the 'stackies' there, wrote with remarkable prescience in his *Journals* of barges unloading bricks at Putney:

In time no doubt all this building material will reach Putney by railway and by steamer; at any rate a wharf will be built and served by steam crane, and then this singular survival of an old activity will pass away in its turn, and we shall tell the young people that we remember it.

Since then many have felt and sought to interpret that sense of nostalgia Bennett expressed, till now quite a literature of the sailing-barge is coming into being. Cyril Ionides was among the first; careful as he was to betray no secrets, it is still possible to locate the story of *A Floating Home* in the waters of the Roach. Frank Carr has written the pioneer history in *Sailing Barges*; E. G. Martin has described her at work in *Sailorman*; Arthur Bennett has sung her praises as a sailing home in *June of Rochester*; Edgar March has shortened the focus down to a detailed picture in *Spritsail Barges of Thames and Medway*; and a professional skipper, A. W. Roberts, of the *Greenhithe*, has made a valuable first-hand contribution with *Coasting Bargemaster*. I have avoided as far as possible ground already covered in these books (and in my own *Last Stronghold of Sail*, which contains some barging stories of the Colne and Black-water) and endeavoured to present as complete a general picture as possible of the last days of trading under sail on the East Coast. For fuller details of the Thames and Medway barge races in particular I would refer readers to Carr and March.

I would also recommend those books to any readers who are ignorant even of the distinction between the sailing-barge, the canal barge, and the London River lighter, or of the great gulf which separates the sailormen of these pages from the bargees of traditional music-hall humour. It should, however, be possible for anyone who cares to examine the end-paper map and diagram and the glossary to get a pretty fair idea of everything described.

In some ways this has been an easy book to write, in others a hard one. It has been a labour of love, and regarded as such by almost every man I have consulted. But there is such a lack of documentation, apart from shipping and Customs registers, that to establish the very basis of a historical framework has often been difficult—to fix dates impossible.

Moreover, owners adopted the perverse practice of giving the same name to several barges, and, as most of the craft were bought and sold several times and so turn up in a number of places under a variety of owners, the job of sorting them out is often a puzzling one. There were, for instance, two craft on the coast named

Old Times (1)

TOP AND CENTRE: Negotiating London bridges under bridge sails.
BELOW, LEFT: Stern of an old-timer (*Progress*). BELOW, RIGHT:
Stumpie (probably *Avon*) at Havengore, 1888

Old Times (11)

LEFT: Swim-headers at Yarmouth, from a nineteenth-century etching

ABOVE: Great Benfleet, from a drawing by C. W. Wyllie. Note sprit to port

LEFT: The stackie *Unity* about to bring up, about 1884

Cambria, Ethel Ada, Gladys, Centaur, Unity, Varuna, and *Violet,* and since the Maldon-registered, Kentish-built *Excelsior* is chiefly connected with Ipswich, while the Horlock family of Mistley owned one Ipswich-built, Harwich-registered *Excelsior* and raced another, the complexities confronting the chronicler are, it will be appreciated, numerous.

Another difficulty concerns the assessment of the size of barges. Where exact tonnage figures are quoted these are the registered tonnages; round figures (as in reference to a "hundred tonner") are to deadweight tons, which may broadly be considered as double the registered figure.[1] In the case of ketch barges or 'boomies' it has sometimes seemed more convenient to classify by overall length, and occasionally grain and brick barges are graded as carrying so many hundred quarters or so many thousand bricks. Bargemen themselves always judge by gross, or burthen, tonnage, a much sounder guide than the register figures often quoted in print, since surveyors became more cunning with the passing of years in decreasing these tonnages, on which dues are paid. For instance, to compare two Paglesham barges, *Ethel Ada,* registered as 49 tons in 1903, was a much bigger craft than the *Paglesham,* registered as 55 tons in 1877.

All this is the reverse of precise, but I have not set out to write a history so much as a story. Maritime antiquarians are as devoted to hair-splitting as any of their tribe. I have been warned by the awful example of a controversy over the exact nature of West Country trows. A major authority, being cornered in a dispute with a minor authority as to the authenticity of one such craft, conceded that she might after all be a trow, yet maintained she was not a true trow!

It is really of no vital importance to know just when every craft was launched or lost (though the studiously inclined will find some building dates in the index), and this must be my excuse for referring rather freely to "old-timers" and "the old days," a period which, according to the context, may cover the years from the furthermost stretch of memory—say, seventy years ago—up to the end of the First World War.

It does, however, matter that the whole glorious life of the East

---

[1] Deadweight tonnage is the carrying capacity in tons weight. Gross tonnage is the whole interior space, and registered tonnage the cargo space alone, a ton in each instance being 100 cubic feet.

Coast seaboard shall not die out and disappear forgotten and un-recorded. Already there are quays and hards, channels and swatches, docks and berths, all down the long indented coastline of three counties utterly deserted or given over to the artificial usages of pleasure yachting, which is the best of sports, but a faint shadow of a substitute for the lusty days when hard and happy men performed astonishing feats of instinctive seamanship, and never paused to consider the merits of their efforts, so natural did it all seem. And natural it was; the unnatural thing is that the slow immemorial dignity of ships on the tideways should be extinguished by the smelly, unseemly (and often uneconomical!) scurry of little lorries along the tarmac.

I have included quite a lot of detail about freight rates and earnings in 'the old days' and modern times, partly because this aspect of barging looms large in the picture to the bargemen who are the real authors of this book, and I wanted to write down their story as they told it, not as a townsman might romanticize it; partly because the rise and decline of sailing-barges has its own place in the social history of the Eastern Counties (and even of London) in general and of agriculture in particular. The interdependence of plough and sail in Essex throughout the nineteenth century cannot be over-emphasized. For instance, a barge mate's pay fifty years ago was seventeen shillings a week, but to be seen in perspective it should be compared with the fourteen to sixteen shillings then paid to an agricultural labourer. Another reason is that these figures supply a corrective to the chronicler's inevitable tendency to don rose-coloured spectacles. This was the life, but those were not the 'good old days.' In 1888 a Great Wakering barge captain, summoned to show why he did not maintain his mother, said he averaged twenty-three shillings weekly, and had a wife and four children.

I admire the men who used to walk from Wivenhoe to West Mersea, row to Bradwell, lump out twenty-five tons of coal, and then find their way home by the same route, but I don't admire the system that necessitated it (though I think I admire still less the couple of stokers who, recently declining a job in one of Horlock's steamships, proceeded to put in a claim for 'disappointment money'!).

The old-time bargemen sailed and sweated and schemed and swore; they toiled unceasingly, not for themselves, not for their owners, but to serve their ships; and they proved that hard work (if

Evolution (1)

ABOVE: The old stackie rig shown in the Maldon *New Hope* (1872), seen at Eves' mills. Compare the long sprit and flat topsail head with the lofty *Phœnician* (RIGHT) (built at Sittingbourne in 1922 for Alf Horlock, of Mistley)

(See Chapters XI and IV.)

Evolution (11)

In London River. ABOVE: An old-time swimmie, off Cubitt Town, with handspike windlass and tops'l innocent of headstick. BELOW: *Reliance* and *Adieu* (both of Mistley) in Limehouse Reach in the 1930's

it also be healthy work to body and mind) is also the greatest of recreations, for to-day the hale and hearty seventy-year-olds who fill these pages wear their years and their adventures and their hardships with a gaiety and grace, a dignity and confidence, denied to the followers of more sophisticated pursuits.

A good life bred a good philosophy. The æsthetic loss as the sails are stowed for the last time is an immense loss, but the loss of human qualities is greater still.

I

THE LAST OF THE SAILING-SHIPS

Ships without Crews—North Europe's Finest Fleet—How much longer?—Technique of Barge-sailing—Mysteries of Barge-recognition—Types and Peculiarities

THE clipper-ships that raced home with the tea from China will be remembered as the ultimate perfection attained by deep-sea sail before its sudden extinction by steam. The ocean-voyaging sailing-smacks, the French and Newfoundland schooners, and the English, Iceland, and Dogger fleets were distinguished by the sheer feats of endurance of the unwashed, frost-bitten crews who manned them. The sailing-barge's appeal to the imagination is of a more intimate, subtle kind.

Purely on their excellence as ships, flat-bottomed craft like these must be ranked inferior to the perfectly moulded 'fruiters' or even the humbler coastal ketches and schooners they chased off the East Coast waters. The men themselves, while needing to be tough, are of no heroic stamp. Their exploits pale into insignificance beside those of the Elizabethan adventurers, or even in latter years of the salvaging Essex smackmen or beach-boat crews of Deal and the Suffolk coast. Yet the very limitations of the sailing-barge provide its essential fascination. Two men and a boy setting out confident and carefree from London River with 150 tons of valuable freight for Norwich or the Rhine, Hull or the West of Ireland; braving the spite of the North Sea one day, poking up a tiny creek the next. There's independence, there's enterprise, there's self-reliance! The very impudence of the undertaking lends it savour. Authorities from Marco Polo to Dr Johnson have shaken their wise heads over the desperate situation of men who go to sea, and my own preference is every time for the friendly, characterful coastal waters over the cold, deep sea and inhospitable wide oceans. Bargemen go to sea, yet keep one foot ashore. They make the best of both worlds, and the variety of their life enriches their calling and their characters.

The joy of the job is that the barge has never carried any crew. A skipper, a mate, and till recently a boy, who was really an apprentice, form a combination to bring out the best in human nature. Each must work; each is a free man. There is no gold lace giving itself airs aft, no grimy complement performing a labourer's function for'ard. No wonder sailormen have developed a philosophy all their own, combining dash and devilry with simplicity, humour, tolerance, and patience. I find a little of the excellence of the two-man team even in the long-distance lorry driver and his mate, or the engine-driver and his stoker. That much remains when a skipper and an engineer chug about the coast with a deckhand's help in a motor-barge. But give two men a sailing-barge to play with and that's really something apart.

One is tempted to speak of the sailing-barge in the past tense, though she is yet with us, for her numbers have dwindled so sadly, from about 2000 in 1910 to about 750 in 1939 and 125 (excluding auxiliaries) in February 1949, that one instinctively prepares to bid her farewell. Happily, that day need not be yet. Even this fleet has no equal in Northern Europe. The Baltic can show nothing to compare with a sight that was to be seen one day in 1943, when nearly half the craft left working met off the Maplin Spit. They had gradually accumulated, wind-bound, lying in Sheerness and the Lower Hope outward bound, and in Harwich and the Colne bound back for London, till one day the weather set them free and over forty craft bound up met over fifty bound down. That was something the like of which will not often be seen again, but for at least a few more years it will still be possible to encounter suddenly and unexpectedly pictures one will carry in one's mind till one's dying day.

In 1949 I made a trip from Colchester to Bow Creek in the *Varuna* to see what it was like to have a 66 horse-power Diesel sprawling its fuel-tanks and oil-pipes all about the aft cabin where old Alf Keeble used to sit and spin me yarns when I first started getting aboard barges during my school holidays. Smoothly and effortlessly we did the whole trip in one tide, and for most of that time all hands were congregated in the wheelhouse smoking fags and looking out of the window. The skipper declared that it put him in mind of standing in the corridor of a train bound from Euston to Glasgow. The Ipswich auxiliaries were dropping down Swin with nothing but their topsails set, but we had the consolation of running into the Essex-men turning up the Whitaker over the ebb to make a harbour in Shore Ends. Led by the *Violet Sybil*, light, came half a dozen loaded Colchester craft. The *Ethel Ada*, sluicing the water off her decks, winded hard by us in a flurry of heavily flogging canvas, and we watched them weaving and threading a criss-cross of tacks till they were hull down behind the Ridge. Presently we met the Ipswich *Spinaway C.* racing down Swin, staysail set spinnaker-fashion from deck to topmast head, and sheeted round the weather spreader. It was blowing, and many craft would have needed hard steering. Her skipper was using no more than a spoke either way, and he put his brake on the wheel to walk to the rail and give us the traditional "Where yer for?" The barge looked as if she were standing still with a torrent of water racing smoothly past her, closing as sweetly round her stern as it opened round her bows, while the *Varuna* tumbled and laboured clumsily under the unnatural urge of her screw. Then later in the dusk of a threatening evening we met the mighty *Greenhithe*, getting her bowsprit down for a wild night's run. The morning would see her off Orfordness, and next night she would be in Yarmouth.

It still goes on, even if in diminishing degree, because the sailing-barge, alone of sailing-vessels, remains unbeaten even by the internal-combustion engine. The last sailormen on the long trek to the North are knocking up four-figure earnings for their skippers in fair competition with the steamers; the men in the less spectacular Ipswich and Colchester work are rewarding themselves on a scale beyond the dreams of the most optimistic trade unionist ashore. It is true these earnings are often made by old barges on which depreciation has long ceased to be reckoned. The *Intrepid* was built by Bayley, of Ipswich, in 1881 for £650; the *Reliance* cost £900 at Ipswich in 1900; the *Defender* £1100 at Maldon in the same year. The 'boomies' *Ada Gane* and *Genesta* were built by Vaux, of Harwich, in 1882 and 1886 for £1700 and £2100, and paid for themselves, including insurance and all running costs, in four and six years respectively. Forty years ago it was actually reckoned a 'sprittie' would pay for herself in twelve months. Against this the modern steel barge *Reminder* cost Horlock's £3000 off their own yard in 1927, Wills and Packham, of Sittingbourne, lost £1000 building the *Phœnician* for £2500 in 1923, and no doubt these figures would be increased threefold to-day. The installation of a Diesel auxiliary and the major reconstruction accompanying it cost

in the case of the *Varuna* in 1949 nearly £5000—four times the
original cost of the vessel.

Yet it would still pay to build barges if there were crews for
them. The very patchiness of present-day trade suits them. When
Horlock's built the motor-coaster *Jolly Girls* in 1936 she was laid
up owing to shortage of work within six months—a serious matter
with a relatively costly vessel heavily insured and carrying a load
of overhead costs. You don't want to be slack with a sailing-barge,
but the crew can make the best of it, giving the mast a scrape and
coat of varnish.

Auxiliaries are now becoming almost universal in the larger
barges, but it will pay to leave some of the smaller vessels purely
sailing-craft for years yet, particularly in the 'seeking' fleets for
which constant work is not assured—if men can be found to sail
them. That is the rub. Men brought up to the life relish its keen,
salty delights, till they can look with deserved sympathy and con-
tempt on the clock-ridden factory worker and count themselves
what by comparison they are, lords and monarchs. "A wet shirt
and an 'appy 'eart" is the bargeman's real motto. But to the
majority of mankind to-day a free life means freedom to attend the
cinema and football match, pleasures which bulk small in a sailorman's ambitions. So they step ashore—for half the money and half
the life.

There are, of course, some Elizabethans in every age, and it is
likely quite a few craft will be under sail in all their glory for long
years yet. But it will always be the twilight of an age, or at best its
Indian summer. Its dawn was perhaps a century and a half ago, its
midsummer sun reached its zenith, we shall see, shortly before the
First World War, and it began to decline in the 1920's.

When the last barge has gone I think the question will often be
asked, What were they really like to sail?—for by then the sailing
of little boats will be everyman's oyster, as indeed it should be. The
questions which will occupy the mind of the thoughtful man with
a fourteen-foot racing dinghy or a ten-ton cutter yacht will be
these: How could two men handle that four thousand square feet of
canvas? How could vessels sail almost equally well quite unballasted,
loaded till the water was literally on deck, and with a straw stack
half-way up the mast? Were they truly weatherly, fast, and handy;
and was some art, since lost, needed to accomplish the astonishing
variety of duties they performed? Perhaps they will even fall back

on that time-honoured coastwise explanation and excuse: The weather must have been different then!

If I could come back to some yacht club in a hundred years' time and answer these questions from a not very profound but fairly representative experience of yachts of most sizes, smacks, and barges, I should say that the barge is the most fascinating vessel of all to handle, if you reckon (as I do) to divide the total fascination by the number of those sharing in it. I dare say a J-class yacht would have been tremendous fun if two or three could have sailed one, but they couldn't. You needed such a staff that it became an organization, leaving just the helmsmanship a pure art to the man at the wheel. A little one-design is fine—what there is of it. A barge is a 150-ton ship shared by a one-design's crew, and that means something. The grandeur of the great thing, with her six sails drawing, fills your heart with sheer exaltation. My little eight-tonner is my pride and joy, but she never gives me exactly that sensation.

As to the technicalities, a mathematician, calculating the stability factor produced by so many cubic feet of buoyant chine against the pressure of so many square feet of straining canvas, could doubtless explain why the things do not turn over. It always seems, looking at them, that they ought to capsize under these conditions, yet they do not—unless you let them stop—and when you are aboard there never seems any likelihood of it. Similarly the mystery of their ability to sail both light and loaded is fascinating. They just do. The best trim of all, of course, is lightly loaded (which they seldom are) with say twenty tons of weight as low as possible in them.

All barges are faster light than loaded, but some are handier loaded than light, being less inclined to 'blow off' when coming about. Barges with long chines excel light. The Maldon *Dawn*, which is nothing to look at, her ends being blunt to an almost perfunctory degree, actually beat her cut-away sisters to win the Maldon race in 1924. The short-chined craft, with fine entries and long runs aft, are sometimes at a disadvantage light, taking a lot of steering, but come into their own when more side is immersed to grip the water.

Barges converted to yachts are, of course, generally lightly ballasted, but, much as I admire some of these, I must insist, in case they should be the last example in years to come of the old craft, that not one ever retains the absolute fitness for purpose which

characterizes the true working craft. Something of the integrity
of the ship disappears with every conversion.

As to the pile of canvas, only controllable because of the unique
qualities of the spritsail rig, it requires a combination of brain and
brawn. One is useless without the other, but the former is the more
important. I believe the modern yachtsman loses some of the fun
of sail because his Bermuda rig is so handy, paradoxical as that may
sound. With a reliable auxiliary to fall back on, he never experiences
the thrilling and rewarding anxiety of knowing he is only under
control if his plans work out as intended. A barge, perhaps more
than any other craft, is often in this position. It is quite normal to be
tearing along, knowing full well that it would be an emergency
job, fraught with danger, to attempt to stop or turn around. Running through the Downs or down Swin for Harwich when the
breeze pipes up, you have to keep going once you have started, till
you are round the Foreland or under the lee of the Stone Heaps.
That is what the Naval officers in the M.L.'s could not understand
in both wars, and they doubtless were often R.N.V.R. yachtsmen. They signalled the bargemen to bring up, and when they
couldn't they thought they wouldn't.

Similarly, when it comes to handiness the barge is a marvel—
within limits. A Royal Corinthian one-design turns up the Crouch
over a spring ebb in a westerly breeze. That sort of talk the barge
just doesn't understand. The yachtsman can thread his way with
impunity in among craft moored thick in a tideway. The sailorman must plan his tacks ahead; it does not pay him to tempt fortune
by cutting close to windward of a buoy or anchored craft with the
tide setting on to them. He thinks ahead, too, in making and
taking in sail, setting the mainsail while she lies head to wind, perhaps before she swings to the tide he intends to use; brailing up
during a convenient moment's calm under the lee of a high building
or passing steamer; dropping a flying jib when the wind is over the
starboard bow; catching her on the port tack to let go the tops'l
sheet.

There is nothing about this fundamentally different from the art
exercised by the yachtsman handling his ship in the congested conditions of the contemporary yacht anchorage or in the tumble of a
seaway, but there is a more constant call for that art, a heavier
price to pay for a mistake. To imagine mistakes are never made is
nonsense. Barges are not infrequently ashore or in trouble through

elementary miscalculations, and if, when barges and bargemen are
but a picturesque and glamorous memory, a legend circulates
among yachtsmen that their seamanship was infallible, it will be
the merest nonsense. But the yachtsmen will do well to equal the
bargemen's imperfect standard.

These legends there will be, and one will, I fancy, concern the
speed of sailing-barges. Their twelve-knot achievements in the
races will be quoted, but it should be recorded that these were not
everyday occurrences. It is a poor yacht of ten tons or over that is
not the equal of a smart barge, so long as both can carry full sail in
smooth water. It is when wind and sea begin to stop the yacht that
the barge comes into her own. In the wind-against-tide lop of the
waters where she belongs, she will march effortlessly past a labour-
ing small craft, though the modern ocean-racer type need still have
little to fear from her if the yachtsmen are prepared to suffer the
flying spray while the bargemen enjoy dry decks and eat their meals
in a cabin as steady and quiet as the dining-room ashore; and, of
course, in landlocked waters, where her tops'l alone finds a breeze,
the barge will make a fool of any other craft afloat.

Another feature of barges which will probably tend to be obscured
is the infinite variety of their types and individual characteristics.
Now the boomie ketches are gone, the best deep-sea barges on the
East Coast are the two steel mammoths of Everard's, the last of the
sailing-colliers, trading to the Colchester and Harwich gasworks,
and the high-bulwarked coasters, often former boomsail barges,
such as Paul's and Cranfield's Ipswich-men. These are craft which
in open water scarcely need their leeboards; they have almost
developed out of being barges at all. The former boomies are the
best barges for passage-making, along with wooden coasters like
Cambria, though in dock their sheering ends and bold bulwarks
are a source of anxiety as the clumsy lighters' heavy iron swims
ride over them. The later steel craft are the best earners, but can be
wet and dirty at sea. Speaking of his Greenhithe, Bob Roberts
observed, "On a passage from the Humber in 1949 I did not see the
capping of our lee rail for three days. She has often put water on
deck light. You only need one leg and a stump to stand at her wheel
in a breeze."

Medium-size barges include spritties by Orvis, of Ipswich, and
the Kentish builders, and—perhaps the beau-ideal for the short passages of modern work—the Maldon 'stackies' that Howard built,

big enough to be at home down Swin, flat enough to slip under
the bridge to the mill, fast enough to rejoice the keenest skipper's
heart. Grouped round these in the Colchester fleet are a few large
types and a few of rather smaller size, though one or two of the
smallest have more of the coaster's cut about them than some of
their larger brothers.

Next come—or, rather, in Essex came, for the type is now confined to Kent—the out-and-out river barges, "straight as a gun-
barrel," with long rudders making them amazingly handy; nothing
to look at, but able to get along in rare style, though awash in a
seaway from stem to stern. Such were the Wakering 'brickies,' the
terriers of the pack. A skipper who took one of this type, the
Monarch, of Sittingbourne, when his coaster barge was on the ways,
said of her: "She was like a plank. I measured her greatest freeboard to the top of the rail going up Sea Reach and it was fourteen
inches. Her rudder was nearly as big as her leeboards. But what a
thing to handle! When we got to Woolwich it seemed a sin to get
into the boat to scull ashore!"

While it is difficult for an amateur to approach the old bargemen's
uncanny knack of recognizing a barge at sea and of deciding her
builder by a glance, the main types are not difficult to distinguish.
The Ipswich and Harwich craft are deep and sea-kindly, with sheering coaster bows. The Ipswich style favoured by Peck and Orvis
have a fine bow and a very elegant stern; these models are pretty as
pictures. Cann and McLearon, of Harwich, favoured a fuller bow
(which a barge needs for dryness at sea). Both these builders
developed a stern which combines a fine underwater run with a
wide, shallow transom; indeed, their products are not easy to distinguish, though Cann's are slightly wider and less rounded in at the
quarters than McLearon's. Howard, of Maldon, whose flat, beamy
beauties are as easy as an old shoe, yet sit in the water to perfection,
also recognized the virtue of this shaped shallow transom, which
generally marks a barge of the best period, in contrast to the deeper
narrow shape to be seen in such old-timers as the *Pride of Ipswich*
(built in 1864 and now a yacht) or the *Unity*.[1] Shrubsall while in
Suffolk followed the Ipswich style, but on going to Greenwich he
widened his transoms, but left them rather deep and oval, which is
no detriment for the racing in which he made his name, but holds
up his fliers when they are laden. His Ipswich-built *Ethel Ada* is as

[1] See plate facing p. 32.

pretty as any of the Colchester craft (though she is by no means the best earner of her size), but the racing *Varuna* and *Verona*, fine craft as they are, are not specially striking to the eye. It is curious that many of the famous racers were nothing much to look at, a very flat profile being favoured.

Cook, of Maldon, went for the stackie's low sides and good beam in the *Dawn*, *Lord Roberts*, and *British King* (now a motor-barge), but made no effort to rival the artistry of Howard in the moulding of underwater lines.

While many barges are marred in appearance by flatness, the Mistley-men tend to have a curiously uneven profile. They were built to load vast quantities of light cargo, and sacrifice a classical sheer for a bit of extra capacity. The most extreme case was *Remercie*, for Fred Horlock actually stopped her builders as they were about to trim down her timber-heads to the proper sheer-line, and had the barge built up to the top of them, giving her the oddest wavy look. The Mistley-built steel barges improved one by one, till the *Blue Mermaid* was a thing of beauty, but even the wonderful *Reminder* was affectionately described by her skipper as a "bladder on the water." It seemed an impertinence to race her against the *Sara* and *Veronica*, he said—yet she beat them. The final test in barge-recognition, qualifying for the higher diploma, is Horlock's *Reliance*. Orvis built her, and embodied his typical stern; Cann had a hand in the design, and gave her some of the fullness he favoured, yet she shows that unmistakable wavy Mistley deckline!

Hull-decoration is equally interesting and significant, representing as it does one of the few surviving examples of popular art. Indeed, it seems that the carved and painted bow and quarter badges, the names incised with curling serif on a resplendent banner, the scroll and paintwork on the broad transoms, will outlast spars and canvas. Such is the love for a little exuberance of decoration that even motor-barges converted since the War retain the traditional patterns in full vigour.

Sea-going decoration has long taken its motives from architecture ashore, and it is not unnatural to find Victorian baroque, necessarily somewhat watered down, borrowed straight from the Victorian pub to decorate the sailorman. Kentish-men preferred the name on a panel surrounded by an infinite variety of scroll-work; perhaps red lettering on a white ground and the final touches in green. Harwich and Maldon barges display a more refined banner, draped on a staff, emblazoned with name and port of registry, the whole painted with care to give an effect of depth. Ipswich-built craft, for some reason, follow the Kentish pattern, but with rather less abandon. Bow and quarter badges, originally intended to take the strain of hawsers forward and strengthen the rail aft, are decorated with great variety. Blue with gold, or black and silver, with red or green for hawser pipes—the variations are infinite. Occasionally the owner's monogram or bob is involved in the intricate scrolls and arabesques.

Bargemen have fallen upon the post-War abundance of aluminium paint with avidity. Silver embellishments at the bow are matched with startling aluminium stove-pipes and binnacles on deck, though in justice it must be added that the older generation decry this innovation. Metalwork, they say, when not 'bright' should be green. The pleasant conceit of carving butterfly chamfers on quarter-boards and stern[1] has completely gone; it took too much labour to justify the saving in weight, the original excuse for its adoption.

Gone too with the introduction of wheel steering is the carved tiller, which always included, amid a wealth of carved turksheads and decoration, the barge's name. As wheels became common the decoration was transferred to the sides of the wooden 'steerage.' Another compensation was found by the big coasters with their brass-bound steering-wheels. They rubbed in their superiority over the river barges, dependent on a cast-iron 'chaff-cutter,' by embellishing the canvas wheel-cover with name, port, and perhaps crossed Red Ensign and bob. Outdoing all others in this was the cover possessed by the *Cock o' the Walk*. On a white field and surrounded by the vessel's name and motto stood in full glory of purple, green, and yellow a crowing cock defying all comers—the pride of Harry Strange's heart.

Of course, the amateur's concern with looks sometimes irritates the man who has to earn his living out of the barge's carrying capacity. Paul's *Serb*, built of odds and ends at Charlton in 1917, is by no standards a beauty, yet she did a power of Channel work before coming to Ipswich, and with her great stowage capacity has her own advantages over some of her dainty sisters when it comes to sharing out for the freight.

The extent to which ports embodied their local traditions in their

[1] See plate facing p. 32.

designs is notable. Fellows, of Yarmouth, built boomies with the
sea-keeping qualities of smacks, as did Aldous, of Brightlingsea, but
they had not enough bottom for sailing light. The few built on the
Humber, such as the *Adriatic*, were as clumsy as the local keels, with
a run like the heel of a boot.

Some barges built down Channel were caulked instead of being
double-skinned or rabbeted, and the Dutchmen made their contribution with the *Fullson* for Burley, of Sittingbourne, the *Antje*,
which was wrecked just outside Harwich harbour shortly before
the First World War, the *Hendrik*, which Harry Stone had, and the
Mistley *St Eanswythe*, as well as Goldsmith's 250-tonners, but,
interesting as it would be to know just what the Dutchmen could
show in a field of shipbuilding so close to their own, not much is
recalled of these vessels' performance.

It is sometimes stated that Essex barges have bowsprits and
Kentish barges do not. That is an over-simplification. Every real
coaster carried a bowsprit, but among the smaller craft bowsprits
are more frequently seen north of the London River—or were, for
many an Essex-man has laid his ashore now that good mates are
such a rarity.

There are two reasons for this. The real Essex type is the stackie,
and with a stack fores'l you needed a bowsprit jib as well. And when
you come out of Harwich in sou'westerly weather you want all the
help you can to thrash up into Sea Reach on a flood-tide, which
again is just when a bowsprit jib helps. The Kentish-men working
through the Jenkin Swatch from the Medway do not encounter
conditions as exacting as faced that Harwich fleet, described in
Chapter VII, and their stemhead staysail rig, while lacking the power
to drive to windward in a sea, has its advantages for working in the
smooth water and congested conditions of London River proper.
Craft like the Yarmouth-built *Fortis*, designed to work under staysail, are not true East Coast types, though they do plenty of East
Coast work.

As always, however, it is dangerous to generalize. Many barges
carry two staysails, one big sail for light airs and for keeping steerage
way behind trees or riverside buildings, the other a smaller working
sail, which is called the "Swin staysail." They may be likened to
the old-time racing cutters' 'long roper' and baby jib tops'l.

Even when one has finished trying to distinguish various types of
barges one finds a multitude of individual peculiarities. Some are

not themselves without a jib; others don't seem to need one. Some
will go with sheets pinned; others must have some flow in their sails
to move them. Some can be loaded mercilessly; others become
sulky and protest at the extra five tons. Some stop in stays; others
shoot ahead and keep way on. Some pay away on the new tack;
others find their course on their own. Some gybe heavily; others
can be relied on to go over "like a feather bed." (It is generally the
wide, stiff stackie type that is heavy on her gear and alarming to
gybe, compared with the more shapely sea-goers, which 'give' to
wind and wave.)

Compared to a keel yacht, however, all have the characteristic
of weaving about under way, always luffing and bearing away
slightly round the leeboard. A yacht will find her own way to
windward; a barge needs continual help at the wheel. Because she
answers slowly, the amateur gives her too much helm, and leaves a
wake like a serpent in pain; the experienced skipper feels and antici-
pates the swinging of the ship's head, checking the movement to
come before the last is finished. He does not use much helm, but
he is always gently using some. The coasters which sail on the chine
rather than on the leeboard are of course the best to steer; craft like
the *Venta* could be left to sail themselves. They will heave to, under
mainsail and backed foresail, or in a strong breeze under foresail
and tops'l sheet. They will come off a lee shore manfully; they had
to in the days when open beaches were used for discharging. And
they do not share the dislike of so many working craft for bearing
away. An amateur with a real sympathy for boats can sail them
adequately, but long acquaintance is needed to sense when the mainsail may (in light airs) be trimmed almost entirely on the sheet and
when the vang must take up its strain. Nor will an instinct for the
right amount of leeboard be quickly acquired.

Every barge's suit of sails (save in Goldsmith's fleet) has its own
varying dimensions and proportions, but most rigging is standard.
I should like to know who was the first to establish almost universal
practice by placing his main brails on the winch to port of the mast-
case; his middles and lowers by the mast-case winch; his peaks on
cleats seized to each after shroud; his tops'l halyard cleating on the
port side of the mast and his tops'l sheet on a cleat on the sprit; his
tops'l clewline on the middle starboard shroud cleat; his foresail
halyard on the fore port shroud cleat; his staysail sheet opposite to
port. Who, I wonder, ordained that first the stanliff and then the

fore starboard and middle shrouds should be bent over the mast head of every correctly rigged barge? And, most fascinating of all, who was the genius among sailmakers who cut the baggy foresail which yet sets to windward without touching the sheet?

Of late years a second winch to starboard of the mast-case has come into fashion for handling the tops'l sheet and the fores'l halyard. Some, alternatively, use a winch in this position to handle jib halyard on the drum, and staysail or jib topsail halyard on the gipsy. Another recent fashion is a tackle in the standing part of the

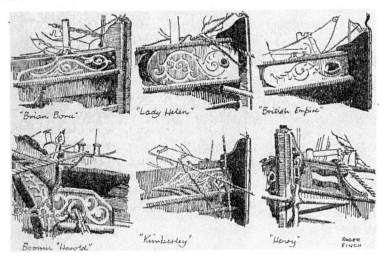

"Brian Boru" "Lady Helen" "British Empire"

Boomie "Harold" "Kimberley" "Henry" ROGER FINCH

BOW-BADGES

topsail sheet purchase to swig out the last inches—a worth-while refinement, save, perhaps, on barges which are often lowering down. Then simplicity of gear is yet more valuable.

Topmasts are fidded to lower, which eases the windage of a barge enormously. They are not, however, lowered for sailing in a breeze, since the tops'l is kept set almost as long as the barge will carry sail. Her handiness goes once it comes in. Sometimes at anchor, however, topmasts are housed to save dragging ashore in a gale. As long as the average yacht is content with one reef the average barge carries full mainsail, topsail, and foresail. In a two-reef breeze the mizzen comes in and a little mainsail is picked up. Only if it really blows does the topsail come down. The big sea-

going coasters are an exception. In bad weather they down tops'l
and keep the mainsail 'set smart.'

Leeboards are handled on the East Coast by standard pattern
winches on the quarters, with a drum for warps, mainsheet, or vang
falls. Sometimes even jib sheets are led aft along the deck to this
handy machine. Some of the smaller old-timers managed with
tackles, and a few Kentish-men have capstans, which are handy for
warping, since the lead can be from any direction without snatch-
block or fairlead.

All in all, barges have never been as well found and looked after
as are those surviving to-day. They are, after all, the pick of the
fleets, for the fittest are naturally chosen to survive. For years good
money has been earned, and it is to the credit of owners (not un-
influenced perhaps by the framing of fiscal legislation!) that profits
have been put back into the upkeep of their craft. A sail up London
River to-day saddens one at the few barges to be seen; gladdens one
at their smart hulls, gleaming spars, and well-tailored canvas. No
longer does one meet the battered tore-outs, with blackened spars
and blue sky showing between the patches on their sails, such as
were common in the bad days of the 1930's, when every buoy was
crowded with out-of-works and Peters of Southend were offering (in 1934) a useful barge, with all gear, recently in work, for £25.
The fine quality of the barges to-day is some compensation for their
sorry quantity.

Craft at Cranfield's mills framed between the stern of *Flower of Essex* and bows of *Dannebrog* and G.C.B.

(See Chapter VI.)

Ipswich Docks

Some of Paul's 'mulies,' showing, centre, *Barbara Jean*, one of the biggest two East Coast barges built. She was lost at Dunkirk

(See Chapter XII.)

ABOVE: Locking into Ipswich Docks in the 1890's, showing *Malvina*, *Unity*, *Carrie Louise*, and (tops'l set) *Victoria*. BELOW: Pin Mill, with the Ipswich fleet dropping down on the ebb, behind craft on the hard

On the Deben (1)

LEFT: *Eldred Watkins*, with Watkins' diamond in her topsail, turning up the Deben, bound for Wilford Bridge, 1930. She is now renamed *Revival* and owned by Woods of Gravesend

BELOW: A busy day at Woodbridge

On the Deben (11)

ABOVE: The boomie *Sussex Belle* passes the Dutch three-masted schooner *Sophie*.
Sussex Belle was lost at Great Yarmouth about 1924, bound from Keadby to Orford
with coal. Anchored in the Roads, she drove ashore in a heavy E.S.E. gale and
broke up. BELOW: Melton dock, Woodbridge, with four craft in

II

OLD TIMES AND OLD-TIMERS

When did it start?—First Records—Cutters, Dandies, and Spritties—Barging 150 Years ago—Changing Channels—Old Customs and Quaint Customers

WHEN did the rivers and creeks of the Thames Estuary begin to know the sailing-barge which, for the purpose, may be defined as a flat-bottomed vessel with leeboards? That is certainly a baffling question.

Was such a vessel known in Colne when Henry VIII inspected the river and thought it such a fine haven? Or when, in 1666, Pepys noted in his *Diary*:

> I down to walk in the garden at Whitehall, it being a mighty hot and pleasant day; there was the King who talked to us a little and, among other pretty things, he swore merrily that he believed the ketch that Sir W. Batten bought the last year in Colchester was of his own getting, it was so thick to its length.

There have been spritsails on London River for 450 years, and there may have been small barges serving local farms and trade on the East Coast rivers down the centuries. It seems strange if there were not, but the first specific mention seems to be Defoe's reference to barges carrying chalk into Essex in the eighteenth century to lighten the heavy clay lands. Marryat, in *Jacob Faithful*,[1] refers to a barge with a lowering mast which "plied up and down the river as far as the Nore, sometimes extending her journey still further, but that was in summer."

If we deduce from this that it was in the eighteenth century that barges began to penetrate down Swin, we are faced with the further problem of deciding whether the original coasters were spritsail or cutter rigged.

A picture exists of spritsail barges in Margate as early as 1786, but I am inclined to the view that this rig was rare in Essex and Suffolk

[1] 1834.

C

before the nineteenth century, if, indeed, it was known at all. I base my view on the following evidence.

E. W. Cooke's etchings suggest that it was not till the 1820's that the London River spritsail barges began to develop in length and set the ingenious mizzen sheeted to the rudder, which is one of the secrets of their handiness and has remained a characteristic feature to the present day, when the ugly fashion of discarding it on installing an auxiliary has come in. Then, no doubt, the handy spritsail rig, which had already been in use for five centuries, soon knocked out the cutter, just as it was to regain its mastery over the ketch, which challenged it for deep-sea work thirty years later.[1] But until these developments occurred the sprittie could not be regarded as a sea-boat capable of tackling the Swin—though it is dangerous to decide what work barges did from their fitness to do it, since within living memory Ben Bennett, of Mistley, was trading from King's Lynn to Harwich with 'gas water' in the fifty-foot swim-head spritsail tank barge *Ivy*.[2]

A sketch by Constable of Ipswich docks in 1803[3] shows not a single barge among the shipping, suggesting that such craft were then uncommon, for probably no picture made later in the century fails to show several. Cotman, however, shows a swimmie at Yarmouth in the 1830's rigged with standing gaff and lug mizzen.

The first picture I have of barges at Colchester shows a cutter at old Hythe Bridge in 1820.[4] At least one of the early Colchester craft, the *Farmer's Delight*, was almost certainly a cutter, since an old account-book records the purchase of grease for her mast over 140 years ago—and a sprittie's mast needed little greasing, even in the days of mast-hoops.

The oldest barge in the 1893 *Mercantile Navy List*, the Maldon *Royal Oak*, built at Limehouse in 1798 and still with Vandervord of Southend almost a century later, was specifically described as "booms'l rigged."

Finally, I feel that had the spritsail been common in Essex in the eighteenth century and before it would be shown in some of the prints and 'prospects' of that time and in the cartouches of the early maps, for its distinctive pattern is attractive to the artist's eye. The absence of leeboards on the vessels sketched in pictures of this period is less convincing evidence, for the leeboard tends to be forgotten

[1] See Chapter IV.   [2] Still working for Salamon, of Rainham, in 1907.
[3] Victoria and Albert Museum.   [4] See *Last Stronghold of Sail*, p. 16.

in non-technical impressions, and was, indeed, often omitted in careful portraits of latter-day ketch barges, as the plates facing pages 81 and 96 show.

Against this, the early Colchester barge *Maltster*, of forty tons register, built at Aylesford in 1807, was certainly sprit-rigged when she was owned by Ben Cackett, of Hockley, in the early years of the present century, though of course she may have been converted in the meantime. (There was also a Colchester *Maltster* in 1757, William Frost master, though there is no evidence as to whether this craft was a barge.)

The first Essex-built barges of which I have record are the *Endeavour*, built at Colchester in 1802, and the *Resolution*, built at Maldon in 1803, and it is notable that other early vessels came from Kent and London. Records of Colchester barges in 1824-25,[1] for instance, list a fleet of nearly two dozen craft, of which only two were locally built, and the name of one of these, *Experiment*, built at St Osyth in 1819, is suggestive, even though *Rebecca* had been built on the Colne the previous year. This old craft, launched in Colchester in 1818, was rebuilt as a 140-tonner in 1868, when doubtless she exchanged her swim-head for a round bow. Her last skipper was the father of Mr Joshua Francis, now managing director of Francis and Gilders, Ltd, of Colchester, who himself made his first trip in her before she was dismantled in 1884.[2]

Then, in addition to the *Royal Oak*, the Aldeburgh *Industrious Ann* was built at Crown Quay, in Kent, in 1799 and registered at Aldeburgh in 1800, and the *Sally*, sold at Maldon along with the *Resolution* in 1845, was built at Horsleydown, in Kent, in 1779. Many of these old craft were doubtless pressed into service for the building of the Martello towers, those massive defences against Napoleonic invasion which still ring the Essex and Suffolk shores after their concrete counterparts which defied Hitler have been blasted away. Work on the towers was delayed because they were sufficiently remote from local brickfields to be unapproachable by the primitive roads of those days. One of Wellington's more resourceful brass-hats pressed sailing-barges into service to unload London bricks on the beaches, and, as this was around 1811, it must have been the first example of 'overside' work.

From all this it seems that sailing-barges spread from Kent and the London River to the East Coast at the opening of the nineteenth

[1] See note at end of chapter.   [2] See Chapter XII.

century, and that most of the early examples were cutter rigged. This does not necessarily mean they were true cutters; they may have sported tiny lug-mizzens mounted on the rudder-head, such as the *Dover Castle* carried to the last. The *Davenport* started with this 'dandy' rig (something between a cutter and a yawl), but they found her long boom such a terror at sea that they shortened it and enlarged her mizzen, and she actually ended her days with no boom at all, half-sprit rigged.

All the barges of this time were swim-headed and budget-sterned —that is, shaped rather like the modern London River lighter. If the evidence of the etching facing p. 15 is to be believed, this style was once common as far north as Yarmouth, but it gradually became confined to the London River, where the swimmie *Atom* was still working from Grays in the 1930's.

Among the first sprities must have been a high proportion of stumpies. This type of craft[1] traded to Essex and Suffolk up to the 1920's, and curiously enough the last wooden barge to be built, the *Lady of the Lea*, in 1931, was a throwback to stumpie style, if one admits this poor little example into the honourable company of sailormen at all. The fully fledged East Coast sprittie, however, was essentially a topsail craft from early days.

So much for conjecture. Now to review what we know about the early craft. *Resolution* and *Sally*, according to the 1845 bills of sale, were 71-footers, 16 feet beam, and 5 to 6 feet deep in the hold. Since their dimensions were identical, this suggests that the Essex model may have been copied from the Kentish. They were described as "square stern sloops, barge carvel built," but were surprisingly long and narrow, most of the early Colchester craft being between 60 and 68 feet long, between 18 and 19 feet beam, and 5 feet 6 inches to 6 feet deep in the hold.

Industrious Ann, of Aldeburgh, was also of this shorter, beamier build. She was 64 feet 7 inches long, 19 feet beam, 6 feet 4 inches height in hold, "a decked barge with leeboards," and was sold by "sixteen farmers of Aldboro' for £50 12s. 6d. with all masts, sails, etc. etc. etc." to "thirteen farmers of Aldeborough, a grocer, John Burrows, of Woodbridge, mariner, and a London contractor," among whom the sixteen shares were equally divided. The sixteen shares perhaps represent a quarter of the traditional sixty-four shares into which a ship was divided, though even so the total

[1] Shown in plate facing p. 48.

value of £200 is surprisingly low compared with £480 paid for each of the Maldoners in 1845, and shows the depreciation in the value of money during the Napoleonic Wars. The London merchant's interest suggests that the *Industrious Ann* was a full-blooded coaster, and there exist actual records of the *Farmer's Delight* trading regularly from London to Colchester, and sometimes to Mistley, Ipswich, Margate, Snape, and Ramsgate between 1800 and 1805.

Quite a picture of these voyages can be reconstructed from a well-preserved volume found among the papers of the Essex family of Round in a Colchester solicitor's office.[1] The barge was sailed by William Beaumont for his father, John Beaumont, who signs a settlement as owner, though perhaps shares were also held by certain others—Mr Fothergill, Mr Sawer, Mr Bawtree, Mr Dixon, and Mr Stonard—who are shown as jointly financing the voyages. Built in London in 1788, the *Farmer's Delight* was registered at Colchester in 1808, three years after this record ends, and vanished from the register in 1833.

She was engaged on an interesting mixture of passage and farm work. The arrival in London for each freight can be traced by the entry, "To boat up the Pool six shillings." The skipper then went shopping, making a varied lot of purchases, some doubtless for re-sale, others perhaps to his 'owner's' personal order, some for the ship. This generally took him about a week, after which he dropped down river, sometimes spending another six shillings on "Boat down the Pool," and loaded "rubbish" (London street manure and general waste for the farms, no doubt), buying this for about £9 a load of sixty carts. This done, he bought a leg of mutton (as sure a sign that he was about to sail as the hoisting of a Blue Peter!), and the next we hear of him is in Colchester, Maldon, Ipswich, or Manningtree, selling the muck for about £12 or £13.

Sometimes the routine is varied with a freight of timber to Maldon, and in 1805 the *Farmer's Delight* made three successive voyages to Ramsgate with bricks. One freight of chalk is recorded, one of ashes, and one of lime, which was taken to Ipswich. Whether the return trips to London were done light is difficult to decide. There are records of shingle-loading, but this may have been for local use, and there are entries relating to "use of granary," so evidently grain freights were done, though they do not appear

[1] Now in the Essex Record Office.

otherwise in the barge accounts, perhaps because the skipper had no trading interest in them.

The account-book opens with the *Farmer's Delight* "up the Pool" on April 8, 1801, and the skipper buying 10 lb. of sugar for 7s. 6d., 1 lb. of tea for 6s., one firkin of tar for 6s., one mop and brush, 2s. 5d., and "four yds bunton," 2s. 8d. There is also an item inexplicable to me: "To an order 1s."

On April 9 he buys sixteen quarter loaves for £1 8s., a cheese for £2 6s., "two letters 1s. 8d.," charges wages, £1 4s., and pays Mr Taylor for paint, oil, etc., and a "suit of colours" £2, £2 for shoemaker's bill, and hands £6 0s. 6d. to "Mr Nowell Attorney"—perhaps for safe keeping?

Two days later he invests 11s. 3d. on 14¼ lb. beef, £1 on new rope, and pays a meter's bill of 1s. 6d. On April 13 Mr Mitchell, attorney, is paid £6 7s. 9d., "Mr George for Mr T. Cooper" 3s. 8d., a pair of spectacles is bought for £1 3s. 0d., a box of candles for £3 9s. 6s., and a telescope for £2 2s. 0d. April 16 is devoted to getting beer on board ("Mr Hebden for porter, £5 15s., Mr Holman for ditto £3 2s."—a regular entry which impressed me with Captain Beaumont's thirst till I tumbled to the nature of his work!); on April 18 come a rand of twine and 4 lb. of butter 7s.

Then I think the *Farmer's Delight* sailed, without loading muck this time, for on May 13 a freight of shingle is bought (presumably in Colne) for £3, and the skipper collects from the owners the sum of £50 1s. 2d., giving him a modest profit of 3s. 9d. on his expenditure of £49 17s. 5d.

June 2 sees him again shopping in London—a mixed load, including, besides the invariable porter, "a rocking horse, £1 16s."; and on June 12 he buys a freight of "muck, etc." at £9 1s. 8d. The leg of mutton comes aboard next day, and £8 in cash is delivered to the owners (presumably in Colchester) five days later.

There is no entry in July, when maybe the *Farmer's Delight* was on the ways, but the routine is resumed in London on August 28, when, having loaded and spent £40 with "Mr Jenkins, sailmaker" (further evidence of a refit), he makes a good passage, and on August 30 is paying 4s. for help up to Colchester, where he enters the Customs House on September 2, and on September 5 charges an "allowance for delivering corn." (What corn this was is puzzling, unless he lightered a freight from a riverside barn to the Hythe in the first few days in September.) A fortnight later he pays £3 for a freight of shingle, but this apparently was not for London, since September is blank and was perhaps spent shingle-lightering. The next trip up the Pool is on October 22, returning a week later to load "quarter hund^d gun stone 2s." and a freight of rubbish. On this and other occasions allowances are claimed for loading, presumably tips for labourers, though possibly 'perks' for the skipper and his mate.

Just a month later the round is repeated, including this time 7 lb. of "Plumbs," 4s. 8d. and a box of pipes, 6s. 6d. There is no note of a muck freight. The final freight of the year—up the Pool on December 20, loading and collecting cash on December 26, and loading rubbish on December 29—shows how little heed was then paid to Christmas, now the bargeman's one annual and inviolable holiday.

In 1802 the *Farmer's Delight* made thirteen round freights, in addition to two short freights of shingle at a total cost respectively of £4 14s. 6d. (including 7s. 6d. expenses on Colne beach and porters for unloading) and £4 13s. 6d. (including £3 for shingle, 1s. for use of two baskets and shovels, and £1 12s. 6d. for porters). One of the rubbish freights was to Manningtree, where help up and allowance to porters cost 12s. Again a freight was done over Christmas.

So it went on throughout the years, items bought including a "Saddle for the Mare £2," "Two lbs Peruvian Bark Mr Foster 1s. 1d.," "¼ Jalop ditto 2s. 6d.," "Bean Tiers £9," a gallon of rum at 16s., "Carriage of a Gun 2s.," "Two bundles Red Sprats 5s.," and a "¼ h'wt oranges Mr Tiffen 5s." Other fragrant-sounding items are a quarter hundredweight Spanish brown and several lots of spruce beer. I am fascinated by the clothing of George Bishop, who gets a "new jacket and trowsers" at 18s. 6d., a great-coat for £1, and, again, later, "jacket and trowsers for George, 18s."

At the end of 1805 it is agreed that "The Accounts up to this time are settled and Ballances appearing in favour of William Beaumont to be his for Master's Wages." These balances were generally about 30s. a voyage, though how the charges are determined one cannot tell.

Wages are set out in 1805 as: five weeks £9; three weeks' victualling £6 12s. On February 6, 1803, £2 was charged for wages, and on March 5, £4 1s., but there is nothing to suggest whether George, the apprentice, constituted the whole crew, save the fact that only two shovels and baskets were hired on Colne beach. Certainly no one else got any "trowsers."

Some curious items of expense are admitted, such as might be questioned by that modern inquisitor, the man from the Inland Revenue, including "house duty and window lights £1 7s." and "expenses for my sister." A "pair of Indentures for George" (bless him!) at £2 2s. presumably mark the official apprenticeship,[1] but "expenses of arrest £1 3s. 6d." is an item which baffles me.

As to the ship's own affairs, items include repairing brass compass, 8s. 6d., job done to leeboard, 3s., hand spike, 1s., grease for mast, 4s., use of beacons at Maldon, 1s., groundage at Ipswich, 1s. 8d., anchorage and groundage at Harwich, 1s. 4d., coast-waiter, 2s., new lead and line, 2s. 8d., repairing rudder iron, 1s., new vane and vane-board, 2s., blockmaker's bill, £6 0s. 10d., and various payments to Webb, shipwright, Jenkins, sailmaker, Heath, mastmaker, and Ridge, ropemaker.

When the *Farmer's Delight* carried her cargoes of muck and porter, paper and candles, cheeses and clay pipes, down on the ebb from Sea Reach at the end of the eighteenth century she perhaps left the Black Tayle and the Horn, or Shoe, Beacon (now the Blacktail and the "Sheers," or N.E. Maplin) to port as they yet do, and ran through the same spitway between Buxey and Gunfleet which has returned to use in 1949 after a century of disuse. But more probably she took another route altogether, which would make the modern sailorman rub his eyes, finding a long-vanished channel through the Maplins to Wakering Haven (Havengore), marked by the Orwell Beacon, and then cutting across to the Bull Beacon, on Foulness, at Shore Ends by a swatchway even then possibly silting up, since it was beginning to be omitted from some charts of the period. From Shore Ends she could have sailed down the Whitaker, avoiding the present Sunken Buxey, then a drying middle ground, to the Spitways; or by steering north-east from the Bull she could find good water to the Swire Hole and the Wallet, where now the Buxey Beacon marks the highest part of that much enlarged bank.

Though it really concerns the days before barges, I cannot resist a digression into the changes in the channels they sailed. In the sixteenth century Burnham was almost certainly on or close to the open sea, and the coast ran north through Southminster and Tilling-

---

[1] Several indentures to barge skippers of four to six years are recorded in the 1820's.

ham to St Peter's Point.[1] Foulness was an island projecting into the sea at the mouth of the Crouch. In 1594 and 1610[2] Burnham is shown as only two miles from the sea instead of five as now, and the Roach joined the Crouch in a wide estuary.

It is the walling of the Dengie Hundred that has transformed this bit of coast. The big Ray Sand grew out from the new walls, split by a channel into which ran the river Asheldon from Southminster. Then the Ray Sand channel (Rays'n) formed itself, cutting off the tips of these sands to form the Bachelor and the Buxey in the seventeenth century. This Buxey, originally a long, narrow sand, flattened and grew to its present oval shape, and the Crouch, which had always been regarded as flowing like Blackwater and Colne into the Wallet (which takes its name from Wallot, or Wallasea, Island), finally became a contributor through the Whitaker channel to the waters of the Swin.

These things, however, would have been but tales handed down to Captain Beaumont of the *Farmer's Delight*, who would also have heard of the old river Gunfleet which ran out at Holland Gap, giving its name to the sand. He himself, however, would have found Harwich harbour encumbered with shoals, picturesquely named the Altar, Cod, Glutton, Bone, Gristle, and Guard, for the dredging away of these was not put in hand till 1845. Changes have been less spectacular within the living memory of the old-timers, and an 1850 *North Sea Pilot* (a much chattier affair than its aloof and formal modern counterparts) gives a picture of a region much as now physically, but seen through very different eyes.

The Wallet, one reads, is a

well-sheltered anchorage in gales off shore, as well as in those from south-west to south-east, for the high sands which bound it intercept all weighty seas, and it becomes completely smooth after two hours' ebb. The precaution should, however, be adopted of giving a good scope of cable on first taking up a berth, for as the bottom is stiff clay the anchors become shod, and will seldom hold again after they have once started.

Many obstructions were said then to exist in the Colne:

The tide is nearly throttled by the overlapping projections, Hound Point and Ooze End, and the navigable state of the river has been considered subordinate to the purpose of the oyster fishery. . . . The oysters

[1] *Short History of the Thames Estuary*, by Muir Evans (Imray, Laurie, Norrie, and Wilson).
[2] Norden's and Speed's maps.

are deposited on the bed of the stream and the result has been that the river has materially lost its depth and vessels are frequently detained in consequence.

Harwich, now a flickering street of lit buoys, was then entered at night by keeping Dovercourt lights in line till Landguard light turned from red to white; "then bring the vessel's head round to north and north-east and anchor under Landguard Fort."

Hamford Water "is available in north-easterly gales for small vessels which have lost their anchors and are unable to fetch into Harwich harbour"; but the most surprising description of all is the Rays'n, which to-day nearly dries. Then it was "very narrow with twelve to fifteen feet in it at low water."

Colchester in 1894 boasted 164 vessels of 4931 tons and seven steam vessels of 239 tons, besides small craft belonging to Rowhedge, Wivenhoe, and Brightlingsea. Ipswich had 113 sailing-vessels, tonnage 6600, and twelve steamers of 892 tons; Maldon (including Burnham) had 140 vessels of 8583 tons.

These, then, were the Essex waters as the old-timers of to-day knew them when first they went to sea. And the men who were old-timers to them?

A typical bargeman of the real old school, if at home on Sundays, wore a blue cloth suit with velvet collar, costing £2 made to measure, a blue peaked cap, and often, in fine weather, stout Dutch slippers with red-plush uppers, bought at five shillings a pair from the Dutch eel-boats then frequenting Hole Haven. These boats also sold cheeses at two shillings each, sixpenny bottles of 'Dutch drops,' mops and brooms, and plugs of hard tobacco. Before the days of rubber boots, Dutch leather sea-boots (thigh-length, thirty shillings) were also popular. They came from Dordrecht. Jimmy Cole, of Erith, recalls that when he was a boy in barges many skippers wore the traditional tarred bowler hat when at work.

The naval dufflecoat of later years had its equivalent in the bargeman's 'lambie'—a long, thick woollen smock, pulled over the head and reaching just below the knees. Moleskin trousers were the rig in summer, 'fearnaughts' in winter, with hand-knitted guernseys, and over them often a canvas or linen smock of tan colour. There were generally a pair or two of mud-pattens aboard for use at winkling or 'eel-pritching' (spearing). In considering the beggarly pay for the freights fifty years ago, it should be recalled that the self-respecting bargeman seldom bought vegetables; he took the bag over the sea-wall after dark instead. And the hare-hunts! With false whiskers on their faces to deceive the keepers, the bargemen helped themselves to any fresh meat that ventured within striking distance of the waterside.

One very noted old skipper, Sammy Cullum, a Salcot man who settled in Faversham and had that pretty little coaster the *Orion* (later *Gold Belt*), always wore a round fur cap winter and summer. But it was one of the Mistley Horlocks who achieved no small fame by standing on Mark Lane one day dressed in sou'wester, thigh-boots, and 'fearnaught' trousers, and the next immaculately garbed, even to a silk hat!

The craft these old-timers knew were very different from their descendants of to-day. Not only were the hulls small, boxy, and leaky—these vessels were strangely primitive in rigging. Boom and gaff rig lasted well into living memory—Edward Haste, of Ipswich, recalls the *Star*, which was not, I think, the Maldon old-timer mentioned in Chapter XI—and lug-mizzens were not uncommon. *Dover Castle*, which finished under the trees at Woodbridge in 1931, carried hers to the last. Seventy years ago tiller-steering was still universal, and wheels were adopted only very gradually after the first was fitted in the *Anglo-Norman* by Stone, of Brightlingsea, in 1882; seven years after the *Alice Watts* was the first wheel-steered boomie launched. The stackie skippers, in particular, protested that they could 'feel' their craft better with the tiller, and I dare say they needed to, for they could see little enough where they were going. More than one man, however, has been knocked overboard and drowned by a kick from the 'rib-tickler.' Until the tiller gave place to the wheel, mizzens in spritties had, of course, to remain on the rudder-head, for the mast on deck would have fouled the tiller, and for the same reason squat cabin stove-pipes were then rigged when under way.

Rope rigging and wooden cross-trees, which could not be topped up and were continually getting broken alongside cranes and ware-houses, were general both in boomies and spritties, and when wire shrouds first came in they were often made with a splice at each end big enough to ship round the masthead so that the wires could be 'end-for-ended' to add to their life, for the first weakening from rust comes always just above the lower seizings. In those economical days precious paint-brushes (a barge was lucky to carry two!) were cleaned by dipping them in mud and painting it out. A skipper who tried it recently told me that, to his astonishment, it proved very effective!

Stayfalls were 4½-inch tarred hemp, and wire was accepted only very grudgingly for this gear, since the early varieties tended to kink, and one or two men were killed lowering for Rochester bridge when the stayfall jammed and the bridge knocked the whole load of gear on deck. The old rope certainly surged well round the windlass, provided a bucket of water was thrown over the barrel first, as is still done when the anchor is let go.

Mainsails were often hooped to the mast, Goldsmith's stumpies being the last to retain this practice, which had much to be said in its favour, for the modern iron jackstay, while neater, is liable to kink, and then the luff will not ride up it when the tack is eased, but jams and strains as the sail is stowed. Handspike windlasses were common and winches were almost unknown, even for leeboards and main-brails. Some barges even raised their leeboards for'd till it came to be agreed that the quarter was a drier and more convenient place than the foredeck from which to work a tackle. Huge wooden blocks were, of course, necessary, but when under way the whole stayfall tackle was often replaced by a special rigging screw and stowed below.

Hatches were battened with special batten-nails instead of wedges, a method which soon made the edges of the hatch-cloths look as if a shotgun had been fired through them, though it ensured a tight, safe stow. A century ago some barges even had the sprit rigged to port, which would cause a sensation now, and rudders were sometimes hollow boxes instead of solid blades.

Many of the quainter customs have died out, but some of the traditions are inviolable. No longer does a mate feel affronted if a skipper lends a hand with the gear forward, nor a skipper expect a mate to ask permission to come aft, but the starboard bunk and lockers are still universally the skipper's and the port side of the cabin the mate's. I have been assured that in any self-respecting barge the skipper's death at sea would be shown by a flag in the starboard rigging, and that of the mate by one to port, but I am glad to say this does not happen often enough for me to generalize. Even in building a barge at Paglesham the starboard side was accorded preference.[1]

[1] See Chapter XIII.

When it comes to rigging, however, sentiment has small say. The Colchester barges which do not often lower their gear are now being fitted with fine plough-steel standing rigging. The *Will Everard* and *Greenhithe* have deadeyes and steel wire lanyards, and the latest Mistley-men have discarded lanyards and dead-eyes in favour of rigging screws. The old-timers' reaction is just what it was when the time came to abandon the hemp rigging which had to be set up afresh after every other trip. "There's no give in that new stuff," they say. "That will tear the life out of them"—but it doesn't.

Note. A Colchester registry of 1824–25, now in the National Maritime Museum, lists *Good Intent*, 68 tons burden, built Cupers Bridge 1793, registered Colchester 1818, T. Jefferies and T. Summersum, mariners, and C. Bones, Jnr., miller, owners; *Endeavour*, 53 tons, built London 1790, registered Colchester 1814, owned at St Osyth; *Union*, 24 tons, built Limehouse 1806, registered Colchester 1807, owned by a "West Mersey" merchant; *Betsey*, built Chelsea 1788, registered Colchester 1817, owned by B. Brown and C. Heath, merchants, Adam Glendinning, Jnr., mariner, all of Colchester, and A. Glendinning, of Bermondsey (perhaps the father of the skippers of *Betsey* and *Endeavour*); *Linnett*, 73 tons, built Maidstone 1797, T. Pilbrow, owner, Joseph Fish, master; *Little Hermitage*, 76 tons, built Maidstone, 1795, C. Parker, of Colchester, merchant, owner, W. Beaumont, master; *Endeavour*, 81 tons, same owners as *Betsey*, James Glendinning, master; *Union*, 68 tons, built Maidstone 1788, registered Maldon 1806 and Colchester 1825, Robert Donne, Brightlingsea, victualler, owner, R. Read, master; *Industry*, built Limehouse 1818, registered Colchester same year, R. Tabor, merchant, owner, W. Wood, master; *Two Brothers*, 89 tons, built Battersea 1816, registered Colchester same year, W. Hawkins, timber-merchant, owner; *Benjamin and Ann*, built Pangbourne 1791, earlier registered Maldon 1813, W. Quilter, owner, Luke Richmond, master; *Amity*, 89 tons, built Vauxhall 1788, registered Colchester 1806, Charles Parker, owner, J. Beckwith, master; *Farmer's Delight*, built London 1788, registered Colchester 1808, Charles Parker, owner, John Finch, master; *Betsey*, 57 tons, built Pangbourne 1799, registered Colchester 1823, William Death, of Brightlingsea, owner, E. Barrington, master; *William and Charlotte*, 54 tons, built Aylesford 1812, registered Colchester 1825, owned by Timothy King, coal-merchant, Ed East, victualler, John Whitley, mariner, all of Colchester, and John Watts, St Catherine's Street, "near the Tower of London," J. Whitley, master; *Experiment*, 31 tons, built St Osyth 1819, registered Colchester same year, H. Ford, Jnr., owner; *Good Intent*, 51 tons, built Ratcliff 1787, T. Pilbrown, Jnr., owner (broken up 1836); *Ebernezer*, built Reading 1807, registered Colchester 1812, S. Overall, West Mersea, owner, J. Lee, master (out of register

1842). These tonnages (which are here rounded off to the nearest ton, though recorded in hundredths) refer to burden. No detail of the craft is given other than occasional references to "square stern," "leeboards," "carvel built," "standing bowsprit," "barge rigged." A contemporary record of apprentice indentures further refers to *Ceres* and *Two Brothers* (see Chapter XIV).

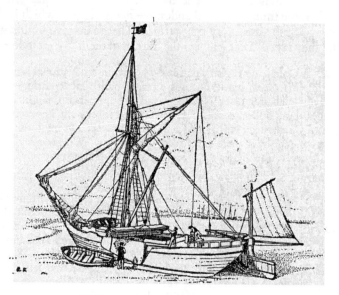

BARGE UNLOADING AT YARMOUTH
From a water-colour by J. S. Cotman,
painted *c*. 1830.

III

FREIGHTS OF TO-DAY AND YESTERDAY

*Hoy Barges and Stackies—Timber and Tarmac—A Rag-
stone Skipper's Memories—Serving the Sea-walls—Up on
the Beach—Wheat, Sand, and Beer*

JUST as coasting sailing-barges have altered and evolved continuously
over the century and a half of their existence, so the cargoes they
have carried have varied according to the changes in economic
conditions.

The passage work in which the *Farmer's Delight* was engaged was
not surrendered to the railways without a long struggle. *Baldwin's
New Complete Guide*, dated 1768, mentioned regular sailings to
Maldon, but these were doubtless by round-bottomed hoys; nor
does another reference book contain any description of 'Wheeler's
vessels' on passage to the town in 1822. *Pigot's Directory* for 1839,
however, specifically mentions "weekly barges" to Southend, sailing every Friday and Saturday, and vessels trading to Maldon from
Coles Wharf, Horsleydown, and also from Kennet Wharf "regularly." In 1854, according to a London directory, the following
weekly hoys were advertised:

To Bradwell: *Weymouth* and *Hannah*
To Burnham: *Endeavour, Good Intent, Tay*
To Southend: *Royal Oak* and *Emily*
To Colchester: *Rebecca, Fame, Osborne, Amity, Industry,*[1] *Cresswell,
     Little Hermitage, John and Richard*
To Rochford: *Meeson, Vickery*[2]

The agricultural work also developed enormously, and was the
mainstay of Essex barges, while the London horse traffic kept up a
continual demand for stacks, which were being carried by literally
hundreds of craft from every wall and wharf between Mucking

[1] *Amity, Industry, Osborne,* and *Cresswell* are advertised as "London and Colchester Packets,
Every Wednesday and Friday from Wool Quay, Lower Thames Street" on a bill dated 1849
of "John Mann, Junr, coal and porter merchant."
[2] Some account of the latter-day goods barges will be found in Chapter XIV.

Creek and Harwich. Root crops often went in the hold and the stack was built on deck, the first tier of hay or straw trusses being lodged on the rails to start the stack with a cant inward, and the whole secured with 'breechings.' You still saw an occasional stackie in the 1930's—a very occasional one. Twenty years before you might have seen thirty running up Swin together.

These Essex-men ran often to the Chelsea Omnibus Company wharf and to Bow Creek, but most of all to Vauxhall, where the barge roads were known as the Essex Tiers. The farm work was so much a regular Essex trade that when Jim Stone, of Mistley, was barge-racing in the twenties some of his rivals brought bunches of turnips with which to taunt him. "Only they meant to wave 'em over the stern at me," he commented, "and I never saw their sterns all day, though they saw some bit of mine."

An alternative freight to hay was 'bavans,' or faggots, loaded "anywhere they were cutting them."

Timber is another freight still much carried, chiefly from September to Christmas, and this also involves a stack, though it is a small one compared with the old-time mountains of hay and straw which necessitated special cleats well up the rigging and a little 'stack fores'l.' 'Rose-upon' barges, such as the *George Smeed* and *Persevere*, with new tops twenty feet wide on their old bottoms only about sixteen feet across, are—or were, for *Persevere* is now a motor-barge—rather cranky with this type of cargo, for a stack barge should have a beam across the bottom not less than three times the height of her side. The *Persevere* came through the Knoll one day dragging half the lee side of her timber stack in the water, and when she was moored on Mersea hard the skipper was rebuked by the timber-merchants for not having a good cover over the top of it. "Suppose it had rained," they pointed out.

As well as distributing timber from import steamers in the London Docks, wood is lightered from Norwegian vessels anchored off Osea Island, in the Blackwater. For this short sail to Maldon hatches are dispensed with, and on one occasion the *Clara* was engaged on this work in a breeze of wind, when, to every one's surprise, she quietly hove-to and sank. The water had been over the coamings! Luckily, timber is a buoyant cargo.

The sailing-barges made a great contribution to the building of the roads, which in turn ruined them. Before the days of tarmac there was a big trade in flints, in which Captain H. Morris was

In Colne and Orwell

ABOVE: Sand-loading at Alresford, showing *Normanhurst* (centre), one of Brice's craft, and the stern of billyboy *Halcyon*. BELOW: A stumpie driving up Ipswich river in a calm. The topsail craft behind is the skipper-owned *Defender* 48

Mistley hard, in the days when the famous racer *Sara* belonged to the port

A great Mistley skipper, Jim Stone, with his racing cups
(See Chapter VIII.)

engaged for some years. As a lad in a City office way back in 1892 he was often sent with Customs clearances to ships in the River, and so became acquainted with sailing-barges for the first time. One evening he got into conversation with the skipper of a little stumpie of Eastwood's, the Kentish barge-owners, that occasionally came up the Roding from Barking Creek with cement, and made a holiday trip with him.

I said to myself, this is the job for me, not sitting on an office stool making out invoices all day long [he writes to me from his retirement in London]. Of course, my parents were much against it. "All beer and bad language," they said. However, the call was too great, and I went to Faversham and got a job for two more trips as third hand, and then mate. Incidentally, there was no beer and no bad language with my first skipper, and he never got under way on a Sunday if he could help it. The two other skippers at Faversham never sailed on Sundays.

There were then 125 sailing-barges and 14 coasters working to and from that little port. Well, after I had been mate in two barges for about three years the barge-owner, Osborne Dan, now long dead, who had large flint-stone pits at Oare and Halstow, took a contract to supply the Essex County Council with flint stone for road-making, to be delivered all over the county from Southend right around to Manningtree and on the beaches at Clacton and Frinton. He had ten barges, and none of the skippers wanted the job, being mostly used only to London River work. My skipper said to me, "Go and see the boss and perhaps he will find you a barge, if you think you would like the job." And he did—the old *Princess Royal*, of London, steered by a tiller. She carried ninety yards of flints. My first voyage to the unknown coast of Essex was made up the Colne in the night—luckily a moonlight night. I well recollect the next day seeing the old *Alice Watts* sailing away down, no doubt on her way to the North for another cargo of coal.

For the next few years I explored, I think, almost every little creek and hard in Essex; and what happy years they were to me! I loved the life, and had an absolutely free hand where I should take the freights. When neap tides were on and lots of the places unattainable for lack of water we used to go to Harwich or Mistley or Wrabness, or on the beach at Clacton or Frinton. If the weather looked like being fine I would send a wire to the coastguards at one of these places, and they would put a light on the mooring-post on the beach so that if we reached there after dark we could sail straight ashore for the spots where the carts came down to unload us, whether night or day, to get us off

D

next high water. Clark, the farmer at Great Clacton, used to find the
horses and carts, and often I have walked over to his place in the night,
to tell him we were coming on at high water, to be greeted by his
barking dogs and a flow of language from him. His contract was,
however, that he had to unload at any time of night or day barring
Sundays. We unloaded three freights at Clacton in one week.

Up the Maldon river a gang of men did the unloading, coming
wherever we were, either by boat or in a cart. Later, when I had a
bigger barge, the *G.H.C.*, and still later the newly built *Cecil Rhodes*,
they took two days to unload us, sleeping at night on bundles of straw
in the hold. I had to send the ganger a wire to say where we were.
We took many a freight to St Lawrence Stone, and as there was no
telegraph then at Steeple Post Office, it meant a five-mile tramp to
Tillingham or Southminster. Once it took me over two hours in the
snow in thigh-boots to reach the former Post Office, the roads were
so deep in snow.

In those years, from 1898 to 1908, we only had one really serious
mishap. We came out of Sheerness one winter morning, wind north-
east, bound for Harwich. Later it came on to blow hard and snow,
and when almost down to the Spitways our rudder-post split, so that
we could not get the helm over very far either way. We tried to hail
the *Gem*,[1] but she was too far off to understand. Finally we managed
to get round, and ran before the wind up to Burnham, and there we
lay till old King and his sons got a new oak post from Maldon and
fitted it up for us. The County Surveyor let us unload our freight at
Burnham, though they had their quota for that district. That was
before the days of the accursed internal-combustion engine.

A great deal of this beach work was done on the open shores of
Clacton, Frinton, and Walton when those towns were being built.
It seems a hazardous business, even though the barges were unloaded in a tide, but they generally got away unscathed. The seas
breaking against them would throw spray over the cross-trees, but
their shallow draft saved them. "They couldn't sink, though they
used to bounce," is one old-timer's impression. In emergency the
brick barges resorted to the desperate expedient of taking out the
plug and sinking the barge to avoid the pounding.

It was a rough trade, but it had much to commend it. It is carried
on now—if one excepts the sand barges that load overside on Colne
Point and at Leigh—only by three of Wakeley's craft, which work
with Kentish rag-stone for the Essex Rivers Catchment Board,
carrying on the Parker tradition.[2] The craft are the motor-barge

[1] See Chapter XII.   [2] See Chapter XI.

Windward (which in her sailing days capsized off Southend in 1935) and the sailormen *Lancashire* and *P.A.M.*, and I think if I could go barging and choose my trade I should be sorely tempted to plump for their carefree life.

Skipper of the *Lancashire* is that redoubtable character Sidney ("Tubby") Blake, who sails sometimes single-handed, sometimes with a lad.[1]

The *Lancashire* came turning up the Medway single-handed one day, "Tubby" shuffling forward every now and again to take in a bit of the mainsail, get the anchor ready, stow the head-sails. On one trip he hangs a bit of dolly-line over the lee bow, drops the head of the tops'l, trots back to the wheel, and falls alongside the tier— half a length short. He catches a line from the next barge and warps alongside, reproaching himself bitterly. "Losing my grip, I am," he groans in agony. "Can't fetch a barge up where I want to any more. Better step ashore."

On another trip he condescends to ship a mate, taking the boy for his first voyage, and goes battering up Swin in weather that keeps every one else at home. The *Lancashire* takes the ground off Leigh on the ebb and pounds so ferociously that the water is soon over the cabin floor. "Shall I pump, Captain?" asks the eager urchin. "Pump, boy? What for? We don't want to waste this drop of water," observes "Tubby," blandly surveying the rising flood. "Get the scrubbers. It's just what we want to spring-clean the cabin."

A young skipper told me of the day during the Second World War when he went, feeling extremely self-conscious, to his first naval briefing conference. Spruced up to the best of his ability, he entered the hotel lounge where were assembled an august concourse of heavily braided masters of ships great and small. They sat in silence, every man concentrating on one figure in a corner of the room. Following the general gaze, the skipper beheld "Tubby" Blake, pipe capsized, white top gracing his cheese-cutter, yarning urbanely and unceasingly (and what yarns!) of the days when barging was barging. But the tales of "Tubby" Blake are legion....

His son, George, was barging as soon as his mother could get back aboard with him. At the age of nine the L.C.C. (for which "Tubby" was working) found him and sent him to school for five years. Then he went mate with his father in the *Southwark*, which

1 He is now Skipper of the Thames Barge Sailing Club's *Arrow*.

competed in the Thames race with Wakeley's bag of manure trade-
mark in her topsail. (The quips of the wags are not for these dainty
pages.) Now he is skipper of the *P.A.M.*, carries a portable type-
writer in his cabin, writes for the shipping journals, and has contributed generously to this book.

What makes the stone work so attractive is that the loading place
is up the green and pleasant Medway, instead of in the infernal
docks of London. Moreover, there is always work without waiting, making it profitable, and a variety of places to visit, spicing it
with a taste of the adventurous freedom of old-time barging.

The rag-stone comes from Benstead's wharves, one at Maidstone
and one between that town and Allington lock. At the former the
stone is shot in by the ton; at the latter it comes in wheelbarrows.
At one time the chips were sometimes mixed in tar, and the result
was poured hot into the barges, having to be excavated with picks
on arrival, even though water was poured on the hold-sealings to
minimize its sticking. The worst of that freight was that even the
butter in the cabin cupboard tasted of tar.

Stone-loading, even a barrow-load at a time, is hard on a barge,
though special boards are laid to save the decks, and the *P.A.M.*
was at one time fitted with a steel floor to her sealing, but this had
to come out to comply with Ministry of Food standards when she
was wanted for some grain freights. Towage is a heavy item at
about £10, but *P.A.M.* has a 44-horse-power Kelvin Diesel auxiliary.
She has been rebuilt and doubled, and with her grey wale and showy
gold scroll-work is a smart craft, and a useful one too, for she will
carry 125 tons dead weight in 5 feet 10 inches of water—540 quarters
of wheat, or 120 yards of stone. At 9s. 6d. a yard, that means £57
a freight, and George Blake has been able to average £12 a week
on his skipper's share—no small improvement on the days, fifty
years ago, when "Chick" Cripps was in this trade. He loaded 90
yards at 1s. a yard, with 4d. a yard extra to Fobbing, which could
only be reached on spring tides. With 30s. for the tow, 3s. 6d. for
dues, and 2s. allowance, he would be left with less than £3 to share
for the freight. The auxiliary eases this work considerably, though
it remains a snag that the gear must be lowered for Rochester
bridge on the way up and again coming down.

From the Medway the work is to whichever part of the Essex
coast is at the time commanding the Catchment Board's attention.
The *Lancashire* was, in 1947, the first barge in many years at Mersea

Strood. With vague recollections of a trip long before, "Tubby" Blake poked his way up Pyefleet, beaconed the channel while he was there, and proclaimed it "dead easy." His son, following soon after in the *P.A.M.*, deemed caution the better part of valour and took a motor-boat, for to get across a rill stone-laden can have serious consequences, especially in a steel keelson barge like *P.A.M.* This is just what did happen to the *Victa* off East Mersea just before the Second World War. She broke her back, and is to-day a houseboat at West Mersea, not far from the scene of that misadventure.

Where, as is generally the case, the destination is an open sea-wall, the ganger foreman is required to clear any stones from the berth and to beacon each end of it, as. well as marking any snags, but George Blake aims always to arrive before the water is over the place where he is to lie. Then in along the wall she goes, and the anchor must be got out to fetch her off again—no light task in soft mud with the forty-five fathoms of chain which are needed, for an eighty-foot barge's stern is not clear of the wall till the first fifteen fathoms are in. On the beaches a farm cart often laid the anchor out, but against the sea-walls it has to be man-handled. A favourite method is to stand astride the stock and walk backward, lifting the fluke with the buttocks. Sometimes on soft mud a hatch was capsized (despite the sailor's superstition against doing this!) and used as a sledge. The dolly-line taken to the anchor over her quarter serves to moor her stern, and the crew usually have to drive their own posts on the wall to hold her in place. The gangers throw the stone out in a tide, chucking it overboard alongside to form a heap the weight of which shoves the barge off before she is afloat. Then it is "So long, lads!" and away to the Medway for another lot.

Sometimes, of course, the barge washes up the wall, and in 1948 the *P.A.M.* was on Cook's ways at Maldon having her chafed chines sheathed with inch-and-a-quarter elm, while George Blake was visiting me of an evening with these tales, and taking my mind off my business with invitations to come and sample it all at first hand.

The Portland stone trade was one of the hardest of all the barges' jobs. Provided the freight was carefully stowed, it was not a bad one for the long Channel punch, as the great lumps of stone kept the weight low in the barge, but there was grave danger of damage if it was lumped in awkwardly. Several craft have been lost through leaks caused in this way, and many more have been caught out, stone-laden. The *Jachin* was abandoned and picked up by French fishermen undamaged, and the *Hilda* turned over.[1] As late as the 1930's a sprittie with stone from Portland for Colchester's new public library was assisted into Ramsgate harbour in trouble.

Wheat has always been a staple for the dry-cargo craft, both imported wheat from the London Docks to the country mills and home-grown wheat away to London from the silos at Fingringhoe, Saltcote, Battlesbridge, and elsewhere. A good deal of flour also goes back to London in Cranfield's and Marriage's mill barges.

Special cargoes are also associated with different places. Moler clay generally comes in Dutch motor-coasters direct from Denmark to the Colchester works, where it is baked into insulating bricks, but during the Second World War a substitute was brought from Ireland to the London Docks and carried thence by barge. A popular freight it was, too, for it filled any chinks in the hold sealing with a handy cement stopping. Up till 1930 Owen Parry's Colchester oil mill used to keep craft busy bringing linseed in and taking oil back, as did similar mills at Lowestoft; and there was a fair cement trade to Colchester, and a still bigger one to Maldon.

The development of the Colne sand trade is quite a barging romance. During the First World War Mr Joshua Francis came to Colchester from Kent, where he had been running tugs on the Medway, to take over the sailing-barge business of his uncle, Mr Howe. He was out for a walk one Sunday when he paused to examine the gravel in Wright's pit at Colchester. Knowing a little of the trade, he took a handful home in his handkerchief and put it in a glass of water in his bedroom. When only a tiny quantity of dirt separated out he knew it to be something good, and he took a paper-bag full of it to London next day. His fellow-travellers on the train laughed at him, urging him to throw it out of the window, but they laughed on the other side of their faces when, on the train down that night, he told them that he had orders for hundreds of tons. His barges soon got busy, and within a few years pit after pit opened on Colne, till now sand is king in this river, almost as much as cement became in the Medway. There is a pit at Rowhedge, two at Fingringhoe, one at Alresford, and one at St Osyth, providing one of the chief sources of London's supply. It is carried in Goldsmith's, Wakeley's, Piper's, West's, Brice's, and Cremer's barges. Many a fine coaster, such as the *Glencoe*, is finishing her days in this

[1] See Chapter VI.

rough work, and the loading of sand off Colne Point still keeps alive the beach work, of which so much was once done hereabouts.

Ipswich specialities are linseed, potash, and fertilizer for the factories, with loam (moulding sand) from Erith for the foundries. Norwich, as well as importing barley and exporting sugar, sent away a good deal of lead spelter in the 1930's. Bargemen, used to laborious shovelling to trim light grain cargoes away under decks, rubbed their eyes to see the *Alderman* down to her marks with a small heap of the spelter on her hold floor.

Wakering, Rochford, and Shotley were centres of the brick trade, and there were many other small brick-fields and kilns.

Middlings and cattle-food material go to Mistley, maize to Ipswich.

No account of freights would be complete without a mention of the beer barges. Meux's *Pimlico*, whose tops'l bore a horseshoe trade-mark, used to work regularly to Ipswich, taking malt back to the Nine Elms brewery; and she was such a smart one that they do say the mate was not allowed down the cabin. The *Kardomah*, with "Shrimp Brand Beers" in big letters in her topsail, brought that admirable liquid to Maldon from Gravesend, and had to make a trip a week, blow high, blow low. Before her time Goldsmith's *Chronicle* and *Majestic* were in this work, as was West's *British Oak*. Another "Shrimp Brand" beer barge, *Black Eagle*, is now a yacht at Maldon. The beer-barge skippers used to be given a small cask for each trip to remove the temptation to broach the cargo. Inevitably the *Kardomah's* skipper was given the name of Beery Bill—and he was a teetotaller!

IV

KETCH BARGES AND PASSAGE-MAKING

Expansion and Eclipse—How Racers set the Pace—The Versatile " Arthur Relf "—Enter the Boomies—'A Schooner with the Bottom cut off '—When is a Ketch Schooner-rigged? —The Sprittie gets her own back—Snape to Dublin!—To Western Ireland and up the Rhine—Tragedy and Comedy of Channel coasting

THROUGHOUT the century and a half that the cargoes mentioned in the last chapter have been carried economic trends had, up to the First World War, been steadily expansionist; thereafter a rather complicated decline set in.

As the potentialities of the sprittie barge came to be seen early in the nineteenth century her numbers must have multiplied with tremendous and increasing rapidity. She kept developing new trades and taking old ones from less handy and less economical rivals, without at first losing any old ground in return for the new fields she kept conquering.

Every farm within reach of the water used her; growing London swallowed up every freight she could carry, and called for more; she served the old world because there was no other means of communication or conveyance to compete with her, and she served the new as it got to work on the roads and railways, the great warehouses, the steam engines and motor-lorries that were to undermine her dominion. Even when the Port of London was transformed by the building of the present docks, what looked like her death-blow gave her a new lease of life, turning her into a distributive coaster instead of a mere river lighter.

The decline of the London horse-traffic, and particularly the end of the horse-buses, caused a falling off in the stack work before the First World War, but in the spacious yet fateful days of 1914 one of the many things that looked set and sure was the undisputed dominion of the sailing-barge over the Thames Estuary and its approaches between the Wight and the Wash.

Throughout the 1920's barging was still barging, despite the motor-coasters' inroads on the long trips, but in the 1930's the 450-quarter hundred-tonners, which had been grand coasters in the days when stackies were counted in scores, were becoming too small for a competitive market, for the tiny loading berths which made them essential were being given up, and the millers were using bigger silos and buying 500-quarter lots of foreign grain. So barges which had for long been the pride of the coast dropped out in the depression of the thirties, when the barge tiers at Woolwich, crowded with idle craft, earned the name of 'starvation buoys'; and their bigger sisters, driven out of the Channel and North Sea work by the competition of the Dutch motor-coasters, had to swallow their pride and be glad to jog back and forth on the short trips to Colchester, Ipswich, and Maldon. Alde and Deben ceased to know the barge at all; Lowestoft saw one rarely, and only a sturdy few continued to ply to Norwich, Yarmouth, and King's Lynn. At the outbreak of the Second World War when a Dover freight came round a majority of Essex skippers would decline it; indeed, it may be said that the variety and daredevilry generally went out of barging about twenty years ago when most of the craft settled down to a shuttle service on a few regular runs.

Up to the middle of the nineteenth century the barge was competing, on the Suffolk coast particularly, with the round-sterned billyboy, her North Country equivalent developed out of the Humber keel. These leeboarded craft, the largest of which were the biggest clinker-built craft in Europe, penetrated occasionally down to the London River, just as the sailing-barges ventured into the Humber, and they were even owned as far south as Ipswich and Snape. They failed, however, to develop the barge's economical versatility, their round bottoms and boomsail rig handicapping further evolution.[1]

Similarly, in the coasting era the barge was able to invade the collier brigs' trade; penetrating up the Waveney as far as Beccles, she has despoiled the Norfolk wherries of a few freights, and has even had a cut at the West Country schooners' work, shocking the Cornishmen by carrying as much with a crew of two as they could with far more gear and three times as many hands.

This all-important versatility is well illustrated in the cargo book

[1] Two which made a brave effort to adapt themselves and survive the competition from the barges are mentioned in Chapter VI.

of the *Arthur Relf*, preserved by her former skipper, Bob Potton, of Foulness. In 1909 she was mixing freights of cotton-cake to Colchester or flour from Yarmouth to London with trips from Alderney with stone, or Le Tréport to Exmouth with phosphate. Two years later she was in the London River ballast trade, but still occasionally putting in a voyage to Par or Pentewan; in 1912 she was cable-laying in the Straits of Dover—and a rough job this must have been, from the faded entries "Left Dover for Gris Nez—Calais for Shelter" and (over and over again) "Come Out and Put Back." The earlier years of the First World War were spent in humble attendance on the London River ballast dredger; then in 1918 she suddenly joined in the work to 'the other side,' taking pitch from London and coal from Goole to Dieppe, Le Tréport, and Calais. This went on till 1920; then it was back to the West Country stone trade, with occasional freights to Boulogne, Nieuport, and Antwerp as late as 1924. Ballast and East Coast freights predominated in 1925, when this interesting record ends.

River lighter, foreign trader, coaster, cable-layer, the *Arthur Relf* was able to switch from one calling to another as occasion demanded without shipping an extra hand or touching a rope yarn about her rigging. It is something no other craft has been able to do. The law of the survival of the fittest has held good afloat as in nature.

The middle of the nineteenth century found the sailing-barge evolving from a rough coaster into a thoroughbred clipper. In 1859 the "clipper sailing-barge *Thames*" was announced in the *Illustrated London News*: "as finished a specimen of barge architecture as ever was built on the river she is named after." Stem-headed and transom-sterned, she was, however, in her rig more like the swim-headers of fifty years before than the heavily sparred, sweet-lined coasters of only twenty years later. The *Illustrated London News* commented then that "there is not much room for the exhibition of naval architecture in a sailing-barge," and seemed more impressed by the fact that "the after cabin is fitted up in a very neat style, with bird's-eye maple and mahogany." During the next few years, however, the Ipswich, Harwich, and Maldon builders succeeded in proving that the barge in fact provides infinite opportunity for the designer's art.

It is customary to attribute this development to the barge races, which started in 1863, but too much can be made of this explanation. It would be truer to say that the races revealed the improvements in barge-building than that they were responsible for them. Classes in the races were generally started to catch up developments which had already occurred, and few of the craft built specially for racing set any lasting fashions in design, much less in construction. But the races did much to promote pride in their calling among bargemen, and recognition of it among the public.

During this time of the barge's development into maturity her family-tree divided, and the sprittie faced the strongest challenge she ever experienced from her new cousin, the boomie, or ketch barge. The schooners and ketches which dominated the coastal trade up to the middle of the nineteenth century had outgrown rivers like the Deben and Colne. For instance, the schooner *English Rose*, according to Mr George Taylor, of Woodbridge, quoted by Dr J. L. Groom:[1]

> sometimes had to wait a fortnight for a tide to get her up to the ferry dock, drawing eleven feet, and Mr Taylor has seen sixteen men heaving on her windlass and literally winding her up the mud till she was a foot out of her marks. When she was bound for the Lime Kiln Quay thirty tons would be taken out of her by lighter opposite Sutton Ferry.

Thus the discovery of a flat-bottomed craft able to go to sea was of great importance; indeed, it is surprising that it was not made sooner, especially in view of the cheapness of hard-chine construction, a form always favoured in time of war.

The sprittie of the first half of the nineteenth century, with her low rails and lack of sheer, was still not a deep-sea type, and there was urgent need for a coaster able to poke up a shallow creek and yet sail boldly down Channel, across to Ireland, or far up the Rhine into Germany. With the possible exception of Shingle Street at the mouth of the Alde, I do not think there is any truth in the suggestion that rivers and bars were shoaling (the charts show four feet on Bawdsey Bar three hundred years ago, just as now), but ships, no doubt, were constantly trying to grow bigger.

Just as the coasting sprittie evolved out of a cross between little London River barges and the round-bottomed sloops, so the boomies grew both 'down' from the coasting ketches, and 'up' out of the spritties. The earliest Essex boomie of which I have record was the Maldon *Elizabeth*, built at Maidstone in 1840 and owned by John Float, of Heybridge, in 1893. She was probably a 'grown-up'

[1] *East Anglian Magazine* (1937).

sprittie, coming from the heart of the Kentish barging country. *James Bowles* (built along with the *Dovercourt* by Aldous, of Bright-lingsea, in 1865) is another barge type, with simple standing bow-sprit, though *Harwich* and *Antelope* (also built by Aldous in 1867 and 1869) show a more distinct variety appearing.

The Ipswich and Harwich builders approached the boomie from the other angle, which again is what one would expect from places where the traditional types of shipping still held sway. At Ipswich, in particular, the old school of building lasted longer than in most places, for the brigantine *Clementine* was launched from St Clement's yard, under Bayley, as late as 1885 for a Newfoundland owner. Thus it is not surprising to find more of the cut of a ship about the first Ipswich boomie, *Lothair*, launched by Robertson at St Peter's yard in 1872; and Vaux of Harwich actually tried schooner rig in his *Stour*, built in 1857, and well described as a "schooner with the bottom cut off." The big mainsail aft, however, is unsuited to a hull with no keel, and ketch rig soon became universal, save in a few three-masters, such as Vaux's *Jubilee* and the Kentish-built *Friendship*.[1] Jib-booms and square topsails were, however, retained for some years, and, by one of those bits of verbal conservatism which are pitfalls to the chronicler, a ketch barge setting square sails continued to be referred to as schooner-rigged.

These craft under reefed canvas could stand up to a breeze at sea in a fashion denied to a sprittie of the period—and, indeed, even to the later spritties which finally ousted them. Even in an exposed anchorage in a breeze one is always conscious of the sprittie's top-heavy rig; in a boomie, to quote one skipper, "when you were brought up you felt you were properly brought up and properly stowed up." So complete did the boomies come to dominate the coastal trade in the latter half of the nineteenth century that builders were busy as far afield as Yarmouth, Littlehampton, and Topsham, in Devon. When the Ipswich spritties *Ninita* and *Lilly* were con-verted to boomie rig new mainmasts ten feet longer in the doubling to accommodate the peak halyard blocks were the only alteration needed to their standing gear. Both these craft, however, later foundered down Channel, which perhaps shows that putting a deep-sea rig into a river barge's hull did not make a sea-goer of her.

Of all the boomies Walker and Howard's London fleet, including

[1] See Chapter XIII.

the famous *Northern Belle*, *Eastern Belle*, *Southern Belle*, and *Western Belle*, were perhaps the queens, but the Harwich and Ipswich fleets came next, probably in numbers and certainly in quality, along with the Shoreham and Littlehampton craft.

Each place particularly recalls the boomies working regularly to it: Ipswich the *Justice* and *Carrie Louise*;[1] Mistley the *Eliza H.*, *Harold*, and *Genesta*; Colchester the *Startled Fawn*, *Antelope*, and *Alice Watts*; Woodbridge the *Reindeer*, *Eastern Belle*, and *Sussex Belle*; Burnham the schooner *Friendship*, the *Malvoisin*, and the Kentish-built sister-ships *Vanguard* and *Thistle*; Maldon the *Record Reign*; Tollesbury the *James Bowles*, *Empress of India*, and *Darnet* (her skipper selling his cargo of coal by the ton to the villagers). Mention of the *Bona* conjures up a picture of the yacht-like standard maintained by her skipper, H. Haste, who afterwards became a Trinity House pilot, while the *Kate and Emily* is recalled as the last to hang on to the old-fashioned hemp standing rigging.

It has been mentioned that at first some boomies were given the rig of the ketches with which they were competing, with jib-booms, figureheads, and (in the case of *Lucy Richmond*) a mizzen topmast. *Lothair*, *Alice Watts*, *Lucy Richmond*, and *Record Reign* had square topsails and topgallant sails, using iron jackstays to enable a gaff topsail also to be set on hoops on the topmast, but *Alice Watts* (1875) was the first of them to exchange the tiller (which most schooners had used) for a wheel. By 1890 square sails were becoming obsolete in coasters, and after this date only a single square sail was used for running, the yard being cockbilled aloft in dock. Standing bowsprits were also by then almost universal, and later boomies favoured the utilitarian 'outdoor' rudder. Early boomies had reef points, and it was part of the mate's ritual to grease the ear-ring before sailing. Later, however, roller booms became popular, a wire from the drum going to the main winch. Once the weight was on the wire the mainsail could be reefed single-handed, and a half-roll was often taken in at dusk to make this possible at night. Like spritties, boomies were partial to their topsails, and these were kept set over reefed mainsails, a mast-hoop being cut from the topsail for the second reef. With two reefs the mizzen

---

[1] *Carrie Louise*, a Shoreham boomie trading regularly to Ipswich, ultimately disappeared without trace in the Channel. A piece of wreckage found near the Varne was thought to be part of her, but even this was never definitely identified. Her former skipper had just left her, and escaped sharing her fate, only to lose his life when the *Robert Powell* capsized. See plate facing p. 32.

came in and headsail was reduced. A wire peak halyard went to the same winch; the other halyards were cleated by hand.

Four men sufficed in the smaller boomies, taking, say, 230 tons to sea on eight-foot draft, five in the larger, which drew up to twelve feet in the case of the *Record Reign*. A feature was a removable galley on deck abaft the mainmast, with a door on each side so that the lee one could be opened. When weather permitted, this was generally preferred to the focs'l for cooking. They must have been dry ships to have allowed this, and it is recalled that *Lucy Richmond* went six months without battening her forehatch.

Freight money, after deduction of expenses, was divided equally between skipper and owner; but the skipper paid mate, boy, and one or two seamen a wage from his share, instead of the skipper and mate sharing the freight money with the owners, as is the sprittie custom.

Despite their small crews, they carried plenty of kites. When David Farrow, of Woodbridge, was in her the *Sussex Belle* had a headsail (which for some reason they called 'Bill White') going from bowsprit-end to topmast-head, and sheeting by the rigging. They stowed all other headsails when that was set "to make one draught of it." In company with the *Eliza H.*, they set 'Bill White' one night after dark and surprised their speedy rival by leaving her sixteen miles astern at dawn.

Ted Marsh, of Woodbridge, was mate of the *Genesta* off and on for years—he kept getting fed-up with Harry Stone's idea of yacht finish, packed up, and then returned for another spell of it—and tells me they had a spinnaker setting to the topmast-head with a boom too long to ship under the forestay. One night the sheet broke as they were setting the sail, knocking Ted up against the windlass and throwing a young Scots seaman overboard. Ted chucked a ladder after him, and got him into the boat just about all in. Back on deck, he found Harry in some excitement and alarm— over the fate of the flogging spinnaker.

They were proud little ships, the boomies, and were monarchs of the narrow seas for half a century. "While I Live I Crow" was engraved on the stern of the *Cock o' the Walk*, whose skipper was one of the six barging brothers of the Ipswich family of Strange— and so she did. The First World War, however, stopped a lot of crowing and a lot of living. The *Cock o' the Walk* and several of her sisters were sunk. *Record Reign* and *Sarah Colebrooke* became Qships, and many more were laid up never to fit out again. *Genesta* and *Mazeppa* struggled on into the post-war years; *Matilda Upton* stuck to her boom a little longer before becoming a sprittie; *Antelope* and *Hesper* were both afloat in the 1920's; *Alice Watts* was trading in 1923, and *Sussex Belle* and *Ethel Edith* till 1927; the *Pearl* lay in Ipswich, where she had been built fifty years before, well into the 1930's. Everard's *Martinet*, the last of all, was actually trading into the Second World War.[1]

But, apart from every other consideration, boomies were really made obsolete by the last word in spritties, as represented in the *Redoubtable*, *Phœnician*, *Cambria*, *Greenhithe*, and *Will Everard*. The wheel had turned full circle since the Ipswich *Ninita* and *Lilly* were converted from spritsail to boomsail rig, and the sprittie, which for a century had been challenging and outclassing every other type of craft, was in at the finish, the last as well as the first fore-and-aft rig in London River.

The boomies died in time to escape the ignominy of conversion into motor-barges (though *Sarah Colebrook* is still at work in the Mersey as M.B. *Bolham*) and are to-day to be seen only as hulks and house-boats or, more happily, converted into fine spritties or mulies, such as *Thalatta*, *Ena*, *Major*, and *Hydrogen*.[2] These latter combine the ketch's mizzen with the sprittie's mainsail.

The voyaging of these ketch barges to-day sounds quite fantastic. In 1891 the *Genesta* was caught on passage from—of all places— Snape to Dublin. It is for all the world as if some one were to go stepping out down the village street, calmly intending to keep walking till he reached the West Highlands. She got as far as Penzance, ran into a full gale, and was towed in with the main boom broken. No doubt they rigged a fresh spar, reset the mainsail, and got going again, all as a matter of course.

In such another blow the *Gloriana*, driving down Channel under Captain W. Rands, missed Portland and shot into Weymouth harbour. When the skipper realized where he was "he just had time to nip her round, dab the anchor down, and miss the bridge."

The *Pegasus* was jogging along from the Humber to Alderney. She hove-to off the Casquets and rode out a gale. The *Empress of*

---

[1] A full account of her foundering at anchor in Hollesley Bay will be found in A. W. Roberts' *Coasting Bargemaster*.
[2] Now all auxiliaries.

India, a round-stern boomie built by Bayley, was hove-to four days in the Irish Channel bound for Waterford. Her jib, taking charge, frapped the sheets into such a bundle of inextricable and indescribable knots that they deposited them in Ipswich Museum, where they are still to be seen.

That this sort of thing was not done without hardship—particularly in winter—is shown by the adventures of the *Malvoisin*, built by Howard, of Maldon, for Meeson, of Rochford. With a gross tonnage of 122, she was 101 feet long, 22·8 feet beam, and 8·5 feet draught. In January 1905, when on passage from Gravelines to Goole, she was ashore in the Thames Estuary. With sails torn and rudder damaged, she was helped by the Margate lifeboat. In 1907 she went to Marshall, at Faversham, and from about 1919 onward was owned by Abbie Anderson, of Faversham. On November 9, 1925, she was caught by a N.N.E. gale in the Downs, bound from Whitstable to Calais, and was assisted by Deal lifeboat. On March 5, 1926, she was again in distress off the Suffolk coast, bound from Hull to Woolwich with materials for the arsenal. Aldeburgh No. 2 lifeboat went to her help, and she was towed into Harwich by H.M.S. *Dee*. Finally, at 5 A.M. on December 7, 1929, she went ashore west of Calais, and broke up immediately. Her crew was saved.

Frank Carr has recorded in *Sailing Barges* that Harry Ward, of Pin Mill, took the first boomie to North-west Ireland with a trip to Ballyshannon; Walter Ward in the *Arundel Castle* performed the unique feat of swimming a six-foot deck-cargo of timber home from Christiania (he was lost in the *Gem of the Ocean* in 1890); and Tom Strange (who later had the *Davenport*) was the first bargeman to reach the Shetlands.

One barge, the Ipswich-built *Eastern Belle*, actually took a freight to Spain. Her crew took her to Rotterdam, where another lot took over, but Skipper David Garnham, of Pin Mill, stayed as sailing-master.

In the coastwise trade flints from the Channel Isles, stone from Portland, and shingle from Orford or Shoreham were useful standby freights, but the boomies ventured much farther afield. Freights up the Rhine, often with china-clay or Apollinaris bottles, were such regular work that there was a captains' room in the offices at Düsseldorf, and many a skipper who could not read or write

Mill Barges at Home

ABOVE LEFT: *Jessie* at Green's, Brantham, no longer served by barges. ABOVE RIGHT: *Lord Roberts* and *Joy* at Stambridge in 1948
(See Chapters VIII and XIII.)

BELOW: *Leofleda* heaving up at East Mills, Colchester
(See Chapter XII.)

TOP: Snape, from which the *Genesta* sailed for Dublin into the gale of 1891
(See Chapters IV and V.)

The Little Ports (1)

CENTRE: Thorington Mill, about 1928

BELOW:
Lord Warden after a stack at Salcot, where the creek is now dammed. On this trip the *Lord Warden's* skipper met his future wife, and they were married in the village church hard by. Their son has been named after the barge
(See Chapter XI.)

English could speak German. Joe Palmer, who had the *Flower of Essex*, was fluent in French and Flemish as well. He was free to dispense with a Rhine pilot, having secured some form of citizenship of a Rhenish town. In his younger days he was mate of the *Arundel Castle* on the Baltic trip referred to above.

A freight of £125 to Remagen sounds quite attractive by the standards of those days, but £25 went on towing, and a gruelling tow it was. Starting at Dordrecht, it took eight days, six barges behind a great paddle-tug which brought up only once a day, at midnight, and then for only two hours. "At 2 o'clock in the morning she would give one blast," "Wings" Chandler, of Ipswich, recalled, "and you had to scramble up quick off the locker-top and have the anchor all atrip, for she gave you no more warning. Her great paddle-floats started coming down *wop* on the water, and away she went." At one place the current was so strong that she could only take the barges two at a time, and at the end of a weary day of up- and down-anchor you could still see the place you left that morning. The return journey was generally made with a freight of bottled mineral water, and the same tow down, with the current, was done in a day and a half.

Often, too, there were freights to Holland, frequently with scrap-iron, returning with tiles or chemicals. "Wings" Chandler also recalled one in the *Davenport* with teak for cigar-boxes. To save dues and expenses, the usual way to Amsterdam was up the coast to Den Helder and down the Zuyder Zee, instead of through the North Sea Canal. But on that inland sea even the smartest boomies and spritties had to give best to the Dutch sloop-rigged barges, with their tall, narrow-headed mainsails, long booms, lofty foresails, and huge leeboards.

The boomies did this work all the year round. In summer some spritties joined in, but in winter Dunkirk was a more usual run, often with linseed cake. Sixty years ago expenses were only £2 13s. a trip, but later, when the French Government took over the docks, such extortions as five francs a day for the right to a fire aboard raised expenses to as much as £15, and this was a nail in the coffin of that trade.

While the boomies were, of course, the most spectacular passage-makers, the spritties also did some astonishing things; indeed, if one remembers the limitations of the rig, perhaps their adventures were actually the most remarkable of all. The Harwich Club was divided

E

into A and B classes, and the 'A' vessels were permitted by the Board of Trade to voyage from Brest to the Elbe, and round Land's End and into the Bristol Channel, till October. In winter the limits were more restricted, and the *William*, of Ipswich, bound for Snape with coal, was lost in the first week of October, getting not a penny from the Club. At least one stumpie voyaged across the Channel; at least one eighty-tonner was seen at Skegness.

"Chick" Cripps, of Colchester, had the sprittie *Klondyke*. He made a good many trips to the Lincolnshire ports, including King's Lynn, where special berths had to be dug for each arrival, and Wisbech, where the tidal scour is so strong that a barge grounding was liable to have the sand washed out from under her and break her back, and the channel is so narrow that it was necessary to tend a craft with a line on the saltings to make her swing each tide. On one occasion after leaving Wisbech he decided to make up his mind off Skegness whether to sail light for London or Hull for his next freight. He made it Hull, as the wind was southerly, lay there three weeks, during which time the *R38* crashed within a quarter of a mile of him, then loaded oil-cake and wheat for Wells, returned light to Hull, and loaded tiles for Yarmouth. And they call them Thames barges!

"Chick" Cripps knew the East Coast so well that he was able to use Wells as a refuge, and preferred the voyage 'down to the North' to the Channel work, which, in his words, "starved barge-men in winter." He recalled leaving Dover for Emsworth, and just getting safely into Newhaven when the wind southered and breezed up. Everard's *Cambria* ran in soon after, bringing her top-mast down as she drove her bowsprit under his quarter. *Grave-lines II* (a small boomie which afterwards became the sprittie *Ena*) came next, struck a grid, and sank; and the *Scot* arrived with her sprit gone. During the 1914-18 War "Chick" Cripps worked a good deal with pitch to Le Tréport and Dieppe, where he once counted eighty barges. He also visited Saint-Valery-sur-Somme with coal, finding a tidal sand-scour similar to that at Wisbech.

The Channel not only starved bargemen in winter; it also drowned them. The loss of the Harwich *Ada* off Portland, with a deck-cargo of petroleum, is notable for the dramatic way it was revealed. In December 1888 the stern-board of a rowing-boat was picked up at Bridport with a message scratched on it: "*Ada* sprang leak. Tried to get to Portland. Send this to Harwich. Layzell, mate. Heavy

sea. Foundered off Portland. Took to boat. Expect all to perish."
The skipper of the *Ada* was Richmond Layzell, and the mate was
twenty-five-year-old Albert Edward Layzell, of Brightlingsea,
where the *Ada* was built. A puzzling find near by was a bottle
containing nothing but the barge's bill of lading. It was surmised
that another message had been written, and that in the confusion
the wrong paper was put into the bottle. A close watch was kept
for further evidence, and a sensation was caused by the finding, years
later, of another message in a bottle in Brightlingsea Creek. Despite
the manifest impossibility of it having drifted there, the wretched
relatives could not believe it was a fake until it was proved to be by
the makers of the paper on which it was written, certifying that
such paper was not made at the time of the wreck.[1]

To end on a more cheerful note: the barging story to end all
barging stories is of George Winn, who, when master of the sprittie
Persevere, sailed down Channel to Portland in weather that kept the
boomies weather-bound in Dover harbour. They were still there
when he came back with a load of stone, so out of sheer devilment
he sailed in through the west entrance, right through the middle of
them, and out of the east entrance!

[1] The tale is told in *Stories of the Colne*, by L. Southern (Southern, Brightlingsea).

CONTEMPORARY MODEL OF THE KETCH-BARGE "THE DARNET," BUILT 1873

V

UP FROM THE NORTH

From Tyne and Humber—Wisbech and Wells—Yarmouth,
Southwold, Lowestoft, and the Broads—Suffolk Rivers—
Barges over the Bar

THE best course now is to follow the barges up the East Coast from
the Tyne and Humber to the Thames. To the landsman with his
atlas 'down' may seem more appropriate, but any sailorman knowing the power of the tide flooding and ebbing in and out of the
Thames Estuary will instinctively speak of 'down to the North.'

The Tyne was a regular stamping-ground of the boomies in the
coal trade, and many an old coastal skipper will murmur even to-day:

> First the Dudgeon, then the Spurn:
> Flambro' Head comes next in turn.
> Flambro' Head as you pass by,
> Filey Brigg is drawing nigh.
> Scarbro' Castle stands out to sea,
> And Whitby Light bear Northerly.
> Huntley Foot, that very high land,
> Is five and twenty mile from Sunderland,
> And our Old Man say: "If things go right,
> We'll be in the Tyne by to-morrow night."

This verse ends with the stentorian envoi, "Damn and bugger the
coal trade."

From Tyne to Yarmouth Roads has often been run in twenty-four
hours, and the *Startled Fawn* has travelled from Colne to Tyne in
thirty-six hours.

In the Humber one meets the spritsail barges, for they were
familiar visitors in this the traditional home of the keels, towing
down through the bridges with a load of seed-cake for Wells,
or starting on the long plug south with a bellyful of 'black
diamonds.'

From the Humber to Yarmouth Roads is ninety miles of difficult
water, with few havens, yet in fine weather the little old-time
coasters thought nothing of tackling it with a headwind. They had

one or two factors in their favour. The prevailing westerlies give a weather shore along this coast, and with the commonest wind, the south-westerly, it is possible to fetch, though south of Yarmouth it involves a turn to windward nine trips out of ten. The flood-tide, moreover, serves for more than six hours, since the tide is later the farther south you get, and thus seven hours of favourable tide may often be counted on. Of course, bound the other way the reverse is the case, but the prevailing winds are then favourable, and the craft were often light. The shoal nature of the shore makes it possible to anchor for a foul tide, whereas down Channel it was often neces-sary to keep sailing, and yet lose ground, and the East Coast's off-shore banks make some recompense for their dangerous nature by providing a bit of shelter to ride the ebb with an onshore wind.

Thus the spritties and boomies, along with brigs and billyboys, schooners and ketches, used to work their way. In among the shoals of the Wash you would find them. I have not heard of barges penetrating to Lincoln or Ely, but Wisbech, Boston, and Fosdyke knew them regularly, as did Blakeney and Wells on the Norfolk coast. Indeed, sugar from the beet factories has caused quite a revival of work from Boston and Lynn in recent years, and the Kentish *Thyra* took wheat to Wisbech in 1949, causing so much interest that the skipper had to set his sails lying alongside the quay to show the assembled populace how it was done.

Wells, where the quay now lies deserted year after year, was a meeting-place of billyboys and barges. The former, including *Sylph*, *Abeona*, *Gills*, *Evening Star*, *Welcome Home*, *Providence*, and *Jehovah Jireh*, arrived from Hull with oilcake (which was also brought from St Petersburg, Riga, Danzig, Hamburg, and Bremen in Norwegian, German, Danish, Dutch, and French vessels), while the boomies loaded trees for Gateshead-on-Tyne, returning with household and gas-coal, and also wheat and barley, in which trades some spritties joined. There were brigs, schooners, and ketches in Wells then. The biggest craft built there was the 280-ton brig *Priscilla*, and the last were the schooners *Peggy* and *Gem* (run down off Dover, malt-loaded, seventy years ago). Local craft included the brigs *Abdale*, *Crest of the Wave*, and *Lady Anne*, but by 1890 out-side vessels[1] predominated, bringing in Welsh coal and patent

[1] Mr Walter Gillingham, to whom I am indebted for these memories, recalls the steel three-masted schooners *Annie Park*, *Cymric*, *Patrician*, *Celtic*, *Charles and Ellen*, *Edith Crosfield*, and *Mary Armstead*.

manure, then cleaning and drying their holds and loading malt for
London or Dublin. The malt trade, however, had gone after the
First World War, and steam had captured the other trades, such as
wheat and oilcake, yet one evening in the 1920's four boomie
barges, *Sussex Belle*, *Zenobia*, *Kindly Light*, and *Ethel Edith*, arrived
together with barley from London. *Zenobia* ran a few more oilcake
cargoes from Hull with the spritties *Scone* and *Cabby* and the billyboys *Sarah* and *Mavis*, which took the last cargo under sail. Motor-
craft did a little up to the Second World War, but now the port is
finished.

Yarmouth, however, really marks the boundary of the barges'
acknowledged domain. In the Roads they used to lie rolling for
days and even for weeks on end—and on at least one occasion not so
long ago Captain Mole in the *Alf Everard* left the motor-coasters
wind-bound there, having the tug tow him five miles to windward
for an offing, and then putting that fine mulie at it. And into the
harbour the barges were towed (even occasionally tackling that un-
pleasant entrance under sail), either to load against the quays of
Yarmouth itself, or to tow on across Breydon Water and up the
Yare to Norwich, past the great pumping mills which stood throwing the water from the dykes with sails that now turn no more.
Here they would meet the hollow-lined, clinker-built wherries,
which were so perfectly at home in these miniature fairways, and,
before 1860, the clumsy square-sailed keels, which probably carried
most of the freight, while the nimbler wherries were in demand for
passenger work.

Yarmouth is also a birthplace of barges. The first barge built
there was *Garson*, in 1864, by Mills and Blake. She finished her
days as Erith Y.C. clubhouse. In the same year Beeching built the
Whitwell, and in 1892 J. H. Fellows and Co. built the *Corinthian*,
but their name is chiefly connected with Everard's steel coasters
Greenhithe (1923) and the *Alf*, *Fred*, *Ethel*, and *Will Everard* two or
three years later.[1]

Lowestoft was the gateway for Beccles and the oil-mills by Lake
Lothing. At least two barges, the *Kimberley* and *Phœnician*, were
made to measure for Mutford Lock, the latter cutting it so fine that
her leeboards had to be removed and her wheelgear unshipped to
get the rudder over hard enough to squeeze her in, and her quarters
were rounded to enable the gates to close behind her.

[1] *Ethel Everard* was lost at Dunkirk; *Alf* and *Fred* became motor-barges.

One of the queerest trades was carried on from these fishing ports before the First World War in the export of herrings to Bruges and Ostend in boomies, particularly the *Britannia* and *Lord Nelson*. The fish was shot in from the quay, a liberal sprinkling of salt was added—and then you did your best to snatch a passage while things remained pleasant.

And so southward to Southwold, that prim and pleasant watering place, with near-by Walberswick, now a quiet artists' colony, and Dunwich, which is but a memory, since every stick and stone of that once proud town is long since swallowed by the North Sea. Yet in these towns, declared Tobias Gentleman, in 1610,

> is a very good breed of fishermen, and there are belonging to those three towns of North Sea boats some twenty sails and of Iceland barks some fifty sails which yearly they send for cod and ling to Iceland.

Early in the last century there were, in addition to fishing-boats, nearly forty trading vessels employing over two hundred men belonging to the little port where, to quote an old rhyme,

> Dunwich Soul and Walberswyck
> All go in at a lousy creek.

Captain Robert Pattman, of the *Loch Torridon*, was a Southwold lad who shipped straight from school in the local 'jackass' schooners, the 120-ton *Woodland Lass* and the *Hearts of Oak*, working from Hartlepool with coal. They were so called because they were square rigged forward like a tops'l schooner, but had a ketch's mizzen. The *Hearts of Oak* used to discharge on the open beach at Dunwich in summer between 1860 and 1870, and the *Woodland Lass*, wrecked at Sizewell Sluice in the eighties, is claimed to have been the last of her kind to get up to Blythburgh bridge with timber. It seems quite an adventure now to sail a dinghy as far as that, but between 1761 and 1884 seaborne cargoes penetrated still farther into the heart of Suffolk, right up to Halesworth, where the old quay and lock basin may still be seen. The Wherry Inn in that town records the type of vessel used. The *Star of Halesworth*, under F. Lambert, was the last Broads craft to load from a coaster at Walberswick and journey up the Blyth.

When the jackass schooners were done with it was the barges' turn to dominate the harbour, as they did well into the 1920's, when the *Leading Light* gave the place its last sight of a boomie's proud gear.

For quite a while at this time the boomie *Lord Hartington* and the sprittie *Dover Castle* were running regularly to Walberswick quay with stone. Old Captain Skinner, of Woodbridge, who was master of the *Dover Castle* (his eldest son John had the *Lord Hartington*), had in earlier years made a practice of buying his own coal and bringing it to Southwold, where he sold it round the town out of the barge. Other regular traders were the *Record Reign*, taking trees to Reydon quay half-way up to Blythburgh, and the *Matilda Upton*, in which Bill Leeks of Pin Mill entered one dark night by the ingenious expedient of sending his own boat ashore with his navigation lights to be placed one on each of the unlit pier heads.

Never again will a sprittie top her spreader to prevent it fouling the stout pole mast of the wherry into which she loads. Never again perhaps will a cargo be brought into this little harbour, which men have fought to keep open down the centuries. Happily the "very good breed of fishermen" remains, even though their activities are now confined to little motor-driven longshore boats. I rejoiced in their company in 1947 when enjoying a fortnight's pleasure-cruising in the *Gold Belt*. I doubt if another working barge will grace that scene—which is hard luck on the artists, for a swarm of them established their easels and had half finished their pictures when early one morning we cleared out. I have often wondered how their memories and imaginations served them when it came to completing the details of the departed *Gold Belt's* gear!

The next two Suffolk rivers, the Alde and Deben, were considerable centres of barge traffic, especially as their entrances made them both a nightmare for the deep, unhandy craft which had used them from medieval times. Though it has been shown that Aldeburgh has known barges from earliest days, only two craft were built in the river—the *Alde*, launched by Walter Riggs at Slaughden (just below the present yacht club) in 1882, and employed for most of her life in stone work from Aylesford to the estate at Snape, and Garrett's *Argo*, built on their own premises at Snape in 1858.

Snape, where Garrett's great maltings stand so boldly beside the little humpty-backed bridge, has been the Alde's chief shipping centre since the passing of the days of long ago when carracks sailed from Orford, and Aldeburgh had its fleet of cod-smacks. Garrett's two little steam-barges *Dawn* (converted from a yacht) and *Eaglet* were used for transporting malt to London and bringing barley back. They were of very modest horse-power, and whenever pos-

sible auxiliary sail was set 'to take the weight off the engine.'
Sailing-barges, however, shared in their work. The *Eaglet* and
Dawn would tow them clear of the river, but the sailormen would
generally reward them by showing a clean pair of heels, and reaching
Sea Reach half a tide ahead of them. The maltings also found a
job for the boomies, for the *Empress of India*, *Mystery*, and *Laura*
brought many a freight of Welsh steam-coal all the way from
Saundersfoot, near Cardiff.

Parker's and Wrinch's stackies were to be found in the Alde, as
everywhere—the *Bluebell* had her rudder taken off by ice one winter
at Orford—and for a short time sand was worked off Havergate
Island. It was not uncommon to see two spritties at Orford quay
and a third lying off in the river waiting her turn, while at Aldeburgh the brickworks employed many a craft, though they owned
none of their own. These bricks were loaded by the last boomie
seen in the river—the *Lord Hartington*—during the 1920's. About
ten years later the *Una* and *Beatrice Maud* were the last spritties to
visit Snape. The final few miles of narrow channel winding through
deceptive mud-flats were always a problem, especially as a loaded
barge needed spring tides; and even in the later days when a motor-
boat was available it was not powerful enough to tow to windward,
but could only help by shoving a barge's head round. Those cheery
friends of Aldeburgh yachtsmen, Jumbo Ward and Jerry Wood,
did a lot of this work, while George Brinkley, of Orford, looked
after the lower reaches. On this last occasion of all, having got the
Una successfully away, they were nearly in trouble with the bigger
and less handy *Beatrice Maud*, which made a determined effort to
nip the boat against the shore, and when they foiled her there
succeeded in ramming the wall with such force that for an awful
moment they were convinced she was going right through it.

Mason's cement fleet at Waldringfield were probably the best-
known craft on the Deben, comprising the *Orinoco* and the Maldon-
registered *Excelsior*, which went to Cranfield's, of Ipswich, taking
their tops'l mark of the white ball with them; *Elsie Bertha*, which
was run down and sunk in the Swin; *Grace*, *Jumbo*, and *Augusta*.
Arthur Catchpole, of the *Elsie Bertha*, would have nothing to do
with the orthodox seaman's cheese-cutter cap and blue jersey, but
was always immaculate in hard felt hat and white collar and cuffs.
With his well-cut beard he looked more like a doctor than a barge
skipper—but to barge-mates he was always just plain "Skatty."

Mason's also owned the little *Kingfisher*, which brought mud up the river to their works. Haste's *Freston Tower* took the last 110 tons of Mason's cement away about 1910, loading with it the dismantled machinery. The *Deben*, which served Woodbridge as passage hoy, was also, as her name suggests, a locally owned craft. She was a round-sterned barge, steered sometimes with a tiller, sometimes with a wheel, sailed and partly owned by Frederick Read. The other owner was John Baker, of Ipswich, a retired shipowner. Later she passed to Paul's at Ipswich, where she was built in 1874. Another Deben barge was the *Lady Ellen*, owned and sailed by Arthur Read. She finished her career as a house-barge at Pin Mill in which lived "Maid" Ward, the well-known crippled ferryman who used to tend the L.N.E.R. steamers *Norfolk*, *Suffolk*, and *Essex*, which plied between Ipswich, Harwich, and Felixstowe.

An almost forgotten Deben freight was coprolite, the Suffolk red crag full of fossilized animal bones, vast quantities of which were shipped to Fison's, of Ipswich, for grinding into fertilizer. A cottager could sometimes dig £20 worth from his garden, and in 1877 10,000 tons were dispatched all over the United Kingdom from the quays of the Deben and Orwell. The pits closed in 1893.

The maltings at Melton and the old Woodbridge tide mill were constantly served by barges, and Parker's craft also did a lot of work on this river. Jack Spitty worked here continuously for a year just after the First World War in the *Lord Warden*, taking a good deal of tarmac to Wilford. Edward Haste, of Ipswich, who started his barging in the family *Haste Away*, was mate of the little *Cygnet* in 1888, in his teens, and went on to command Cranfield's *May* for twenty-one years, and after that the *Beric*, recalls that Harte's Dock, just above the mill, was the boomies' favourite place for discharging coal and loading trees. Trees were also loaded by crane at the ferry dock, and were a regular return freight for the coal boomie *Reindeer*. *Eastern Belle* and *Sussex Belle* loaded ballast back, a poor freight, but reckoned "just enough to fill the grub locker." *Empress of India* and *Masonic* are other boomies remembered at Woodbridge.

Hay was loaded at Ramsholt quay by Wrinch's, and a few freights were taken to Woodbridge during the First World War for the Army. Road materials were taken to the East Suffolk County Council yard up by Wilford Bridge, and even one or two boomies managed this long poke inland, for which one had to wait for spring tides, as there was only water to Melton on neaps. The old

Ipswich *Nautilus*, caught trying to chance it, sat on a pile which came through the bottom. The shipwright sawed it off in order to get a patch on. He handed the piece to the skipper with the comment "You'd better keep that. It's the soundest bit of wood in her." *Sara* and *Agincourt*, a Kentish stumpie trading coastwise and regularly reported anywhere between Lynn and Plymouth as a tops'l barge in trouble with a broken topmast, regularly used to trade with wheat, but barges in the Deben were sufficiently scarce for the millers to be always eager to fix a freight away.

The Newsons have for two generations been pilots at Bawdsey, at the mouth of the Deben, and there were formerly two pilot-hufflers at Waldringfield for the tortuous upper reaches, Ted Marsh and Nelson Oxborrow. They certainly earned their modest charges. Sailing through the difficult entrances of the Deben and Alde, in particular, must have given many a sailorman an anxious moment, especially as before the days of motor-boats the pilot could not get out if wind and tide were in, but anchored his boat in the channel and waved a flag towards the direction the barge was to steer. If the wind was 'out' the barge was thrown head to wind and washed in on the racing tide; there was no room to turn. Though some of the bargemen came to know these entrances well enough to do without a pilot, most of them paid him nevertheless on the principle that "We pay you to be there in case we may want you"—an attitude some yachtsmen might imitate.

Jack Spitty told me of one nasty morning when he arrived off Shingle Street in the *Victa* in company with two other barges, stone-laden from the East Swale. The smother of white breakers on the bar looked so appalling that none of them felt like being the first to have a go. The *Victa*, a good seaboat like so many 'rose-upons,' lay hove-to pretty quietly, but the others had to keep sailing about, and one had two men at the wheel to steer her. At last he decided there must be water enough, and, letting draw, tore in, the other two at his heels. On another occasion Spitty loaded a freight of sand from the Horse, inside Bawdsey Haven, which Neil's, of Wandsworth, called the best sand they ever had. But it took six tides to load, since the Horse does not come adry on neaps, and it was not worth all the trouble.

A commoner freight was shingle from the bar, where the banks are so high and steep that the shingle was run *down* a plank in a barrow into the barge. The last of the Deben barges, *Tuesday* (survivor of a Kentish fleet named after the days of the week), kept it up till shortly before the Second World War. Old Captain Skinner, who in earlier days had a share with Cox, the coal-merchant, in the local boomie *Lord Alcester* (built at Littlehampton), carried many a freight for Woodbridge bypass road in the *Tuesday* at cut rates in competition with the motor-barge *Justice*—and was never paid for it. At the last she was left driving up and down, with hardly a bit of sail left. One day they found her old skipper lying dead in her cabin. So ended barging on the Deben.

OFF FLAMBORO' HEAD

VI

THE PROUD LADIES OF IPSWICH

Grain-ships for Grandeur—Short Spindles and Long Spindles—
Mulies—A French Experiment—Shipyards of To-day and
Yesterday—Cow-dung and Horsehair

HARWICH is the one great natural harbour on the East Coast, and since the Orwell has always been the one river in Essex and Suffolk with ample water (thanks partly to nature and partly to far-seeing harbour commissioners), Ipswich has for centuries occupied a privileged position in the coastal trade.

Defoe, describing a visit over two hundred years ago,[1] waxed enthusiastic over

the greatest town in *England* for large colliers or coal ships employed between *Newcastle* and *London.* . . . They built also there so prodigious strong, that it was an ordinary thing for an *Ipswich* collier, if no disaster happened to him, to reign (as the seamen call it) forty or fifty years and more. . . .

There were, as they then told me, above one hundred sail of them belonging to the town at one time, the least of which carried fifteen score, as they compute it, that is, 300 chaldrons of coals, this was about the year 1668 (when I first knew the place). . . .

The loss or decay of this trade accounts for the present pretended decay of the town of *Ipswich*; the ships wore out, the masters died off, the trade took a new turn; Dutch fly boats taken in the war and made free ships by Act of Parliament thrust themselves into the coal trade in the interests of the captors, such as the *Yarmouth* and *London* merchants, and others, and the *Ipswich* men dropped gradually out of it, being discouraged by those Dutch fly boats; these Dutch vessels, which cost nothing but their capture, were bought cheap, carried great burthens, and the Ipswich building fell off for want of price, and so the trade decayed and the town with it.

There is an ominous hint of days to come in all this, for two centuries later Ipswich barges held almost as proud a position as had the colliers before them, and again the Dutchmen (subsidized this

[1] *A Tour through Great Britain.*

time, not captured) carried great burthens, discouraged them, and, as the masters died off and trade took a new turn, the building fell off for want of price—though luckily modern Ipswich has sufficient other irons in the fire to avert decay.

To this day, however, Ipswich-owned barges remain, for style and seaworthiness, the pick of them all. They do not need the shallow, beamy hulls favoured by Colchester and Maldon, because they have not to squeeze under bridges into shallow mud berths, and stack work is beneath their dignity. But they have to tackle the Swin and the Wallet—or often nowadays with the Old Spitway such a death-trap, the Barrow Deep and East Swin—every trip, and that calls for a sea-kindly hull, able to get along. Because this is a deep-water harbour, there are no quaint tales of hovellers to interest us, and the passage work was years ago taken from sail by Paul's steamers. Ipswich gasworks and power-station are grown-up affairs, attended to by deep-sea colliers, though Harwich still accepts a few hundred tons of 'black diamonds' at a time from the sailormen.

But, in ample compensation, this continues to be the home of the coasters. Down in Harwich harbour they lie to their anchors in the tideway, with feathers still ruffled. Jibs are hitched out along bow-sprits, topsail sheets are pulled out as the outward-bounders shelter under the Stone Heaps, or in fine weather feel the eternal swell of the Rolling Grounds, eager to carry the ebb beyond the Naze and be up to the Spitway or round the North-east Gunfleet by low water. The new arrivals, deep with wheat for Cranfield's, potash for Fison's, loam for the foundries, middlings, maize, or cattle-food, await slack water as near the breakwater as a westerly breeze will take them over the ebb, or proudly carry a southerly up to Pin Mill, where their grandeur dwarfs into untidy insignificance the motley fleet of pleasure craft.

Once into Ipswich docks they preen themselves till the veriest landlubber must pause to stare in wonder and admiration. Elsewhere the ebb tide deposits the grandest ship upon the friendly but undignified mud; here Cranfield's showy streamers, and Paul's smaller bobs, both scarlet, carrying respectively a C and an X, are reflected high water or low in the unruffled mirror of the big tideless lake. No wonder the Ipswich-men with their well-found craft take a special pride in the stow of a staysail, the gleam of a varnished hatch, the glitter of a polished binnacle.

It was not always thus. Up to a century ago the Gipping ran down under Stroke Bridge to become the Orwell, filling and emptying with the tide as do Blackwater, Stour, and Colne. Then a new cut was made, down which the tidal stream to-day runs, and the present docks were dug from the marshy saltings on the old river's banks.

Stoke Bridge remains a front door into fairyland for the ship-lover. I walked round the docks on one of those still, solemn November afternoons when the weak light and first hint of evening mist make the scene seem like some dream survival of another age. Over the bridge ran the noisy buses and silent trolley-cars which swoop through the narrow streets of this town. Above it, where is now Kenney's builder's yard, I saw the site of a long-forgotten yard where Mason's spritties *Augusta* and *Grace* were the last built, in 1874. But according to local tradition the earliest Ipswich barges of all were the booms'l rigged *Primus*, *Secundus*, etc. (numbering up to *Octavius*!), built over a century ago by one Colchester.

Hard by the bridge Cranfield's mill barges clustered, by general consent the smartest craft on the coast. A few hundred yards farther, beyond the Customs House, whose columns lend character to the scene, a mixed batch of craft lay unloading middlings, and opposite was many a fine 'furriner,' Sully's *Hydrogen*, the London and Rochester Trading Company's *Pudge*, Horlock's *Repertor*, Everard's *Lady Mary*. Paul's *Lady Jean* and *Lady Daphne* (which in 1928 sailed herself right into Crow Sound in the Scillies, after her crew had been taken out of her by a lifeboat off the Lizard) lorded it along the quay, their foredecks sheering almost precipitously up to their coaster windlasses. Almost all were flush-decked craft; some 'short-spindles,' some 'long spindles,' as the bargemen differentiate between those with wheels abaft the cabin skylight and those steering from the more conventional position by the main horse.

Several of these craft were auxiliaries, but it was heartening to see the number of new white sails awaiting their first dressing, even on craft where the mizzen was replaced by wheelhouse and exhaust-pipe. I do not admire the bobtailed effect which seems to be thought natural for an auxiliary barge, nor the shapeless square wheelhouses which are preferred to the whaleback shape that looks so much more in keeping, and the mizzen is a real loss. The auxiliary *P.A.M.*, for instance, has to drop her foresail altogether to turn up the Medway, and in a hard breeze she sails with the helm hard down, which does no one any good. However, I consoled myself with the reflection that even in the great days of sail no better cared-for collection of craft can ever have been gathered together.

As if to accentuate the lordliness of the assembled company, two of Piper's cockneys, *Fortis* and *Brian Boru*, lay cheekily in their midst. Half unloaded, their battered hulls lay listing, showing the ballast-men's rubbing-bands on their blunt bows. One had left her topsail sheet pulled out, and they made the quaintest contrast with their neighbours, *Spinaway C.*, *Petrel*, and *Gladys*, which lay moored abreast like a trio of guardsmen, stems level to an inch, each sail a perfect stow, each spar new varnished, each hull fresh painted and splendid with gilded scroll-work on the carved sterns.

Yet looks are not everything. Stepping aboard the *Brian Boru*, I heard from her young skipper that for all her rough gear, with the iron bolt-heads sticking out of worn cleat and rail, for all her squat profile, for all her decks sheathed with short thwartship lengths, for all her primitive chain-and-barrel steering, innocent even of a wheelbox, he wanted no stiffer, handier, abler craft. Her rough work with the P.L.A. dredger[1] would soon knock the shine off the grain-ships' flaring ends and smooth sides. And did not the *Fortis* have her never-to-be-forgotten day when she not only won the staysail class in the Thames race, but led the whole fleet home, bowsprit-men and coasters too—the only staysail barge ever to do so?

But to resume our tour. Away on the other side of the dock one could see the site of St Peter's shipyard, where the first Ipswich boomie, *Lothair*, was built in 1872 by Robertson, who came from Woodbridge. Robertson built those first boomies big, for *Lothair* was 101 feet, his *Alice Watts*, so well remembered at Colchester, was 100 feet, and his *Lucy Richmond* 106 feet.

Down towards the lock is the shipyard where Robert Peck built the boomies *Ethel Edith* (88 feet), running till 1927 and now lying hulked at Pin Mill, *Ivy P.*, and *Flower of Essex*. The *Ivy P.* finished her days trading in the Irish Sea. In December 1936 or 1937 she was in distress in Wicklow Bay. The Wicklow lifeboat took the crew out, but some Ramsgate fishermen from a trawler sheltering in the harbour went out and sailed the barge in, earning themselves a nice Christmas salvage.

In 1896 Horace Shrubsall followed Peck, to make this the most

[1] See Chapter XIV.

The Little Ports (11)

ABOVE: One of Wakeley's at St Osyth. LEFT: *Lancashire* ('Tubby Blake's yacht') at the Strood, Mersea. BELOW: The spritties *Juniper*, *Unique*, *Gazelle*, *Gascoign*, and *Duke of Kent* at Shuttlewood's, Paglesham, about 1929

Contrast in Ends

The massive bow and stern of *Will Everard* (LEFT) and (BELOW) the fine head and cut-away quarters of *Mirosa* (a typical example of the work of Howard of Maldon)

BELOW: *Ethel Maud* (here seen acting as Committee Boat at West Mersea regatta) is another product of Howard's yard

ABOVE: *Alice May* (now a yacht) is a fine example of a wooden coaster

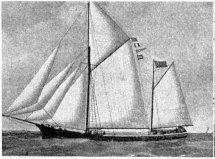

Harold, noted for her handiness
(See Chapter VIII.)

Genesta, a beautiful little ship, which was
kept up like a yacht (See Chapter VIII.)

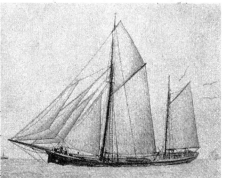

Matilda Upton under reefed canvas

Pearl, showing the curious old-fashioned
way of setting the flying jib with halyard
to mainmast to ease strain on topmast
(See Chapter VI.)

ABOVE: *Genesta* in the great gale of 1891.
(See Chapter IV.) RIGHT: *James Bowles* under
squaresail (See Chapter XI.)

RIGHT: *Eliza H* under
reefed canvas

ABOVE: Schooner
Friendship, owned at
Burnham, but trading
mostly to Rye

81

RIGHT: *James Bowles*,
Tollesbury 'schoolship'
and local collier

RIGHT: *Ida*, showing
square topsail and
mizzen staysail

ABOVE: *Alice Watts*, for forty years
a collier to Colchester gas-works

RIGHT: *Flower of Essex*, a beautiful
little tiller-steered Apollinaris
trader. She was originally dandy-
rigged, and finished as a sprittie

prolific shipyard of all, with four barges building at the same time and fifteen shipwrights employed. From his ways came *Violet* (not to be confused with the Maldon craft of the same name), *Lloyds* (a paper-carrier), *Rowland*, *Ethel Ada* (the vessel now working from Colchester, not to be confused with the *Ethel Ada* launched the same week by Shuttlewood, of Paglesham), *Violet Sybil* and *Nellie Parker*, those two well-known Bradwell-men, *Klondyke*, whose coasting exploits have been mentioned in Chapter V, *Augustus*, *Anglia* (George Ventris's old ship, now with Paul's), *Challenge* (a big mulie built for the stone trade, and one of the Weymouth barges), *Venture* (still with Cranfield's), and *Teaser* (working with Cunis in 1933).

In 1901 Shrubsall, who also had a yard at Limehouse, moved from Ipswich to Greenwich, where he is remembered for the racers *Verona*, *Veronica*, and *Varuna*,[1] and R. and W. Paul, Ltd, took over the yard. This firm, old-established Ipswich shipowners of square riggers and latter-day steamers as well as of barges, here built the *Marjorie*, *Audrey*, *Doris*, and *Jock* (1908). This was the last new building in the yard, but in 1912 the *Robert Powell*, which had washed up on the beach running for Newhaven stone-laden, was brought here and rebuilt as the *Wolsey*.

Paul's *Gravelines* was originally the *Hilda*, but was sold to the French port and renamed. Three barges (*Gravelines I, II,* and *III*) recall the Frenchmen's experiment with spritties, which was apparently short-lived, for *Hilda* was soon back in her old home, retaining her new name. These fine craft are a far cry from *Julia*, *Princess*, and *Ann*, which are the oldest Paul barges remembered. The firm also owned boomies. Harry Stone had their *Ida*; but he was fond of going places, and the owners liked to have a sight of their ship, so they parted company, Harry taking the *Moss Rose*.

Below the dock gates lies the most famous of all the Ipswich yards, St Clement's shipyard, where ships have been built all down the centuries; as one would expect, for here is a natural site, the slipways giving on to deep water. First of the barge-builders was W. Bayley, who, in addition to owning nearly a hundred craft, built many. The last round-bottom ship to be built in Ipswich, the brigantine *Clementine*, was launched here as late as 1885. She had been preceded by the boomies *Park End* (103 feet), *Moss Rose* (94 feet), and *Blanche*, and was followed by the *Zenobia* (85 feet) and *Alert* (85 feet).

[1] See Chapter XVI.

F

W. J. Curtis also occupied the yard, building the boomies *Mystery* (90 feet), *Reindeer* (97 feet), and *Unity* (85 feet), whose hulk, long used as a timber lighter at Heybridge, is now at West Mersea. After Curtis came Orvis and Fuller, builders of the boomies *Matilda Upton* (86 feet, later converted to spritsail rig) and *Pearl* (85 feet, last of the Ipswich boomies), and many spritties, including *Petrel*, *Spinaway C.* (still with Cranfield's), *Reliance* (for F. W. Horlock and Co., Ltd), *Coronation* (now a London and Rochester Trading Company motor-barge), *Vigilant* (which went to Horatio Horlock, later becoming a yacht, and now a motor-barge), and *Ardwina*, the last barge built at Ipswich.

With Mr R. P. Orvis, whose grandfather was the first of his name here, I looked out down the tideway from this ancient shipyard. Lower down, by the Cliff Brewery (which once had its own barge, the *Cliff*), was the lower yard, also worked by Bayley and Orvis, from whom Dan Marine took over. After Bayley's day, but before that of Orvis, the yard was worked by G. P. Gildea and Co., builders of the boomies *Lord Hartington* (85 feet, and still registered with Sankey and Sons in 1927), *Lord Shaftesbury* (84 feet, with Walker and Howard in 1927), *Lord Iddesleigh*, *Southern Belle* (85 feet, for Walker and Howard, but with Paul's in 1927), and *Hilda* (83 feet), built in 1895 for her skipper-owner, C. King, who sold her to Paul's on his retirement. She was ultimately run down and sunk in the Lower Hope.

All bar Paul's and Orvis' yards have long been closed, but on the old St Clement's slip, blocked high off the ground, lay the *Kimberley*. Watching the shipwrights adzing under her bottom— red-painted, like all of Cranfield's—fitting a new piece in her sheer-strake, and offering up a massive new stemhead, I heard something of the old days when the Ship Launch Inn was open for coffee at 5 A.M. and for beer at 6 A.M. Of the old shipwrights it was said that a man could take a thin shaving from end to end of a sixty-foot spar in one piece. Mr Orvis recalled a barge picking up a tree in London for thirty shillings to be shaped up into a complete sprit for £7. From old Tom Simmons, a Maldoner whose Essex speech had lost nothing of its edge from a mere fifty years' living and working in Ipswich, I heard of billyboys of long ago, the *Jehovah Jireh* and *Sarah*, and the latter-day steel-built *Halcyon* and *Mavis*, which could actually outsail the barges; of pitch-pine being rafted up from Groom's, at Harwich, and hardwood laid out in the Knolls, where

Ransome's now have their plough yard; of the days when four sawyers in two pits supplied the yard's cut timber; when twelve-hour days were accepted, and a man might walk ten miles to work; but when old Mr Orvis would toss half a crown into a sail that was being dressed and it would buy drinks all round.

"Of course, that wasn't six till six in our time," one old-timer gravely assured me. "When I started here fifty years ago we began at six and finished at five." So much for the folly of romanticizing

ST CLEMENT'S SHIPYARD, IPSWICH

the good old days, though, in fairness to the ship-builders, they profited little by these conditions, for you will seldom find a barge-builder who made a fortune unless he was owner as well.

Orvis' craft were built single-skin and rabbeted, the firm having an immense steam-chest to enable such massive planks to be bent. Cann's, of Harwich, preferred two-skin construction,[1] the outer

---

[1] Not to be confused with the 'doubling' of old barges to give them a new lease of life. A two-skin barge when doubled is thus actually three skins thick—and when they rebuilt the old Ipswich *Sextus* it is said they found seven layers!

skin being oak and the inner pine. In each case the water was
kept out by tar and hair inserted either into the rabbet, or between
the skins. In the real old-timers they used cow-dung. In addition
to being builders, Orvis' owned the *Eliza Patience*, and had part
shares in the *Rosebud* and the boomie *Pearl*. Some of their craft were
built to order and some as a speculation, and, like Howard, of
Maldon (who built the *Emma* from the left-overs of the *Record
Reign*), they sometimes laid down a little one from the pieces over
from a bigger craft. Their *Tit-bits* (now a house-boat in Bradwell
Creek) betrays her origin by her name. *Hector* and *Sophia* were
other Orvis miniatures of this type.

As I left the yard, picturesque like all such places with its clutter
of old gear and sails, the ebbing tide below the slip was revealing
the sunken wreck of Cranfield's *Excelsior*, bombed at the mill during
the War. Near by lay the *Emily*, a stand-by barge for lightering,
her upper-works painted utility grey in contrast to the show of
colour and varnish on the fully commissioned barges. She looked
forlorn and rather pathetic, as if she was surprised that her shapely
hull should lie neglected, and I thought how much she and I would
enjoy it if I could have set her topsail and taken the ebb-tide away
down to Pin Mill. What yachts these Ipswich-men would make,
with their deep holds and shapely ends!

Paul's and Cranfield's are now the only barge-owners at Ipswich,
but there were formerly several other fleets. Packard's (now
associated with Fison's, the chemical fertilizer makers) had the *Fossil*,
Nautilus, and *Ammonite*. About 1876 Thomas Haste had the *Robert
and Thomas*, then, in succession, *Haste Away*, *Freston Tower*, *May*,
Kimberley, and *Memory*, which is now working for Christopherson's.
Watkins, with his cement-works at Stoke, had the *Eldred Watkins*,
Novator, *Ethel Ada*, and a part share in the *General Jackson*; while
the *Felix* was Felixstowe-owned.

These barges engaged in trades which have disappeared from the
Orwell, bringing coals to Ostrich Bay and the districts of Halifax
and Nova Scotia, where East Indiamen were built; to the old
landing-places of Sloppy Lane Hard, Freston Hard, and Cathouse
Quay; to Pin Mill, where Webb, the shipwright, works on the
barges on the hard; picking up a stack and a few tons of carrots or
mangolds from a farm on the banks of this beautiful river, or collecting a freight of bricks from Pattrick's works behind Harwich
harbour, which it is now time we visited.

HARWICH BUILDERS AND OWNERS

*Vaux, McLearon, Cann, and Norman—Fleet that recorded a
Career — One-inch Freeboard, for Safety! — Colchester's
Colliers—187 Barges in one Club*

EVEN their rivals will be prepared to admit that the Harwich-built
barges have always been the most admired of all. The Harwich
model was the sea-going shape *par excellence*; Harwich construction
something to swear by. Even the Kentish men say "go to Harwich
for building a barge"—though they add (which Essex and Suffolk
men hotly contest) "and to Sittingbourne for a suit of sails."

The ancient Harwich naval shipyard, just on the seaward side of
the town pier, where ships of the line had been built down the ages,
went in for barges in the days of Vaux, father and son, who were
followed by McLearon, again for two generations. Here were built
many fine boomies, of which one of the first was the schooner[1]
Stour—an unusual development of the barge, also represented in the
three-masted Kentish-built *Friendship* and *Emily Smeed*. The Mistley
spritties *Remercie* and *Redoubtable* were also products of this yard.
Most of these craft were by Vaux, for McLearon's ownership started
in 1895 and lasted till 1927.

But the finest barge-builders of all time were J. and H. Cann,
whose yard was near the gasworks, in the creek away behind the
present train-ferry pier. While Cann's built at least two boomies—
the *Carisbrooke Castle* (86 feet) for Walker and Howard, and the
Mazeppa (88 feet), which after being Harwich-owned was registered
with Ward, of Ipswich, in 1921—this firm's most characteristic
product was a powerful sprittie, a long succession of which went
down the ways between 1877, when the *Florence* (whose hulk is

---

[1] Ketches included *Trim* (95 feet, 1881, lost in 1907), *Gloriana* (101 feet, 1871), *Hesper* (124
feet, 1879), *Ada Gane* (106 feet, 1882), *Alcyone* (95 feet, 1884), *Genesta* (1886), *Britannia* (86
feet, 1893, converted to half-sprit rig, lost off Gorleston, Suffolk, 1929), *Dunkerque* (86 feet,
1894), *Alice May* (1899), *Dannebrog* (1901), *Ena* and *Thalatta* (all four last-named were converted to spritsail rig, and are still at Ipswich), and *Major* (1897).

now the club-house of Pin Mill Sailing Club) was launched, and 1914, when Marriage's *Leofleda* was the last of her line. The names of some of the best are recalled in the local tag, 'The *Kimberley May Haste Away*, and bring back the *Memory* of *Freston Tower*.'[1] Old Mr Cann, father of John and Herbert, founded the firm as Parsons and Cann after an apprenticeship at Brightlingsea, but he was killed in 1889 when he was crushed by some timber which was being un-loaded from a railway truck. There were two barges on the ways at the time, which his sons took over, John being the shipwright and Herbert the business manager. The secret of the quality of their craft seems to have been the extreme conscientiousness of their characters. Stories illustrating this are legion. The *Orion* (now *Gold Belt*) was once having a pitch-pine keelson put in, when John Cann found a tiny spot of sap in it. The owners were satisfied, but he insisted on scrapping it, and it was cut into planks for a new sealing which she still has. A Leigh bawley was built of elm which proved faulty. The fisherman sent a bit of her bottom back to Cann in a match-box, and was told to return the boat to Harwich, where she was replanked with oak, the result being—since virtue is sometimes rewarded—orders for several more of her kind.

Cann's barges were built from half-models. John would bring his latest design to Herbert for an opinion. After it was approved he would still see new improvements. "I'll have a bit off here," he would say. "She looks a bit thick there." Thus do masterpieces evolve. At least one of his barges was built with an inch or two of curve in her keelson, not with a view to retaining this shape as in the racer *Sara*, for this was ruinous to a loaded barge in a hard berth, but so that the keel might be left true and straight by the inevitable hogging which every sailing-craft experiences. Very few barges were built from lines, exceptions being the *Lady Jean* and *Lady Daphne* (by Short's of Rochester), Everard's Yarmouth 'ironpots,' and Stone's Brightlingsea craft.

The brothers' first job on starting a barge was to cut out the deck-planking (Oregon pine or pitch-pine, though the latter was regarded as rather slippery). As the deck went on last, the timber for this all-important part was well seasoned when wanted. But all the firm's

[1] The list, as near as Mr H. Cann could reconstruct it in 1948, was *Florence* (1877), *Muriel* and *Eureka* (1880), *Una* (1882), *Glen Rosa* (1884), *Haste Away* (1886), *Irex*, *Freston Tower*, and *Dorothy* (1889), *May* and *Mistley* (1891), *Susan* (1892), *Felix* (1893), *Ethel* (1894), *Centaur* and *Kitty* (1895), *Beric* (1896), *Edme* (1898), *Marjorie* (1899), *Kimberley* (1900), *Gladys* (1901), *Resolute* (1903), *Memory* (1904), *Edith May* (1906), and *Leofleda* (1914).

timber was kept carefully stacked for this purpose. When the bottom joints were butted a saw-cut was made along the join to ensure a perfect fit, and after the edges had been dressed with tar and hair the work was pulled together with chains, cramps, and wedges. On a warm, sunny day the wedges were knocked finally home, and the squeezed-out tarred hair adzed away.

Most of the Cann barges were built in winter, to keep their hands employed, and it was a commonplace to build barges as a speculation. McLearon's *Thalatta* and *Ena*, in 1906, failed to find a buyer till they were as black as tar; then Paul's summoned up the courage to take the *Ena*, and *Thalatta* promptly found a Harwich purchaser in Groom.

Many of the earlier Cann craft were ordered "hull, spars, and blocks" (including the *Felix* for Smith, of Felixstowe, at £1050), the sails often being ordered at Brightlingsea, but later the brothers insisted on delivering their barges "fitted out to the knives and forks." Pennick made the sails in the loft in Cann's yard.

Farther up the harbour Norman and Sons built, in 1873, the *John Wesley*, of 184 tons registered, the biggest boomie ever launched at Harwich, which ended her days as Sully's hulk *Crowpill* at Bridgwater. Norman also built at least one sprittie, the little 23-ton *Muriel*, for Groom and Sons, best known among the owners of the 'seeking' fleets of which Harwich was the home.

John Turner Groom and his wife Lydia were the early registered owners of the Groom barges, followed by their sons William and James Robert. William Groom ensured he should not be forgotten on the waterside by recording his own career in the names of his craft. The *Justice* marked his elevation to one bench, the *Alderman* to another; the *Major* celebrated his attainment of that dizzy rank in the volunteers; the Sandwich-built *Mayor* the ultimate honour of his year as chief citizen of Harwich; *Dannebrog*, the Danish honour as Knight of the Dannebrog, for he had consular connexions with that country, as the *Consul* reminds us. It sounds a bit vainglorious to-day, but doubtless seemed rather less immodest in those days of sturdy individualism.

Groom's also had the *Beric* (named after a cousin), the *Laura*, and the *Hand of Providence*, a Maldon-registered barge dating back to 1826, and in early days were for a time owners of the *Arnold Hirst*[1] and the billyboy *Opal*, not to be confused with a Harwich sprittie

[1] See Chapter XII.

of the same name. One of their smallest barges was the little *Fairy* of 25 tons register, their largest *James*, of 59 tons register, which caught fire and was sunk by soldiers from Landguard Fort. Dr J. L. Groom, of Woodbridge, still has the letter in which William Groom claimed for damage, and the military counter-claimed for the cost of powder and shot.

After William Groom's death the barges began to be sold off about 1912, when there was a slump. Some were actually scuttled off Patrick's Wharf to strengthen the sea-wall, and in 1918 only seven were left. These were sold in 1924 to the London and Rochester Trading Company. *New Trader, Aline, Eastwood,* and the old *Sextus*, built at Ipswich in 1849, had been used for shipping ballast from Landguard to the timber schooners discharging in the harbour. One day one sank, and from then on a freeboard of one inch was insisted on! The Rochester firm had to take them to secure the vastly superior *Alderman* and *Mayor*. They were soon broken up, but the *Mayor* is still at work, having in 1948 undergone a complete refit, including the installation of an auxiliary, and *Alderman* was lost in the Second World War on Government service in the Clyde. (Her origin, by the way, was less grand than her name; for Groom sent a barge-load of timber to Shrubsall for her building during a slack time at the Greenwich yard.)

Lothair, built for John Watts, of Harwich, in 1872 (and named, no doubt, after the hero of Disraeli's novel published two years before), was the centre of a minor *Marie Celeste* mystery when, after a gale in November 1880, she was found abandoned off King's Lynn with only a dog and a man's hat aboard. Whether the crew were washed out of her, or whether they took to the boat, was never determined. She survived the First World War and was ultimately lost on the St Andrew shingle bank off Harwich, stone-laden, the skipper mistaking his buoys entering the harbour.

Her sister-ship was the *Alice Watts*, named after the owner's daughter, and complete with a figurehead strikingly resembling her, even to the curly black hair. This figurehead was later removed and presented to Colchester gasworks, where it was set up in the yard, but, alas, it had to be removed because it frightened the horses and dogs!

For forty years the *Alice Watts* slogged up and down the coast between Colchester and Newcastle, carrying tens of thousands of tons of coal to the gasworks, and doing the round trip in a week at least once. Her skipper, James Meachen, in due course acquired her from Watts. He was a member of one of the most famous of all boomie-barging families, for his son, James Arthur Meachen, was skipper of the *Startled Fawn* (lost in the London River in the 1920's) and his nephew, Herbert, had the *Gloriana*, all three very well known in the Colchester gasworks trade; indeed, in 1893, Mr J. S. Pike, the gasworks manager, is shown as managing owner of the *Startled Fawn* and the *Hesper*, which was sailed by a stone-deaf skipper, Ralph Hatcher. James's father, Joseph Meachen, had the *John Watts*; another son, Arthur James Meachen, was in the Mistley-owned *Garson*; and yet another Meachen, Ruderham, was skipper of the *Brightlingsea*, which was taken over by his son, W. B. Meachen, when he transferred to the *Active*, in which the mate was his nephew, G. W. Mynheer, who later had the Ipswich *Eliza Patience* and *Pearl*, which he owned.[1]

Among the other chief Harwich owners T. Middleton, the ship-chandler (whose eighty-year-old son still keeps open the old shop in King's Quay Street, recalling the days when every breeze of wind brought him more trade in a day than now comes his way in a month), had the boomies *Carlbury*, *Gloriana* (lost in 1882), *Mizpah*, *Valonia*, *Laura*, and *Dorothea*. The Vaux-built *Mary Lyne* was owned jointly by Middleton, Fulcher (whose wife's maiden name she bore), and her skipper, Captain Redwood, who went down in her when she was lost in 1882. The boomie *Sunbeam* was sailed and owned by W. T. Whitmore, of Harwich.[2] She was in her day the most expensively built barge afloat, and was not many months old when she was sunk and completely wrecked off the Spurn lightship near the mouth of the Humber. The Whitmore brothers, Holmes,[3] John Wells,[4] and Robert Lewis (a half-brother of Lewis, of Wood-bridge),[5] were other Harwich owners. Gane had the *Elsie Owen* and the *Ada Gane* (later the *Askoy*, and later still the *Leigh Hall*, and one of the few boomies to be converted to a yacht), Mann owned the Vaux schooner-barge *Jubilee*, trading often from the Tyne to Poole, thence to Antwerp, and back to the Tyne.

Round at the back of Harwich, in Dovercourt, John Pattrick's

---

[1] For disentangling this remarkable family's commands I am indebted to Dr J. L. Groom.
[2] The Whitmore brothers also owned the *Fearless*, *Flower of Essex*, *Glen Rosa*, *Justice*, *Edith Mary*, *Gladys*, *Hesper*, *Princess May*, *Tintara*, *Teresa*, *Una*, *Florence*, and *Dunkerque*, and a share with Rands, of Ipswich, in the Brightlingsea-built *Harwich* and *Dovercourt*.
[3] *Gladys*, *Ethel*, and a share in the *Genesta*.
[4] Part of the boomie *Mazeppa*.   [5] *Irex* and part of the *May*.

brickworks maintained four craft, including *Onward* and the little *Alice*, of 22 tons register, specially built to load the mud on which she sat. These craft were sometimes employed carrying the septaria, or cement-stone, from the heaps in Harwich harbour to Pattrick's works.

But to enumerate all the Harwich owners would be impossible, for in 1910 the Harwich Barge Alliance Insurance Association numbered on its books 83 A-class vessels and 104 B-class, though included in these numbers were most of the Mistley, Ipswich, and Deben craft, and some from farther afield. The list is of interest because it shows the values then set on the vessels. The most highly prized in the A-class were: the Shoreham *Athole* (£1500), the Ipswich *Boaz* (£1600), the Littlehampton *Clymping* (£1600), the Harwich *Hetty* (£1500), the Ipswich *Kindly Light* (which had the complete hymn "Lead, Kindly Light," painted on the panelling of the cabin) and *Leading Light* (£1500 and £1650), the Ipswich *Nell Jess* (£1650), and the Faversham *Olympia* (£1800); and in the B-class: *Alderman*, *Defender*, *Dorcas*, *Edith May*, *Mayor*, *Memory*, *Princess*, and *Water Lily*, all at £1200, and the *Vigilant* at £1250. Most of the barges were then valued at between £600 and £900, with the Colchester *Cambria* and Ipswich *Charles and Ann*, *Tertius*, and *Tit-bits*, and the Maldon *Three Sisters* valued at only £375, and Middleton's *Good Intent* at £300. This Club's list for 1927 numbered 59 vessels, of which the most highly valued were the *Olive Mary* and *Raybel* at £3200 each. About two dozen of these vessels were left, either as sailing-craft, auxiliaries, or motor-barges, in 1949.

Harwich should, however, be seen in the panorama of barging, not only as the home of the boomies and the birthplace of the finest sprities, but as the gathering base of the great fleets. Before the decay of coastwise sail, the huge harbour was literally full of craft of every kind during an easterly spell of weather. From Ipswich and Mistley the barges gathered to form great fleets, and only twenty years ago seventy lay there one day waiting to get away for London. One, the *Royalty*, had lain there five weeks, and it had blown so hard that the *Redoubtable* had dragged both anchors ashore. They were fed up with it (no one who has not been wind-bound knows what impatience that experience provokes), and, though it still blew hard sou'-westerly, thirty mustered together one day and left the harbour. Only four made Sea Reach, the *Redoubtable*, *Vigilant*,

Pall Mall, and *Mildreda*. Fred Cooper, who was mate with the celebrated Captain "Gosher" Smith in the *Mildreda*, told me of that day. A Shrubsall racer, she was not a powerful barge—indeed, they used to belay the jib-sheet on the weather bitt-head because the lee deck was too wet to work on—but "Gosher" swore that if she went back into Harwich it would be stern first with the gear blown out of her. They were off the Naze at high water and made the Shears on the low water. It was the *Adieu's* maiden voyage, and her crew could do nothing with her, but had to run back with several others into Harwich. Some finished up in Colne, some in Shore Ends, the *Norman* in the East Swale with both leeboards gone.

To-day as I drove along the Harwich road beside the Stour, only the *Petrel* was to be seen turning quietly down the river; the *Redoubtable*, *Edith May*, and G.C.B. lay at Mistley quay, and in the harbour one auxiliary swung to her anchor. The Felixstowe ferry chugged stolidly across a deserted waste of water.

"BERIC" REBUILDING ON THE ST CLEMENT'S YARD,
IPSWICH, 1949

VIII

THE HORLOCKS OF MISTLEY

*A Seaport unspoilt—Champion of Eighty Years ago—
Growth of a Fleet—"The Essex Man of the Suffolk Coast"
—A Bargeman's Holiday—Last of the Line—The Memories
of Jim Stone*

THE Stour is the one Essex waterway unfavoured by yachtsmen.
They fear its mud-banks—not without reason; for what, from
Mistley's commanding hill, looks a grand expanse of water, two
miles across when the tide is at the full, is, to the man in the boat, a
narrow channel wriggling through a vast expanse of flats. And—to
quote a succinct comment: "You can't see the buoys in the Stour
unless there happens to be a cormorant sitting on them."

Nevertheless, when one comes into Harwich it is worth sometimes
resisting the call of Pin Mill up the Orwell and, leaving Bloody
Point and the barracks of Shotley to starboard, to sail by the packet-
boats at Parkeston and the rusting ranks of laid-up naval craft, for
Wrabness is a happy anchorage, Erwarton is worth adding to one's
collection of ports of call, and, best of all, Mistley, with its sister-
town of Manningtree, just up the river, casts a spell on every sailorman. Here the maltings line the quay, where the railway trucks
shunt sleepily, and behind the road rises sheer over the roofs of the
maltings and one looks out on eye-level with the fluttering bobs of
the barges at the quay.

Georgian houses and pubs recall the strange influence on the town
of the Rigby family in the eighteenth century. Here, in 1703, came
Richard Rigby to spend a fortune on the building of Mistley Hall,
thirty good houses, granaries, quays, warehouses, coalyards, and a
large "malting office."

In Mistley Hall were entertained Garrick, Walpole, and many
another figure of fame and fashion, and in 1774 the famous architect
Adam prepared an elaborate scheme for a "sea bathing establish-
ment" with hot and cold sea-water baths. Thirty years later, in

1807, Arthur Young described at Mistley "the little dockyard with ships building in the very bosom of a hanging wood—a lively, beautiful scene of singular and pleasing features."

To-day Mistley's charm is of a quieter kind, though the wooded hillside still sweeps down sheer into the river in "lively and singular" fashion. The classical towers remain an elegant survival of the only church the Adam brothers built, and the characterful swan, ever bending his neck in the pool around him, a solitary reminder of the bizarre vision of a fashionable spa. He could not be more fitly placed, for swans are ever cruising in the near-by Stour, nosing round the grain-laden barges, gobbling at the droppings from the elevators and the sweepings off the wooden decks.

The name of Horlock is synonymous with the Mistley waterside. Back in the eighteenth century these Horlocks were big farmers at Rettendon, Battlesbridge way, and owned a few barges. Great-grandfather Horlock had a dispute about a freight and decided to stake his all at law. Or, rather, he tried to go to law without staking his all, and made over his farms to another party so that he might not be destitute if he lost the case. But it does not pay to be clever with the law, and the too-ingenious litigant found that, though he won his case, he had made away with his land only too successfully, and was left with nothing but a few old barges. From such an inauspicious start the destinies of the Horlock family came to be coupled with the Mistley waterside.

But plough and sail have long been near neighbours in Essex, and the one-time farmers seem to have taken like ducks to the waters of Manningtree river in the distant days when billyboys, schooners, brigantines, and barquentines made the quay picturesque with their pattern of spars. The names of these vessels have mostly passed from memory, though the *Rainbow* and the barque *Mistley* are recalled. John Finch owned a billyboy named the *Alconet*, the swim-head stumpie *Marie*, and one named (according to recollection) the *Sunfly*. The Mistley hoy in the mid-nineteenth century was the billyboy *Elizabeth*, a cutter-rigged vessel, round-bottomed, but with leeboards. She is recalled as "round as an apple both ends," yet somehow she got through the water so successfully that she could beat any other vessel in the place. (This is also a reminder of the way the sailing-barge developed, for she would have had short shrift from the *Reminder* and *Redoubtable*.)

There was Jimmy Allison's brig *Economy*, which had "a berth made a-purpose for her," and which is recalled to have run practically the whole way from Sunderland to Harwich under bare poles in the "November gale" (1884) with Captain Reason as skipper. (The *Rainbow* went one better when, having reached the North and actually got the tug's rope fast, it came on to blow so hard she had to slip, run all the way back, and discharge her grain again at Mistley quay.) Bill Carrington had the schooner *Lydia*, which lay by the wooden quay with her great jib-boom poking nearly into the paint shop over the way (a barge of the same name came later); Poole, of Lawford, owned jointly with Mann, the local grocer, the barquentine *Frances and Jane*; and there was Brooks' brigantine *Mistley Park*, recalled in a story (which sends the old 'uns into fits of laughter still) of the skipper's adoring but nautically innocent wife crying out from the quay, "Oh, I see the *Mistley Park* a-coming with her flying gaff tops'l set." Built in 1845, the *Mistley Park* was still a lighter with Paul's in the early 1900's.

There was not a buoy in the river—but they found their way, four men in the boat towing on the end of the jib-boom to yank their heads round as they stayed. The barges were such tiddlers that they still talk of "the big old *Ocean Queen*," though she was only 130 tons.

Such, then, was the scene at Mistley in 1848 when Richard Horlock was one of the town's sixteen shipowners. By 1865 the family fortunes were prospering sufficiently for a barge to be built, and it was named *Horlock*. Soon after came a foretaste of the fame that was to be won seventy years later, for in 1868 Richard Horlock's two sons won the first Thames barge race for big topsail barges with his *Excelsior*.

Turning to more modern times, one of Richard's grandsons, Fred Horlock, had, just before the turn of the present century, a quarter-share with his uncle Robert in the *Pride of the Stour*. On that was founded the firm of F. W. Horlock and Co., Ltd, whose bob, the white Maltese cross on the blue field, has become one of the best known on the Essex coast, thanks largely to the firm's participation in the Thames and Medway barge races, in which, with Parker, of Bradwell, they championed the cause of the Essex-men against the cockneys and the men of Kent. From the *Pride of the Stour's* earnings Fred Horlock had built in 1900, by Orvis, of Ipswich, the *Coronation*, which he sold at a profit to buy the *Reliance*, which is still with the firm. In 1903 the *Resolute*—blown up in the Second World War

—was built by Cann, of Harwich; this year also marked another interesting milestone in the development of the firm.

A local industry, the Xylonite works, now developed into B.X. Plastics, Ltd, was calling for acids in large quantities, and as this was brought in large glass bottles by rail the loss from breakages during shunting was formidable. Fred Horlock saw that water transport was the answer, and bought for the purpose an interesting vessel, the *St Eanswythe*, an iron barge built in Holland to win the races.[1] She had slightly round chines and long outside bilge keels like a steamboat, and although she never achieved her object she was a flier. The wiseacres foretold that the acid would eat her up in a few freights, yet she made her trial trip without breaking a bottle, and kept it up for thirty years, though steel drums later replaced the bottles, and finally the firm began to mix its own acids. Some work to B.X. Plastics has, however, been revived as recently as 1949.

Before this the Mistley work had mostly been taking malt and home-grown wheat to London, with some freights of bricks from the Sudbury brickyard. These were brought down the upper reaches of the Stour, through Bures, Nayland, Stratford St Mary, Dedham, and Flatford in the lighters which are so familiar in Constable's pictures of this his native and beloved countryside. The mills up-river, almost all now closed (though Hitchcock's, of Bures, still retains its barging trade through its associated mill at Fingringhoe, on the Colne), were also served by barges, which unloaded foreign grain into these lighters at Mistley and loaded flour in exchange.

Stack work was less common than among the Maldon barges, perhaps because the big maltings established by Brooks and Edme did not trouble about sending away straw in this way. Brooks now owned Groom's little *Fairy* for the river, and for sea-work the *Lydia*, replaced in 1892 by the *Swan*, which was later sold to F. W. Horlock and lost on the Barrow; but their big cattle-feed mills called for many cargoes of maize, meal, cake, and bran, the light, bulky nature of which caused a special type of craft to be developed.

In 1908 the *Remercie* slid down the ways to join the fleet, and at this period—as everywhere, the heyday of the Essex coasting trade —one needs pause again to survey the scene. In addition to the vessels mentioned, Fred Horlock had acquired the *Jumbo* and *Minerva*, and his brothers H. F. ("Raish," to use the friendly vernacular

[1] See Chapter XVI.

abbreviation of the more stately Horatio), A. R. (Tony), and E. A.
(Alf) Horlock had the *Marjorie, Dorothy, Princess, Kitty* (since sold
to Colchester), *Percy, Volunteer* (now a yacht), *Maria, William
Hordle, Horlock, May, Wellington,* and *Vigilant*[1] in which "Chubb"
Horlock (Tony's son), now part-owner of Sully's *Oxygen*, made
such a name.

Cromwell and Lionel Horlock had the famous *Sara*, later acquired
by Everard's for her prowess as a racer (but still with a Mistley
crew!), and *D'Arcy*, which was managed by F. W. Horlock and
Co., Ltd, before ending her days. Cromwell Horlock was for many
years skipper-owner of the Maldon-built *Defender*, till he parted
with her in 1949, taking the *Xylonite*, and Lionel was skipper of
Sully's *Beatrice Maud* and *Scotsman*. *Sara* was, incidentally, noted for
her handiness as well as her speed, and claims to be the only barge
ever to turn to windward up the Yare all the way from Yarmouth
to Norwich.

The story of the *Sara*'s racing exploits has been told by Mr R. L.
Horlock,[2] and as she is certainly destined to become a legend on
Mistley waterside, and indeed throughout London River, his account
is well worth quotation.

> The 1902 race was won by the speedy Shrubsall-built *Imperial*, built
> at Ipswich, but sailed by a Mistley crew, whilst the *Sara*, completed
> only a few weeks previously at Conyer, was second. Mr A. H. Horlock
> was of the opinion that the *Sara* was the superior vessel, and his crew
> thought that if they sailed her they could win, so he and his father
> bought her. *Sara* was entered in the 1903 race and her crew's belief was
> fully justified in the event. She won the race at the record average
> speed of nearly 11 knots, completing the 55-mile course in 5 hours
> 11 minutes 10 seconds, and this was in spite of an accident within five
> minutes of the start that might have put her out of the race. The mast-
> rope broke and part of the mainsail tore. Before it could go any further,
> however, two of the family effected a temporary splice and stitched up
> the mainsail as well as they could. In the same year *Sara* was second in
> the Medway race.
>
> Although the family continued to own her, she was not just a racing
> machine, but was fast loaded and worked up to Yarmouth regularly.
> *Sara* did not race again until 1928. In that year Lionel Horlock, who
> owned her, sailed her in both the Thames and Medway races with a
> crew of only four, but unfortunately she was dogged with bad luck.

[1] A winter's barging in *Vigilant* has been described by Commander E. G. Martin in *Sailorman*. *Vigilant* later became a yacht, but has since been turned back into a motor-barge.
[2] *Spritsail*, spring 1950

Harwich leaving the Schelde

Pearl, with roller reefing
(Compare earlier rig in plate facing p. 81.)

*Boomies as
the Camera
saw them*

Loading
Apollinaris
water at
Remagen,
Germany.
The front
craft is a
sprittie

96

Beam and quarter views of *Britannia*. Last of the Vaux barges, she
was later converted to half-sprit and lost at Gorleston in 1930

'Starvation buoys' at Woolwich, with idle craft awaiting work
during the hard times of the 1930's

The London End

Sully's *Raybel* and
the Ipswich-men *Lady
Jean* and *Tollesbury*
lying on the buoys

Building

ABOVE: *Marjorie* ready for her broadside launch at Cann's Harwich yard in 1899. CENTRE: Half-model of *Aveyron*, built by Robertson of Ipswich, 1881. BELOW: *Kimberley*, just after launching at Cann's, 1900 (See Chapter VII.)

Trouble

ABOVE: *Esterel* washed up Walton beach in October 1939. LEFT: The end of the *British Oak*, off the Knoll, seen from the *George Smeed*, 1948 (See Chapter XVII.)

BELOW: *T.T.H.*, West's coaster, lost her rudder on the Gunfleet in 1935, and was taken into the Colne by two lifeboats

In the Thames match, which was sailed on a Thursday, the mizzen sprit snapped as the *Sara* rounded the Mouse lightship to windward at the half-way mark. Worse followed: the iron band holding the topsail sheet block out on the jog of the sprit broke and then, for full measure, the bowsprit jib went to pieces as she came up to the Nore. Thus she finished the course under foresail and mains'l alone, and even then there were only three barges who could beat *Sara*!

At Gravesend the next day all the damage had to be made good before sailing round to Gillingham for the next race. However, Saturday saw *Sara* in the Medway match, and at the half-way mark she was coming up fast upon the leaders. Unfortunately at the turn she fouled the *Miranda*, but no protest flag was hoisted. The language of the *Miranda*'s skipper could not stand repetition, even amongst bargemen, and as Fred Horlock afterwards commented, "it was not fit to put in a sandwich." The mishap did not delay the *Miranda*, but it broke the *Sara*'s bobstay; the topsail had to be rucked and the jib downed until one of the crew went over the side and rove a new bobstay. Despite the considerable delay thus caused *Sara* passed all her opponents and finished the course at Chatham Pier twenty-five minutes ahead of the *Portlight*. The protest was not upheld until Captain Horlock was going up to collect the cup, so it came as a miserable anti-climax after winning the race by such a margin.

In the following year the champion barge was sold to Everard's, and although they increased the size of most of her gear and she was raced right up until the last war with Mistley crews, the *Sara* did not beat her own record and it stands until this day. Many consider *Sara* to have been the fastest barge ever built, and fortunately she is still trading, although the fitting of a steel keelson recently is said to have somewhat spoilt her.

The Stone brothers (eight of them, and all sailormen!) had the fine two-hundred-ton boomies *Harold* and *Eliza H.* (Jim Stone) and *Genesta* (Harry Stone), in which they brought in coals to Mistley and took away wheat, as well as trading to 'the other side' and coasting down Channel; and the sprities *Excelsior*,[1] *Centaur* (now of Colchester), built for Charles Stone, *Jachin* (later *Venta*), *Florence*, and *Mystery*.

The Colchester steamer *Gem* had now taken over the hoy trade from the billyboy *Elizabeth*, bringing the town's porter and paraffin, its grocery and ironmongery, and, as well as the cargoes peculiar to the place, the usual timber and stone were coming in for building, and chalk and 'London mixture' for the land.

[1] See Introduction.

G

At Brantham Mills Green Brothers had the *Valentine* (still with Cory's in 1933) and *Jessie*, loading 330 quarters (about 60 to 70 tons). These little craft used to work to London mills above bridges. Once when they were short of a freight the skipper of the *Jessie* fixed for a trip to Dover, and Billy Green, horrified at such an undertaking, had to bribe him out of it with a sovereign. Their last craft was the *Orion* (sold to Cranfield's in 1939, and later renamed *Gold Belt*), which was one of the last of the 90-ton coasters. She was a coaster in miniature, and the authentic sea-going lines applied to so diminutive a hull made her a particular delight to the eye.

Among the farmers, Wrinch, of Erwarton, was to the Stour what Parker, of Bradwell, was to the Blackwater; indeed, one might call him the Essex-man of the Suffolk coast. He owned a wharf at Vauxhall, to which the straw from his lands and the farms on the near-by rivers was sailed for an Army contract by a fleet including the *Farmer's Boy*, *Butterfly*, *Primrose*, *Snowdrop*, *Victoria*, *Bluebell* (in which Captain Harvey, of Holbrook, took the last stack out of Harwich), and *Cygnet*—that pretty little fully rigged 25-tonner, tiller-steered, which used to fill the yachtsmen's hearts with covetousness as she dodged about the Stour and Orwell well into the 1930's, and is now ending her days as a lighter in Burnham river. She was a fascinating little toy, was the *Cygnet*, and one Sunday Fred Cooper and another skipper, having nothing better to do, commandeered her, lying half-loaded in Felixstowe dock, and spent a happy day sailing her round Harwich harbour. Edward Haste recalls that on her first trip down Swin from Frindsbury, where she was built by Gill on the lower yard, she nearly sank, and they were very glad to put her on the mud in Holbrook Bay. She relied on enlisting a mate from among the school truants, her first being 10½ years of age, and Haste himself next at the age of eleven. It is interesting to note that at Frindsbury a sprittie yacht-barge has been designed in 1948 almost exactly to *Cygnet's* dimensions, but with more 'side' to give headroom below.

Wrinch's barges at one time sported metal 'ramping-horse' vanes, with long bunting tails, but maybe the mates objected to shinning up aloft to clean them, for the fashion did not last long.

Too often in telling the tales of the Essex ports it is a matter of making the best of a sad story from the 1920's onward, but Mistley sailing-barges enjoyed a glorious Indian summer. F. W. Horlock resumed their building in 1915 with the *Redoubtable*, which deserved her proud name, turning to steel construction in their own yard after the War. In 1924–25 came the *Repertor, Portlight*, and *Xylonite*; and in 1927–30, *Reminder, Adieu, Resourceful*, and *Blue Mermaid* (mined on the Hook in the Second World War—blown to pieces with her crew as she sailed peacefully on a fine summer morning, every stitch set—a horrible end for a lovely vessel).

Among other Mistley-built barges was the *Colne Valley*, built half a century before for George Morris, of Colchester. *Blue Mermaid* was actually the last sailorman to be laid down in the country, if one excepts the little *Lady of the Lea*, which was hardly a true sailorman. Horlock's craft were designed with huge cubic capacity to suit the light cargoes needed for Brooks' cattle-foods, a trade which, alas, came to an end when the wharfside warehouse was gutted by German incendiaries early in the Second World War.

Conditions in the river these modern barges work are very different to those the old-timers knew, for the eel-grass has disappeared here as elsewhere, though in the Stour it lasted right up to the end of the First World War, when (it is claimed) effluent from the Manningtree gasworks killed it. After investigations the company shot the offending chemical into a gravel-pit, though no doubt it still found its way into the river. While the loss of the eel-grass has, in most places from Mersea to the Deben, merely spoiled the fishing, in the Stour it has had another effect, for the vast carpet of fronds, up to sixteen feet long, so held up the tide over the acres of mud that it had to run fiercely in the clear channel. Then you could not row a boat against the spring ebb off Mistley; and so swift was the tide that coal spilled from the colliers' shoots there was rolled along the river-bed and fetched up on Ballast Hill (the shingly point at the end of the reach below Horlock's yard), where it was a regular occupation to gather sacks of it.

To-day the tide drifts sluggishly all over the bare muds, and the old billyboys would sadly miss the hearty streams they knew. It is interesting that the Stour grass is now showing signs of returning, though it is likely to be outpaced by the coarse Dutch grass,[1] which, sown by way of experiment, is spreading everywhere, to nobody's benefit.

The steel barges marking the last stage of sail in the Stour are not, to the bargeman's eye, as pretty as the more 'sneaky' type of

[1] *Esparta Townsenda.*

craft, being bulky to the verge of boxiness, but they are heavily
canvassed and wonderfully able, for *Reminder* actually came straight
off the building-ways to win the Thames and Medway races in 1929.
Now she and *Resourceful* have lost all their original character on
conversion into full power-craft, and the *Adieu* is to be next to suffer
this fate. They will join the M.B. *Spithead*, an ex-1914–18 landing-
barge. *Redoubtable* and *Remercie* had auxiliaries in 1947 and 1949,
but retain their sailing-gear. *Reliance, Repertor, Portlight, Xylonite,*
and *Millie* remain sailormen, but it is likely that only the old *Millie*
will end her days without a screw through the quarter. Marcus
Horlock, the present managing director of the firm, and son of
Fred, is in love with ships and sail, but at Mistley, as elsewhere,
they aren't breeding sailormen any more, and the merchants
clamour incessantly for power craft, indifferent to what sort of kettle
contains the machinery.

Marcus Horlock can remember, not so long ago, seeing his
Resourceful towing eight sailormen up the Stour on a calm summer
morning. (His admiration at the beauty of the scene was tempered
with anxiety as to the cylinders of his 100 horse-power Diesel!)
Forty years ago there must, sometimes, have been a score of craft
up on a tide, turning and tacking, 'filling and backing,' poking,
rowing, and kedging. Soon a barge turning to wind'ard will be a
rarity, here as elsewhere.

Then let us share the memories of the greatest old-timer of them
all—Jim Stone.

Jim Stone, one of the eight sailormen brothers of Mistley, made
his first barging trip in the *Yulan* at the age of thirteen. As he was
eighty when, with unfailing memory and humour, he spun me
these yarns in 1948, that must have been in 1881. They were taking
broken glass to Dort (Dordrecht), and he recalls that as they came
into the Roompot (at the mouth of the East Schelde off Veere)
they saw the boomie *Davenport* ashore there. The *Davenport* asked
them to help lighten her—a pretty job, as it meant getting heavy
bags of nitrate of soda into the boat; but they did it, the redoubtable
"Wings" Chandler, of Ipswich, who was mate of the *Davenport*,
carrying his bags two at a time. Away went the *Davenport* to
Zierikzee, and the *Yulan* to Dordrecht, whence she returned with a
cargo of gunpowder.

It was a fine, breezy introduction to the bold, free, strenuous days "when barging was barging" and the distinctive pattern of the lofty Essex sprits was a common sight over low Dutch dykes; and Jim Stone evidently liked it, for he shipped next aboard the *Excelsior*. Sometimes he had to sleep on the floor with his fingers in the pump well, that the incoming water might be detected in time, but he stayed in her for fourteen years, becoming master.

Then came the *Jachin*, that fine model of a coaster built by Howard, of Maldon, my humble service in which (after her re-building as the *Venta*) I have described in *Last Stronghold of Sail*. I was happy to hear him praise my old ship as one of the finest coasters ever launched. He recalled how they used to lock the wheel and go below to dinner, letting the *Jachin* sail herself as straight as an arrow; how one night he set up her lights off Margate and was off Southampton before dowsing them—a tidy night's sail; and how they used to forget about her leeboards once they got out of the river, for she would sail as well without them, and, in fact, would not lie on them if they were down, but let them float about. (His brother Harry went one better in the boomie *Genesta*, sometimes unbolting the leeboards altogether and stowing them in the hold.)

The *Jachin* then was owned by four partners. Harry Stone had a quarter, and other shares were owned in Southampton and Tolles-bury. "When we had to go from Mistley to Exeter and back for a £40 freight, it was a fine job satisfying all those owners," Jim Stone recalled. William then took the *Jachin* (Roberts and Cresswell were other skippers who had her before she was sunk at Seaford and re-built by Shrubsall, who sold her to Harvey, of Rochester), and Jim, after a spell in the *Florence* and *Mystery*, took to boomies, first the *Eliza H.*, then the *Harold*, which he described as the handiest boomie ever launched, able to pick her way anywhere a sprittie would go. In *Eliza H.* he did a number of coal freights to Mistley from Sunder-land, and in the *Harold* worked to Brussels via Antwerp. One cargo out was empty boxes, and back with white lead and glass for Farmi-loe's. He recalled that one summer he could not get a freight for the *Eliza H.*, which carried five hands, unless he was ready to accept £75 to go to Amsterdam and take a cargo to Truro. He took it; following up with clay from Charlestown, near St Austell, to Antwerp, then slates to London, wheat to Southampton, and thence to Guernsey to load stones for Mistley. What a summer's passage-making! Who would want to have a yacht of his own in those days if he had leisure enough to ship passenger on a two-hundred-tonner carrying on like that? I am almost glad such temptations don't come my way nowadays!

One Monday morning Jim Stone boarded the *Eliza H.*, lying in Harwich, and, though it was blowing easterly and most craft were wind-bound in the harbour, he put to sea. He was back the following Sunday with Sunderland coals for Mistley, and the skippers of the craft still lying wind-bound could not believe it till they came and saw the *Eliza H.* unloading at the quay.[1]

On another occasion he was bound from Sandwich to Dunkirk, already short-handed, when the mate came aboard so merry that he told him to get below and stop below. The skipper and the boy sailed the ketch to Dunkirk, and as they came between the pierheads he called his wife, who was making the trip with him, to the wheel. "But I can't steer this ship," she protested. "Oh, yes, you can," replied Jim; "only don't take any notice of what those Frenchmen call out to you from the pierheads. Do what I say." So they made port.

After the *Harold* Jim Stone took the yacht-barge *Thoma II*, that lovely creation which Howard of Maldon, in 1909, modelled on the *Record Reign*. When *Thoma II* first began to sail from Maldon quay, six men used to heave on her lines. Jim Stone, who had her 32-foot mast replaced by a 45-foot spar, and added another 12 tons to her 28 tons of ballast, stepped aboard and ordered "Let go." "You'll blow ashore," observed Howard. "You haven't even got a head rope on her." "Let go," said Jim. Then he set the fores'l first—a manœuvre to shock any bargeman. "Heave out your tawps'l," came next, and under tops'l, fores'l, and mizzen she sailed off from the quay "like a little smack." "You're a proper old blowhard," was Howard's grudging tribute, and by that name the builder addressed the skipper ever after.

Once, down Channel, Jim Stone was at the *Thoma II's* wheel when, in the small hours of the morning, she suddenly spun up into the wind and lay there flogging. Her rudder had broken off under the counter. The owner wanted to close the land and hail a tug, but Jim Stone declared they had still a good ship. "We're just right to lie about at sea for two or three days and nights," he cheerfully assured the anxious owner. Then, making land, they reduced mainsail and, jockeying her with heads'ls and mizzen, took her right into Weymouth without steering-gear of any kind.

[1] Compare the similar feats of the *Alice Watts* (p. 88) and of the *Record Reign* (*Last Stronghold of Sail*, p. 125).

The owner hankered to scrap her sprit in favour of booms'l rig, but Jim Stone would not have it. After his day she was changed to standing gaff, and was a familiar feature of the Essex coast well into the 1930's; but, while the change may have made her more elegant, · I cannot believe she set her sail as smartly.[1] She was in Kingstown during a royal visit of 1911, and Jim Stone has a picture of the King being rowed ashore on that occasion. It warms the heart to see a sprittie's gear sticking up in the midst of all the swank and panoply of that event.

After leaving *Thoma II* Jim Stone came to Horlock's fleet, taking a leading part in the barge races,[2] till he retired from sea-going more strenuous than skippering Marcus Horlock's *Owl*. Now as that staunch little ketch jogs down Channel the.sight of Portland Bill, the Needles, or Beachy Head recalls to him voyages long ago in the *Harold* and *Eliza H.*, and to him the Channel again becomes alive with coasting barges, schooners, and ketches, though to the eyes of us of the younger generation nothing is to be seen but the tall, monotonous triangles of the modern jib-headed yachts, and the low trails of the steamers' smoke.

[1] *Thoma II* was again in commission in 1950, with spritsail rig, including mast-hoops which contribute to her very stylish appearance.
[2] See Chapter XVI.

IX

IN THE BACKWATERS

*Exploits of the Ditch-crawlers—The Days of Push and Poke
—Hufflers and Huffling—The Walton Archipelago*

THE exploits of the coasters are at one end of the scale; at the other
are the ingenuities of the ditch-crawlers. How 120-ton sailing-vessels
were persuaded up long and tortuous creeks and rivers in head-winds
without a tug is as remarkable as the way those craft used to defy
the open seas and round far headlands.

In the Ipswich and Maldon rivers barges could turn up to the dock
gates or the quay; at Yarmouth and Lowestoft there have been steam-
tugs from early days. Colchester has had motor-tugboats since 1924.
One of the last barges up without that aid, while Tom Eves was
actually getting his motor-boat ready, was the 240-ton ex-boomie
Hydrogen, whose mate, Harold Butcher (himself a Brightlingsea
native, son of George Butcher, skipper of the ketch *Majestic*), tells
me they took five tides to get her from Wivenhoe to the Hythe, and
a week to get down again. A barge of that size needed a tug; the
smaller craft of earlier days could get on fairly well in places where
there were plenty of hands. Sometimes trace-horses were available;
if not, two or three men on a track-line can move a lot of weight,
especially as close-sheeted mainsail and topsail would generally help
up some of the reaches. Moreover, in the days when the rivers
and creeks were truly alive, and "help one another" was a
maxim carried out without question or hesitation, the two or
three official haulers generally found some casual help available and
readily given.

But the central figures in this sort of activity were the hufflers,
who, the etymologists tell us, derive their name from the way they
used to station themselves on the 'huffs,' or bows of the swim-head
lighters, and are no relation to the 'hovellers,' or beach-sharks, of
Deal.

Often retired bargemen themselves, they were respected and
well-loved friends of the sailormen, versed in every subtlety of the

waters they worked, cunning in all manners of ways to coax and humour a barge in a tight corner.

Where there was no help at hand, as in Fingringhoe's snake-like creek, it often became necessary to lower the gear on deck and shove the dead weight of the barge along with booms, but Saunders, huffler at Battlesbridge, prides himself that he used to get craft after craft up the last reaches of Burnham river without ever lowering down. That is where the long-chine craft, such as Cook, of Maldon, built, show their merit. They will 'pick up' and go ahead in getting under way or coming about; after sailing two or three lengths they will wend again. The short-chined fliers, which delight at sea, are less able here, and the round-chined Goldsmith's 'ironpots' are the worst of the lot—"Two feet to leeward for every foot ahead," in Saunders' words.

The good huffler drove a post in the mud to check or guide a barge wherever it was needed, as well as beaconing his channel; he had his own marks to advise him just how much water there was at any one of a score of places; he knew the run of the 'gutway' at every twist and turn, and every point where the tide ebbed across the channel and was liable to set a barge ashore—or, worse still, to set one end of her ashore, for a whole barge on the mud only loses her tide, but if her head goes on one side, leaving the stern free to swing athwart stream on the other, the chance is that she will, if loaded, break her back across the gutway. A barge turning up a channel only about twice her width wends every time with her bows out of the tide and her stern in it. Then the danger is that, even with the mizzen's help, she may fail to twist her head to windward of her tail, and will sail into the bank against the helm.

Not many years ago the *Maria* tried to find her way down from Battlesbridge unaided and, caught by a cross-tide, went ashore across the gut. She survived; but you could row a punt under her on the low water, and her butts were two inches open. She lifted half-full of water, and they had to dry her sodden wheat as best they could. Bob Eves had the same thing happen to him with a 40-ton stack in Salcot Creek, where the gut of the channel is so sharp that the barge made a bridge you could walk under. She was a leaky craft at the best of times, and they surveyed the scene with gloomy forebodings as to the amount of pumping likely to be necessary before they got to London. To their astonishment, however, the old barge did herself a power of good in dropping her belly, and when she refloated she was tighter than she had been for years!

Bad berths have also to be known by the huffler; to ebb adry across a telephone cable or ferry hard would be obvious folly, but a few bits of rag-stone spilt in unloading may prove equally fatal, for a boulder the size of a doughnut can wreck a barge on a hard berth. In her motoring days the well-known coaster *Northdown* sat on a bit of stone at Battlesbridge mills, and the water covered two recently installed engines worth £1000 each—but that was not the huffler's fault.

Hard ground is the chief danger, soft mud is another. In the Wade in Walton backwaters craft would sometimes 'suck down'— that is, fail to lift when the tide came round them. The flat bottom formed a vacuum in the mud, and could not be torn from its embraces even by vigorous waggling of the rudder. The farseeing huffler slipped a light chain under the barge before she grounded in such places, and this was pulled back and forth to make a blowhole through the mud. If this was not done the trick was to take a maul up the rigging and give her a sharp tap on the masthead. The vibration often did the trick, and up she came with a tremendous sucking gurgle. This practice is not to be confused with the technique of the skipper of an old 'ironpot' who kept a seven-pound hammer on the cabin-top. When she was sailing unusually sluggishly, he would rush forward with the hammer and strike her a literally resounding blow on the nose. He declared that after this treatment she invariably travelled better—"particularly to windward in light airs."

At least once a barge has been held down in the Wade for a tide, the water running on the decks, and only raised by another barge being laid alongside on the next tide, all hands stirring the mud under the chine with booms, but I have not heard of one being actually sunk. Of recent years the berths at Colchester Hythe quay have 'slobbed up' with soft tenacious mud, and one or two craft have caused a scare by remaining fast in it as the water crept up to the hatches. All have been got free in time, but at least one has missed a tide up to the mills. Barging decreased in Walton backwaters before 1914, though the *Maid of Connaught* was up at Foundry Dock in the 1930's. Tom Bloom, who was till 1946 cox'n of Walton lifeboat, did a lot of piloting in these waters (having served a few years in Horlock's Mistley-men as a youngster), and estimates that there were then four barges a week in and out. The tidemill was working eight pairs of stones, the near-by windmill four pairs. Into Windmill Dock and Tidemill Dock came the barges to collect their 'cotchels.' Tom Bloom recalls hauling the *Gertrude May* into Windmill Dock a foot out of her marks with six men handling two wires on her windlass. Near by, on what is now the yacht club hard, the Harwich boomies (*Lothair* and Forster's *Emma* are remembered) unloaded coals, and the Kentish-men brought granite from the Channel Islands. *Warwick Castle* (one of Walker and Howard's Littlehampton-registered craft) and *Queen Mab*, from Sittingbourne, were among the last arrivals in this trade. Smeed Dean's Kentish spritties were up all the creeks with rag-stone for walls and roads, returning light, and the Essex-men were busy serving the farms far up the creeks at Kirby, Oakley, and Beaumont, where the quay, according to Captain Morris, is built of timbers from old London Bridge. You can hardly find those old wharves now. In 1947 I had to drive my sailing-dinghy through dense reeds to reach Oakley dock, yet thirty years ago Keeble's farms here were served entirely by water, both for inward and outward goods.

Tom Bloom described how they got the craft away when winds were foul. Two or three men on the windward wall would haul the barge to them and pay away line as she sailed the better tack. Checking her on the lee mud, they would pull her head round and help her back to windward again. Sometimes they carried a kedge and stubbed this into the wall so that the crew could haul up to it on the dolly-line. Then, as she sailed away, easing her line, they ran forward to plant the anchor again in the right place for the next tack. It took a hard blow to postpone getting under way, and rarely did they lower down the gear. In fact, when one skipper decided to lower down and start to 'poke up,' the huffling party were quite put out, for, hidden behind a bend in the wall, the barge seemed to have vanished entirely.

Only three barges actually belonged to Walton. Alan Stanford, of Beaumont Hall, owned the *Beaumont Belle* and the little *Gleaner*, of 28 tons register, specially built for Beaumont Cut, and, in 1938, owned as an auxiliary at Skegness. Still smaller, by six tons, was the *Hector*, belonging to Hector Stone, of Kirby.

Several barges a week, mostly Kentish-men, used to load sand 'overboard' from the Pye Sand at the mouth of the backwaters. At this time the Pye stood up steep and sheer from Dovercourt Bay, and loading could be done even at high water. To-day, whether because of the loss of those freights of sand or from natural causes, it has become a flat sunken bar which seldom shows even at low water; one result being that the tide flowing over it has washed away 150 yards of saltings from the north point of Horsey Island. Tom Bloom remembers, too, the Kentish-men—the Gorfs and Farringtons in particular—on Walton beach with stone for the groynes. The *Victoria* he recalls as the last in this trade. They would never stop more than one tide (if any stone was not unloaded, away they went again with it), and often managed two freights in a week.

There were several hufflers in Walton backwaters. David Lay served Landermere, where he lived; Jack Scone (and Bob Smith before him) took you to Kirby. You brought up above or below Kirby Creek, according to which you wanted, for neither would poach on the other's 'huffles.'

David Lay is perhaps the best remembered of all Essex hufflers. "Good morning, my dear," he would observe, rowing up in his punt. "You got here, then?" "Yes, we're here, David." His punt made fast, he would start a jogging dance about the barge's decks, which, together with his characteristic flow of conversation, never ceased until the job of piloting was done. "We shan't *never* do it to-day" would be his discouraging start, preparing for the worst. Then, as the barge got under way, "Let her luff, my dear," he would cry, "let her luff just the breadth of a half-a-sovereign. No, no, a *half*-a-sovereign, I said. Bear away a li'l' mite. Now do you let David take her. All right, my dear, David has got her now." So it ran on. At night he would leave a lamp in his window, and when it showed in the right place through the panes came the encouraging command, "Bear up, my dear; bear up for the harbour lights."

Perched up along remote sea-walls and tucked away in tiny docks, the barges were often beneaped, but David Lay came to them every tide, day or night, paddling his punt, whether there was any real chance to get away or not. A bit of poaching passed the bargemen's time away on these occasions, and when such opportunities were not available a few seagulls often went into the pot. Once, in 1905, Bob Eves was frozen in Oakley dock for seven weeks, and when things like this happened David Lay would always suggest postponing payment for the 'huffle' till better times.

There were generally three or four spritties somewhere in the backwaters forty years ago, and by helping each other the crews managed to pull and poke in and out of John Salmon's, Landermere

Hall, Joys, Beaumont Cut, Oakley, and Kirby, to mention some of
the names of these havens, many merely enlarged drainage outfalls.
Bill Kirby, of the *Water Lily*, used to tell a tale which epitomized
the humorous, happy-go-lucky nature of the trade to these places.
Arriving at a truly rural berth one day, he hailed a farmer's boy for
advice where to moor. "Well, I down't rightly knaow," called
back the man ashore, scratching his head. "The larst owd booy as
come here, I think he jest stood an' howded her."

David Lay's whole living was made from the huffling and from
tending John Salmon's little yacht. I doubt if he was a rich man,
though he was a happy one who has left happy memories. It is,
however, recalled that he liked to keep five-shilling pieces, and that
when he died he left "nigh on a peck of crowns."

Jack Scone it was who kept a donkey and was kind enough to
lend it to a bargeman wanting to take his water-cask up to the village
for filling, so at least one young skipper used to empty that cask
out in Hamford Water for the pleasure of riding Scone's poor old
moke half across Essex on the pretext of fetching water.

Eagle's, the Walton farmers, were among the big barge-users,
and another was Colonel Davis, who at one moment would threaten
a fearful retribution on all bargemen who dared set foot across the
wall on his preserves and the next would take them home to cele-
brate. His house had a pond by the drive, and after such an evening
the Colonel would grandly explain that to clear this hazard it was
necessary to keep the gate-post 'on' with a certain tree. On one
occasion he went farther and accompanied his guests to act as pilot.
A little jostling and elbowing *en route* landed the Colonel in his
own pond, from which watery situation he surveyed the scene,
rebuking himself with apologetic self-deprecation: "Why, I'm a
fine pilot," he proclaimed. "I'm in the pond myself."

The Mistley huffler was universally known as "Jimmy Mustard,"
because on going aboard a deep-sea ship he judged the berth by
whether mustard was served. If there was no mustard Jimmy con-
demned the ship and would not sail, and, indeed, when salt beef and
biscuit formed the staple diet something to help it down was of some
importance. He and the other Mistley pilot, Nutter, were both
really deep-sea men. "They talk about the Swin and the Wallet,"
said the latter disdainfully. "Now, if those fellows were to speak to
me about the Indian Ocean I could enjoy some conversation with
them."

Ted Marsh, the Woodbridge mud-pilot, used to sail craft down to Waldringfield, fair wind or foul, and even work night tides in the winter when the yachts were out of the way. Tom Kirby, in the *Nellie Parker*, once paid him a nice compliment. "I wouldn't want your job," he commented. "No. You've got a better one," said Ted. "It isn't that," replied the skipper. "We sail these craft for years to get to know what they will do. You have to know what they will do before you step aboard." And, indeed, to coax one day a sailing-barge and the next a 300-ton Dutch motor-coaster up a twisting channel was an exacting responsibility. Ted always took the wheel, also handling a setting-boom over the quarter. "I could never give another man orders quick enough," he said. The only time he was really alarmed was when he boarded one of the few stackies to use the Deben. "Just follow the stack," the skipper advised the pilot with a grin.

Chaney, who 'huffled' the occasional barges up Salcot Creek, had the reputation of making use of them to keep his channel dredged. Barge after barge used to get ashore in the creek, for which he would apologize profusely, adding, "Well, well, she won't take no harm here; and that so happens the way she lies she'll serve to scour that old point that's been growing up. If that had to happen that might have been in a worse place."

Many a time a sailorman must have been thankful to get out of these quaint corners and have sea-room and steerage-way once more. But the strenuous co-operative efforts of mind and muscle which got the craft in and out are a delightful part of the whole pageant.

> Below the lonely sea-wall,
>   Beside the straw-thatched rick,
> Beside the red-bricked maltings,
>   By Strood and hard and wick,
> In quiet estuary, where sea with river meets,
> There rise our lofty topmasts;
>   There lean our canted spreets.

X

A LONG LIFE AFLOAT

Bob Eves, his Memories and Notebooks—Grain to Colchester,
4½d. a Quarter—'Big Logs' and Small Parcels—Running the
Gauntlet—Huts, Gate-posts, and Oysters

BOB EVES, of Wivenhoe, has seen as much as any man of these Essex
backwaters in days when spritties used them. He has been skipper
of a dozen barges engaged in local trade, and to-day, at 79, after
retiring recently from barge-towing on the Colne, he is still active
about Wivenhoe quay, looking after the local yachts and the old
Cap Pilar in her last berth. Bearded, and with the sailorman's gold
rings in his ears, he wears no other rig but a seaman's blue serge and
cheese-cutter—and what rig is there to exchange for that? He
makes a particularly valuable contribution to this record, because he
has kept all his barges' discharge books, giving actual details of
freights done and rates paid, except in the case of three craft in which
they went to the bottom of London River.

After he had served a spell as mate in the *Ann Elizabeth*, Bob Eves'
first couple of commands were the *Denton* and *Robert*, both owned
by W. C. Murrell, a London owner of craft constantly working
from Essex. In these and the next three, *James*, *Peace*, and *Audacious*,
all owned by Henry Howe, of Colchester, covering the period up
to the turn of the century, he was busy in the agricultural work
which characterized the barging trade of that time—away with
stacks, in with manure; with some cargoes of flints for the roads of
pre-macadam days, and grain when the Colchester rate was 4½d. a
quarter. All these early craft were tops'l rigged, round-bowed
craft, and *James* was of 550 quarters—no mean size for that time,
and 100 quarters bigger than the *Peace*. In 1901 Bob Eves took the
480-quarter barge *Keeble*, whose immense curved tiller, retained
after most other barges had changed to a wheel, makes her so easily
recognized in many a photo. She and the *British Empire*, a fine 600-
quarter craft still working for Francis and Gilders, Ltd, were his last
commands for Howe.

His next four were of W. R. Cunis' fleet, then thirty-five strong.
First came the *New York*, a 550-quarter barge, which had taken third
place in the Thames race in 1878; then the *G.W.*,[1] a 160-ton barge
loading 700 quarters, in which he was run down and sunk in Northfleet Hope. Next came the *Torment*, and lastly the *Terror*, which was
also run down and sunk in the Albert Dock, and soon after ran on a
grid at Woolwich and sank again. Cunis had two other barges,
Ada and *Shamrock*, sunk on the very same day, and to make matters
worse they were all among his biggest and most valuable craft. All
were safely raised in due course, none the worse—and neither was
Bob Eves, three times sunk in two and a half years.

By this time sand for the tarred roads (with which the name of
Cunis is closely associated on Colne) had ousted flints as a freight,
and Bob Eves was also doing a lot in the rough timber work. In
the *Keeble* and *G.W.* particularly, he was trading largely to Maidstone with tree-trunks from Mistley, St Osyth, Heybridge, and all
over the place. Freights were reckoned at so much per load—8s. 3d.
to Maidstone by one pre-1914 discharge book, or up to £1 a load
for Lowestoft. Once he took aboard eleven loads in one tree (a
load being 40 cubic feet). They got it aboard with the sprit, and it
pulled two cranes over trying to get it out. A photo in Bob Eves'
home shows the *G.W.* with 150 trees aboard, five high above the
hatch-coamings. This trade came to an end after the First World
War.

Bob Eves' old discharge books, a well-thumbed collection of
penny notebooks which he has had the sense to treasure, throw a
vivid light on the rates paid in the old days. In 1903, for instance,
he had to load at three separate places in London for Colchester,
taking 49 quarters of linseed at one wharf, 40 quarters of cotton-
seed at the second, and 39 quarters more at the third—the whole
job, at 2s. 6d. a quarter, amounting to the princely sum of £12
after expenses. The stackies got 5s. a load of 36 trusses for straw and
7s. for hay, and it needed good stuff to stow forty loads and make a
£12 10s. freight of it. To-day the modern stackies are knocking up
£60 a trip to Ridham Dock on the East Swale from Colchester,
with no loading and unloading to be done by the crew.

Bob Eves got so tired of timber-loading (this was sawn stuff, not
to be confused with the rough timber, or 'big logs,' referred to
above) at Heybridge, at the time when you had to empty one lighter

---

[1] The *G.W.* foundered finally in 1947.

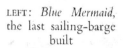
LEFT: *Blue Mermaid*, the last sailing-barge built

BELOW: The Maldon *Oak*, a round-stern barge

ABOVE LEFT: *St Eanswythe*, a speedy Dutch-built Mistley acid-trader

ABOVE: Meeson's little *Rainbow* converted into a yacht

ABOVE: *Paglesham* in a strong wind

LEFT: *Antje*, a Dutch barge converted into a sprittie

LEFT: The Mistley *Resolute*

RIGHT: *Remercie*, showing the bulky Mistley shape

LEFT: *Hyacinth*, one of Howard's Maldoners, passes in light airs

An 'ironpot.' Goldsmith's *Calluna*
(See Chapter XV.)

Marjorie winding. The mizzen sheeted to the rudder presses her
stern round while the rest of the canvas flogs

one day and two the next, that he shipped for a time in Alf Layzell's boomie *Llama*, a Channel trader built by Vaux, of Harwich; only, after the way these things turn out, it was still timber work, and the owner began to dispense with a stevedore when he got a man so used to the work!

The *Llama* was five-handed, and the skipper was pleased with £100 for a freight from Surrey Dock to Truro, taking a month—not a lavish reward, but then the mate of a boomie was paid fifty shillings a month and the third hand eight shillings a week. The regular choice for a boy going barging was two shillings and sixpence a week and his keep, or ten shillings a week and feed himself. "You went to sea for your grub and worked cargo for a living," is how the old sailormen put it. One old-timer recalled how the third hand was lost overboard, and, according to the general custom, the skipper went to the fo'c'sle to collect his gear and sell it for the drowned man's family. There was absolutely nothing there but an old Army greatcoat; the poor devil had been lying on bare boards.

Sometimes, however, there was a good freight in compensation. The building of Colchester barracks in the first years of the present century kept the *Peace* busy with £8 freights of brick-rubbish from the Wakering brickfields; one freight could generally be loaded and delivered in two days. In bad weather, when work in the brickyards was held up, a gang loaded the barges; in fine weather the crew had to load their own, for which £3 was paid—and earned, with all that wheelbarrowing and trimming. One of Bob Eves' quaintest freights was fifty gates and a hundred gate-posts from Sadd's, of Maldon, to the Southminster railway. "Where do you want them?" Bob asked the ganger on arrival in the Crouch. " 'Chuck 'em all overboard; we'll pick 'em up,' he said," recalled Bob, with a chuckle. "We chucked 'em over all right. You ought to have seen them chaps scramble about to get them." Sometimes Sadd's sent such small parcels for different jobs that the mate sculled them ashore in the boat, pitched them over the wall, and marked them by a withy with the delivery note on top. "I suppose they picked them up some time," Bob reflected.

During the First World War the *G.W.* was not allowed to go into the cross-Channel trade and pick up her £100 per freight of coke, but did a good deal of explosives work to the East Swale. One of Bob Eves' worst nights was spent lying moored beside a

H

burning ammunition dump in which great explosions kept occurring. Forbidden to go ashore, forbidden to row off clear of it in the boat, he finally got below, shut up slider and flushing-board, and turned in, declaring that if he was to be burned alive he would burn in comfort. The military and naval patrols were in both wars hopelessly obstructive to the legitimate coming and going of sailing-barges, and *G.W.* was often in trouble entering the East Swale. When shouts went unheeded shots followed, and Bob Eves used to stand on his cabin ladder and steer with only one hand exposed to reach the wheel. When he left her she still had bullets embedded in her stem. "*Whew* they used to go, and then *plonk* as they hit you," he recalled with a grin.

But the Army provided Bob Eves with what he reckons the best freight he ever had: two huts from Yantlet Creek, opposite Southend —one to Shoebury, one to Foulness. For this £60 was paid in 1922. In those days foreign oysters were coming to Brightlingsea by barge for re-laying, and in 1924 the *Terror* brought 350 barrels from King George V Dock. Nowadays fleets of lorries bring them, though what saving that is on the £15 paid for the barge freight mentioned, goodness knows.

Bob Eves' last ship was the *Paglesham*. She was owned by A. J. Meeson,[1] of Battlesbridge, but Bob Eves fixed his own freights and managed the barge entirely. The first time he called on Mr Meeson for settling, that old-time countryman waved aside all the barge's books, telling the skipper he did not want his house cluttered up with a lot of paper. "If I can't trust a man I don't employ him," he declared. A pleasant partnership.

Running a barge meant standing up for yourself with the charterers and merchants, and on one occasion Bob Eves found only fifty tons of barley to load instead of the hundred tons for which he had been chartered. He refused to allow the barge to be touched until he was paid for the full freight, and the difference of opinion ended with a joint protest deputation arguing it out in the owner's house.

At last, in 1934, came the time to retire from sea-going, and Bob Eves bought a motor-boat on the Colne, towing barges and doing a bit of lightering of sand for the blockhouses built on the sea-walls in the Second World War. After ten years of that he finally came ashore, and can conjure up for those who sail the little 14-foot

[1] See Chapter XIII.

Wivenhoe one-designs the day in 1897 when he saw the *Victoria* capsize, racing in a private match with *Satanita*, *Conqueror*, and *Arrow*, or of the similar mishap which befell the stackie *Renown*. Both craft, he recalls, were taken in tow capsized, and both righted themselves when their gear touched the ground.

XI

THE STACKIES OF MALDON

*Howard the Artist—A Sailmaker's Treasury—Sixty-foot
Sprits—Straw and Muck—Parker's Bradwell-men—Spittys,
Kirbys, and Goymers—Tollesbury's Colliers—Woodrope and
Old Hall*

WHILE Ipswich and Harwich were bringing to perfection the
coasters, Maldon was developing the flat beamy type of barge, ideal
for stack work and for reaching the mills up shallow creeks and
rivers.

I have said that Cann's Harwich barges are the most admired of
all among bargemen, but that need not blind us to the fact that
Howard, the chief Maldon builder, was no less of an artist in his
own field; indeed, his artistry was really the greater, because of the
limitations of that field. His task was to make a thing of beauty out
of a craft which must be broad, flat, and low-sided, for any pronounced sheer made too hollow a foundation for a stack.

What he could do, given a free hand, is shown by the *Record
Reign*, the loveliest barge ever built, *Thoma II*, the best of all the
barge-yachts, which was a copy of her, *Jachin* (later *Venta*), one of
the most perfect of all the coasting spritties, and *Emma*, an out-
standing smaller version of the same ideal. But it was in the stack
type that Howard really excelled. The insurance limits for the
Maldon Club were only from Orfordness to the North Foreland,
but within those limits the craft had to be both nimble and nippy
to turn away up London River with the hay and straw half-way up
the mainmast.

And nimble and nippy they were, even if they were also woefully
wet in anything of a seaway. Indeed, it is a pity no Maldon craft
were ever put into the classic races, for they might have surprised
some of their proud sisters. They would have been handsomely
beaten in light airs, for they were moderately canvassed, but the
Maldoners will tell you that once it begins to blow a little the
racers have to shorten sail and the stackies begin to travel past them.

The first barge Howard built was the *Surprise*, in 1879 (owned by Strutt in 1907, and not to be confused with Rankin's Kentish-built craft of the same name), and from then on they came off his ways in a long succession. Often there were three building simultaneously, and at harvest-time, the refitting season for farm barges, as many as sixteen craft have been in his yard together. *Defender*, *D'Arcy*, *Violet*, *Mirosa*, *Ethel Maud*, to name a few which yet survive, all bear the mark of his hand—a wide, shallow stern-frame, great beam, shapely ends, easy draft and low side, and a profile unmarked by any flamboyant flare or sheer, yet all sweet curves, utterly different from the flat, square, plank-like productions of lesser builders. Wrinch's *Butterfly* even had a song in her honour:

> As dainty as a butterfly, as fair as a queen,
> The prettiest little stack barge that ever was seen.

Howard's craft, however, though they bear a strong superficial family likeness, are astonishingly different under water. Billy Austin, who has spent most of his life in the *Mermaid* (now a yacht) and *Mirosa* (which is kept up like one), commented, "They don't begin to be alike, those two. The *Mermaid* was all chine. This one hasn't got any." The explanation is that, moved by the constant urge to make each an improvement on the last, Howard built only two identical, *Violet* and *Hyacinth*, for Bentall, brother of the Maldon ironfounder who created the famous yacht *Jullanar*. During the twenty-eight years he had the *Mermaid* Billy Austin reckons he delivered 80,000 tons of cement to Heybridge, besides other freights, mostly chalk and lime.

A qualified naval architect, Howard designed all his craft on paper, being one of the first men to build flat-bottomed craft from lines. As the design evolved he would declare, "I can see her in the water now!" and before the launch his impatient genius would often prompt him to comment, "I can improve on that one next time." He only built a half-model when a customer was unable to read the lines, but even so the walls of his office were lined with models of barges and smacks—for he excelled in this field also, building the famous Brightlingsea clipper *Sunbeam*. Some of his original drawings are still preserved, but after his death during the First World War all those priceless models were put on the fire! He was always a greater artist than a business-man, and it is characteristic of him that the lovely *Record Reign* was laid down to satisfy his creditors.

Though she was built for Heybridge lock, the beautiful counter stern and clipper bow he added prevented her going in save on big tides, and the footways on the gates, hinged to lift and lengthen the lock, recall that tight fit to the present day. Similarly, the later spritties such as *Jess* had such fine quarters that their carrying capacity was reduced by many tons when 'snug loaded,' as bargemen describe cargoes which can be tucked below hatches. Most of Howard's craft were of oak, single-skin rabbeted, but a few (including the original *Surprise*) were double-skinned of soft wood.

The products of the other Maldon yard, Cook and Son, are less immediately attractive to the eye, being longer on the chine and less 'yachty' in the shaping of their ends, but they are not to be despised. The *Dawn*, still with Francis and Gilders, actually beat the Howard barges in one Maldon race, and *Lord Roberts* certainly does not owe her owners, Rankin's, of Rochford, much money. Another Cook barge, *British King*, was cut down to a Rochester motor-man after being capsized in collision with the Whitstable *Savoy* in 1935.

The Sadlers were the old-time Maldon sailmakers. The trade ran in the family, which established businesses at Ipswich, Brightlingsea (reopening Paterson's old loft), and Burnham. The original Maldon business was taken over in 1914 by Arthur Taylor, whose son, Fred, has carried it on for the past twenty years. Though some sail-makers, including Whitmore's of Ipswich, now stitch barge-sails by machine, in Taylor's ancient loft, next door to Howard's old yard, the process goes on much as it has for a century. In fact, the only notable technical innovation has been the replacement of a seven-inch hemp headrope to the mainsail by wire. All the stretch of the canvas now takes place downward, but in the days of the hemp headrope a new sail was held at the sprit-end by a temporary snotter, which was removed when the sail had 'grown' enough for the eye in the peak to slip over the sprit-end.

Fred Taylor's drawing-books are a fascinating treasury. Here are sketched sails of barges, smacks, and yachts now long forgotten—square tops'ls for the old ketch barges and spinnakers for little raters —and here it is possible to trace the gradual change in fashion. Some of the later stumpies had sprits up to sixty feet long in a ninety-tonner, and mainmasts so long that they reached over the taffrail when lowered, and it is this sort of gear, crowned with a square-headed tops'l, which is shown in the *New Hope*. The high mainsail suited stack work, since a working area was left above the stack.[1] As stacks went out tops'ls were enlarged, and mainsails made more square, with the foot as long as the head. The tendency was for eager skippers, influenced by racing fashions, to order each new sail a little bigger than the last, though now, with skippers so frequently changing craft, repeat orders are usual. The old high, narrow sail-plan ("spinnakery," to quote Bill Raven, who has been sailmaking at Maldon for fifty years) must have been easier to sheet, but was clearly less powerful than the modern style. One delightful little fashion in the old tiller-steering days, when mizzens were set on rudder-heads, was a mizzen staysail, stayed to the tiller. Thus a complete little sloop turned as the helm went up or down. The staysail balanced the 'rib-tickler' and helped steering.

Taylor's records show that the practice of bowsing forward the topmast is not done to enable a tops'l which has 'grown' to be sheeted. The later drawings for new sails show the topmast curved till the truck is two feet out of the plumb, but in the old ones it is vertical. The cutting away of the lower luff of the tops'l to clear the mainmast doubling has only come in at Maldon with this fashion of carrying a tops'l forward, though it is shown in photos of Kentish barges of fifty years ago. Whitmore, of Ipswich, preferred his customer to set the sprit and topmast up just as the skipper liked it; then he would measure 'the hole.'

Fred Taylor can fit practically any barge from these records, but sometimes a trip to the sprit-end with a tape-measure is necessary. This used to be worth a shilling to an agile mate; latterly it has been increased to half a crown. One young hopeful tried to make his own terms while he was up there, threatening that if they were not accepted he would tie the end of the tape before coming down! " 'Tie it where you like,' I told him," recalled Bill Raven. " 'I'll soon get up and unhitch it!' "

In addition to the Sadlers, Whitmore, of Ipswich (to-day the last barge sailmaker in that town), Pennick, of Harwich, and Taylor, of Maldon, Goldsmith's had their own loft at Grays, Hibbs made barge-sails at Brightlingsea, Gowen, the yacht sailmaker, formerly made some at Mersea, and in the 1890's J. H. Lott was the Southend sailmaker. Bill Raven in younger days used to visit the Colchester bargeyard, and "Yankee" Bill Phillips looked after repairs for the Bradwell fleet, for which Clem Parker often bought sails from the

[1] See plate facing p. 17.

big yachts. The *Astra's* mainsail was also cut into sails for Paul's
Ipswich-men when that yacht belonged to Hugh Paul. Nethercott,
of Ipswich, today makes sails only for yachts, but had a great name
for barge work in the old days. He made *Sara's* suit for the great
race of 1903.

So much for the builders and sailmakers. Evidence has already
been given that the sailing-barge was known from early days on the
noble Blackwater river, which has seen every type of coastal craft
down the centuries from Roman corn-carrier to Geordie brig,
from Danish longship and medieval carrack to eighteenth-century
schooner, hoy, and billyboy. During the golden age of barging,
however, hay and straw were king in the Blackwater, just as was
cement in the Medway; and the name of Keeble is as much the hall-
mark of Maldon as are Horlock and Stone of Mistley or Strange of
Ipswich. Old James Keeble, hay and straw merchant, had two
nephews, Jim (now an octogenarian, with a fund of memories
which have contributed to this chapter) and Ebenezer (in whose
memory the Maldon Race Cup was given).[1] They carried their
uncle's produce afloat, and built up a fleet which included at one
time and another the *Sunbeam*, *Eva Annie* (now a hulk at Leigh),
Emily, *Keeble*, *Ready*, *Burnham*, and *Diligent*. In later days E. J.
Keeble sailed the *Saltcote Belle*, Alf had the *Varuna*, and S. A.
("Hobb") still carries on the good work in the *Dawn*.

Sadd's, the timber firm whose connexion with the Blackwater is
a very ancient one, had besides the *Record Reign* the spritties *Emma*,
Falcon, and the counter-sterned *Oak*, while among the millers
Eves (now Hasler's) had the old-time swimmies *City of London*
(built way back in 1825) and *Brothers* (1843), later the *New Hope*,
and, last of all, the *Jess*, built for them by Howard and sunk by
the s.s. *Malines* as she lay at anchor in Harwich harbour in fog.
Her hulk lies still at Pin Mill. Baker's had the *Minerva*, and May, the
maltster at Saltcote, just above Mill Beach (often confused with
near-by but distinct Salcot), had the *Saltcote Belle*, built by Howard
after his old *Star* had finally set.

Nearly all the other Maldon craft were owned by farmers or hay-
merchants and were busy with stacks to London, with an occasional timber freight back to vary the usual muck. There were
Thompson's *William and Elizabeth*, *Rose*, *Ann Elizabeth*, and *Two
Friends*; Henry Stevens, of Purleigh Hall, had the *Albion*, and later

[1] See Chapter XVI.

Keeble's *Burnham* and *Eva Annie*, their cabin-tops painted black and white like chess-boards; James Cardnell, of St Lawrence, owned the *Mayland* and *Mundon* (named from the near-by creeks where they did so much work), *Faith* and *Defence*.[1] The Kentish-built *Mundon* was one of the few Maldon-owned barges built with caulked seams, ship fashion. *Three Sisters* was the only one so built at Maldon to my knowledge.

These craft, along with Charlie Gutteridge's, of Vauxhall (which for barging purposes was, as has been mentioned, a little outpost of Essex), made Maldon the real heart of the characteristic old-time barging of the days of plough and sail. Surprisingly, there seems to have been little hoy work to the town in living memory, though George Hales[2] recalls at least one freight of a commodity much associated with it—two hundred barrels of paraffin oil which he unloaded one Friday, having only discharged a freight of stone the previous Monday.

Finally, the little 'miniature' of the Blackwater must not be forgotten. She was the *Energy*, built at Brightlingsea, of only eighteen tons register, trading mostly between Bradwell and Maldon. Her crew were paid by the week, as were Eves' men, though the general Maldon custom was to work on shares.

Registrations are not a very helpful guide, for many Maldon-registered craft were scattered elsewhere, and many 'furriners' were owned in the port, but for what it is worth it seems that in 1885 there were about seventy Maldon-registered barges.

Over on the south shore of the Blackwater, Bradwell was the home of the picturesque Parker fleet—picturesque because the old barge quay, crowned with its towering crooked posts, with the green hill rising behind, is the loveliest of settings for a barge; because of the nature of the barges' work, trading to places with names like Deal Hall, Pigeon Dock, and the Hoo Outfall round the great wall of Bradwell; because of the colourful personality of old Clement Parker himself—for though James Parker was a Bradwell barge-owner in 1850 (William Hatch was another), it was in Clem's era that the place became famous. Often clad in tropical attire, complete with pith-helmet, he would come clattering down in his pony and trap from his farms or from the bargeyard, which was on

[1] Her loss on the Buxey is mentioned in Chapter XIII.
[2] His racing exploits are mentioned in Chapter XVI.

the site of the present water-tower and café above the Green Man, to inspect his barges at the quay. Woe betide the skipper whose craft was unkempt! As one of his former skippers, H. Bell, has recorded[1]:

Clem's fleet was undoubtedly the best kept of any. Rope, paint or varnish were to be had for the asking, and in fact, any material that added to the sea-worthiness or to the smartness of appearance of these craft was never denied one, and great was the competition among the crews, only they would be the last to admit this. Great latitude was allowed as to the colour scheme, no order ever being issued from the house at Bradwell, and the result was—perfect uniformity, the only departure being Bill Polly, when he had the *Strood*, and Tas Paine in the *Dover Castle*; *Strood* having grey rails and the *Dover* having scraped and varnished quarter-boards.

The colour scheme was: Windlass black with woodwork mast colour, coamings mast colour, rail, black with a gilt or yellow line and scroll work of the same, white quarter-boards and French grey decks. ... Once every year each of these barges would load freight to Bradwell, and if the time was from May to September they, when unloaded, would spend a week 'on the ways.'

The mast would be lowered, sails unbent and taken up the hill to a small meadow which was "Yankee Bill's" domain, who would go over the gear with a small tooth comb for the smallest chafe or rent, after which the crew would stockholm the ropes and dress the sails with a mixture of red and yellow ochre, cod oil, and sea-water. "Yankee Bill" was reputed to be the world's worst sailmaker, but he kept those sails in perfect condition. He was an excellent workman, but as a designer he left a lot to be desired. He would not realize that a sprittie is very sensitive as to where her centre of effort comes. I have known skippers tie a piece of spun-yarn round the standing part of the forestay fall as a mark for the best position of the block, and this would be moved half an inch at a time until the best rake of the mast was found —that was our usual practice in the *Veronica*. When one remembers that it was a threefold purchase, the infinitesimal difference that one half-inch could make to the rake shows to what lengths we would go to get the best out of those lovely craft.

"Yankee Bill" spoilt the *Veronica* first by cutting a topsail too high in the head, and after that, when a new mainsail was required, by cutting the peak too high. She was never the same after that.

It was an inflexible rule that every accident, no matter how trivial, must be reported. One day a first-rate skipper arrived with a tell-

[1] In *Spritsail*, summer 1949.

tale bend in his anchor stock. It did not escape Clem Parker's eye.

"You've hit something," he observed. "Well, yes, but it didn't do a mite of damage," the skipper expostulated, but in vain. Clem Parker brooked no exception to his rules. "I'm sorry," he said, "but you know the orders. You're sacked." In fact, however, the owner was the loser and the skipper the gainer, for he shipped at once in a better craft elsewhere.

Clem Parker's barges were unique in carrying their bobs—his Oddfellows' mark of the heart and hand—on flag halyards. Down they had to come when the barge was alongside the quay. Jack Spitty, at one time skipper of the *Lord Warden* and the *Victa* (formerly the *& Co.*, built up to a six-foot side and later wrecked at East Mersea) and now landlord of the Chequers, at Goldhanger, has told me that Alf Horlock rebelled against this fashion when he sailed the *Veronica* in the races. Her bowed topmast soon let the bob droop, so he had his mounted on a spindle, and the rest followed suit. Though he came ashore in 1923 at the age of twenty-six, Jack Spitty, son of the redoubtable smack skipper of the same name and great-nephew of the famous "Righto" Spitty,[1] yet tasted the spacious days of barging, seeking his own freights at the London offices of Gilders, Sully, and Clarke. He worked sometimes up Salcot Creek, seldom visited by barges, and on one occasion came right up to the White Hart, where no craft will be seen again, for the creek has since been dammed to save flooding. His son's name, Victa Warden Spitty, recalls and records his barging days.

While the *Water Lily* was by common consent 'flagship' of the Parker fleet, the racer *Veronica* was the fleetest; indeed, she was perhaps the fastest flat-bottomed craft ever launched, though when Jack Nunn, sen., had the *Princess* he could always beat *Veronica* to windward, working or racing. *Veronica's* run started just abaft the mainmast, and she was a flier at work as well as in the races. She once finished loading a stack at Burnham at midday and started unloading it next afternoon at Woolwich. *Triton* (which was destroyed by fire one hot week-end at Nine Elms) was noted for her handiness.

When the fleet broke up *Violet Sybil* and *Nellie Parker* went to Wakeley's, who carry on much of the traditional Parker work,

[1] See *Last Stronghold of Sail*, p. 99, where I plead guilty to a confusion between "Righto" and Jack. Aaron, of course, was "Righto's" nephew.

including the wall-stone, sand from Alresford, and English wheat from Saltcote mill, under the management of Victor Parker. *Nellie Parker* was given an auxiliary, and in June 1947 was towing *Violet Sybil* when the pair fouled Southwark Bridge and both sank. They were raised and repaired, *Nellie Parker* then being bought by Captain Frank Whiting, of the *Northdown*. *Verona* remains at work under Shrubsall's bob; but these are the last survivors of the Bradwell-men, for *Veronica* raced herself to pieces for Everard's, *Duchess* was lost at Dunkirk, and *Daisy* on the Maplins. *Champion* was sunk in collision off the Mid-Blyth buoy, and *Fanny* is now a house-boat. I hope her present occupiers do not know too much about all the sludge freights Tubby Blake did in her.

The Kirbys were another great Bradwell barging family. Tom Kirby had five sons, each of whom came to him in turn as mate, and when the youngest took his own craft the old man had to come ashore at last—a family record by no means unparalleled on the East Coast. One of those sons, Bill, had the *Water Lily* till shortly before his death in 1948. This craft was built for the Spittys from the proceeds of the sale of the licence of the Bradwell Inn, The Case is Altered; she later passed to Parker and to Wakeley's, and, almost completely rebuilt on Pin Mill hard, was offered for sale in 1948 for over £7000.

Mr T. Goymer, who farmed West Wick, at Bradwell, tried his hand for a time in competition with Parker, the quay being divided between them. The *Bradwell* was built for him, and he also bought the *Dover Castle* and one of the many *Mary Ann*'s (an antique which was a continual failure), as well as hiring the *Denton*. The venture, however, was not a happy one, perhaps because he was of too unassuming a nature to control his skippers. At any rate, when his son (who to-day farms Muggeridge's, at Battlesbridge) was put on to the barges' books as a lad, it only took him a few months to see that the craft were all losing money, and when the local school-master, called in to test his theories, ruled that "the boy's right" telegrams were sent to the skippers to return home, and all the craft were laid on the mud in Bradwell Creek for sale. So generous to themselves were the skippers with 'expenses,' Mr Goymer recalls, that they would often hand in only a sovereign or a sovereign and a half as the owner's share of a freight.

While the Ipswich *Tollesbury* (a Sandwich-built coaster which saved over two hundred troops at Dunkirk) was originally owned by Fisher, in the village whose name she bears, the Frosts were the chief Tollesbury owners with a fleet of boomies. The Brightlingsea-built *James Bowles* (named after the original Tollesbury owner) was their first ship, in which William Frost brought his sons up to barging. Then came the Kentish-built *Darnet*, the Ipswich-built *Empress of India*, and the *Lord Hamilton* (one of Walker and Howard's Littlehampton 'Lords'), which was the best of them all, with such features as a proper lavatory and galley. Joe Culf, of Tollesbury, also had the *Mary Kate*.

Jim Frost, who is now, at the age of three score years and ten, the grand old man of barging in this grand old village of yachtsmen and smackmen, had one of the most bizarre escapes imaginable in his boyhood. He was to have shipped as boy with his brother in the yacht *Mignonette*, which in May 1884 sailed from England to Australia, but, as his brother could not go, he also was prevented, and his place was taken by a nineteen-year-old lad named Richard Parker. There were three other hands, including E. Brooks, of Brightlingsea. Off Madeira the yacht foundered, and the four of them were eighteen days in the boat under the tropical sun. In their extremity, two of the men killed that boy and drank his blood—an act in which the Brightlingsea man would not join. The whole story emerged in a sensational trial when the couple were sentenced to death, which was commuted to six months' imprisonment.

Spared from that grisly experience, Jim Frost became one of the best known of East Coasters and a surveyor to the Harwich Barge Club. His craft used to bring coal on to Tollesbury hard, where it was unloaded into carts and dumped in the streets for sale at sixteen shillings a ton, of which the carter was paid one shilling. The crier with his bell informed the village in good broad Essex that "The *Darnet* is up Woodrope with a cargo of coals. Give your orders to the Captain, who has also brought a freight of Sunderland dishes." Out came the housewives with buckets and baths to gather their share and collect their orders. Bagged, the price was £1 a ton.

On one voyage to Colchester—where, incidentally, he brought the Co-operative Society's first water-borne coals—Jim Frost remembers seeing seven boomies waiting to unload. One queer freight he took was the jib of a crane, four feet longer than the barge, from Fambridge to Keyham. "We had seventy tons of ballast to steady her below decks, and two bowsprits sticking out on top that time," he recalled. Queerer still was the complete removal of a chapel from Colchester to Bursledon, in Hampshire—"pulpit and all; everything bar the parson." Jim Frost cast an interesting light on coasting under sail in giving the opinion that the worst harbours to take on the East Coast were Scarborough, Whitby, and Bridlington, and, down Channel, Bridport.

The old *James Bowles* is (or was till recently) still lightering at Portsmouth; the rest all met violent ends: *Darnet* in the Wash; *Empress of India* on the Caistor Sand; *Lord Hamilton* on the Goodwins, her crew spending no less than sixty hours in the rigging; and *Mary Kate* off Alderney.

Tollesbury Creek still sees a few smacks and yachts up it, though never a sailing-barge, but another old-time harbour near by is now so deserted that its former busy days are practically forgotten. This is Old Hall Creek, running up into the finest wild-fowl marshes in Essex. At its head stand a couple of cottages. That is all—now. But till thirty years ago those cottages were a licensed inn, The Hoy, with a signboard showing a ship in full sail, and there was once considerable traffic up to the brickworks, coal-yard, and lime-kiln carried on there by Richard Banyard, grandfather of R. E. Banyard, whose verses adorn these pages. The barges and ketches owned and chartered by his grandfather, Mr Banyard tells me, fetched chalk from Purfleet for the kilns, and coal from Newcastle. The boomie *John and Martha* was lost on Spurn Head in the gale of 1884, Captain Brand, of Mersea, and his crew being saved. Here traded the stackies owned by Seabrook, of near-by Tolleshunt d'Arcy—the *D'Arcy*, *Defender*, and *Pride of Essex*—loading roots, straw, and hay for London at a charge of one shilling, and one shilling and sixpence to unload the muck they brought back.

Maldon river is a rare place for dry stories of the humour and eccentricities of its characterful natives. As well as being the last barge to be tiller-steered (as late as 1930 or 1931), the *Eva Annie* was the first (and last!) stackie to sport a 'wheelhouse.' That was how her skipper, "Balsham" King, described it, but when a boat-load of bargemen rowed off from Woolwich one day at his invitation to admire it they found it was actually a cabbie's umbrella mounted on the 'rib-tickler' in such a way that he could turn it against the driving rain.

George Cooper recalls how one day when he was mate of the

Maid of Connaught, stretching up under the Maplins in a breeze, they came up on the *Eva Annie* staggering along under her stack, and luffed out past her in a squall. "Balsham" had his umbrella in action, and demonstrated it proudly. "Wherever I go, Cooper," he panted, shoving the tiller hard up to the weather rail, and then darting down his deck with it as she bore away, "whever I go, the beauty of it is my bloody wheelhouse comes with me."

STACK-BARGES LONDON-BOUND

XII

THE COLNE

David Francis, Passage Barge Skipper—The Lop-sided "Exact"—Wivenhoe's Contribution—Aldous and Stone of Brightlingsea—Sawyer's Boomies—Howe's Black Tops'ls— The Colchester Concentration

COLCHESTER has of recent years stolen Maldon's barging glory. Throughout the old days described in the last chapter, however, the picture in the Colne much resembles that in the Blackwater, though for some reason there has never been any regular barge-building at Colchester, and surprisingly little in the other Colneside shipyards.

Best known among the old Colchester stackies were George Littlebury's *Eureka*, which later went to Horlock's and is now a yacht-barge in the Medway, and *Unique*. Bentall's *Hyacinth* and *Violet* were later added to Littlebury's fleet. W. C. Murrell's Bermondsey craft were as much at home in Colne as were Gutteridge's, from Vauxhall in the Blackwater. The Harwich boomies' work to Colchester gasworks has already been described,[1] and Moy's, the coal-merchants, had the old *Rebecca* till she was dismantled during the Colchester earthquake of 1884, when Hythe quay rocked and the man at the masthead sending down her gear shouted to his mates on deck to stop shaking him.

With three barges in the 1820's[2] Charles Parker seems to have been the first Colchester owner of note. One of his skippers, Joseph Beckwith of the *Amity*, then became owner of the town's hoy barges in their heyday, and the Francis family, members of which sailed for him, in their turn became owners of the present-day fleet.

Through the eyes of David Francis quite a picture of local barging in the Beckwith era can be built up. He is best remembered in Colchester as skipper of the *Gem*,[3] that celebrated hundred-ton

---

[1] Chapter VII.   [2] See Chapter II, note at p. 45.
[3] Built of iron at South Shields in 1881, the *Gem* was registered at Colchester the same year. She was 80 feet long, 16 feet beam, and had an engine of 20 horse-power.

At Colchester

ABOVE: Loading baled straw for the Kentish paper-mills, 1946
BELOW: *Mayland* starts the long 'poke' up to East Mills, 1949

End of an Era

May and *Kimberley* loading wheat from the *Abraham Rydberg*, Ipswich, 1939

sailing-steamer which was the last of the Colchester passage boats from 1902 to 1914, and later went coasting here, there, and everywhere.

Oh, the tales of the *Gem*! "I can see David still, trotting down Hythe Hill with a lump of coal under each arm, singing out to them to get the mainsail set," one old-timer chuckled untruthfully but picturesquely. She poked her way into one corner of Holland and could not turn round, but had to come out miles stern first till they could swing her. She loaded in another Dutch backwater and then had not enough water to get away, so they had to tow a string of borrowed lighters with part of her cargo till it could be restowed. She fetched the machinery for the sugar-beet factory at Cantley, in Norfolk, and the manager insisted that, by way of acknowledging her services, she should take away the first cargo of sugar to Ipswich. So she did, and, as luck would have it, the boat got adrift on the hatches and tore the cloths, wetting the precious freight. None of it worried David Francis. Only one of his yarns of the *Gem* showed him perplexed. That was when he shipped a new engineer and rang down "full astern" as she came alongside Poole quay. The engineer gave "full ahead," and she rammed a schooner, which started to settle by the stern. "The schooner skipper hopped on to my bows and came up on one side as the engineer came up from below on the other," said David. "That was too much. 'I'll talk to you beggars one at a time,' I told them. 'I can't cope with the pair of you. One of you buzz off and come back when I've done with the other.'" With three lads as his crew young David Francis was back and forth between Colchester, Mistley, and London "like a hand-saw." "The four of you don't add up to one grown man," the Mistley pilot complained one day after totting up the inconsiderable total of their ages. But the *Gem* is really outside the scope of these tales.

One of David Francis's first berths (after he had served a while in the Harwich packets when they were still paddlers) was in the Colchester boomie *Jabez*. Left at the tiller in a flat calm off Flamborough Head one scorching day, he had a fancy for a swim, and went overboard. The horrified skipper, coming on deck, picked up the mainsheet and threatened to use it on his backside as he came aboard, which David Francis countered with a threat to swim ashore on Flamborough Head. Not till the skipper saw he was in earnest did a truce result.

I

At the end of that trip there was a quarrel, David and the other lad having been promised the mate's money till a man was found. The promise was not kept, and the two lads took the boat from Hythe quay, rowed down to where the boomie lay above Pyefleet, cleared out their gear, and left her. The skipper shipped a new crew, and the *Jabez* sailed—into the never-to-be-forgotten gale of 1881, to disappear with all hands. She is believed to have capsized, timber-loaded, though it is said no other boomie ever turned over.

Soon afterwards David Francis was mate in the Rochester barge *Caprice* (in which Littlebury, of Colchester, had a quarter-share). There was a lot of work taking rape-seed from Hammersmith to Dunkirk then, and after one such trip the *Caprice* and the *Pride of Ipswich* came out of the French port together and ran up the Gore Channel off Margate neck and neck. Here they parted company, the *Pride of Ipswich* standing on for London, the *Caprice* running over the Ridge and up the Rays'n into Colne, which she entered just eleven and a half hours out of Dunkirk—a fine day's sail.

Then came the first command, the Colchester *Exact*, so named because, after being built on beer-barrels in a field at the Hythe in 1859, she would only just go under Hythe bridge, then a pile structure. It was a queer bit of building altogether, for it was not until she was framed up that her builder, Carrington, began to have doubts about his measurements, his faith undermined by the comments of the onlookers. And, sure enough, a check measurement showed she was too wide by several inches. Whereupon they took down one side, shortening the floors and moving in the chine keelson and timbers. The other side they left alone! Even then, when she was launched, she jammed between the bridge-piles, and, rather than crush her shoving her through, they took her back to her berth. That night Carrington, the builder, and Benjamin Beckwith, the owner, sallied forth with adzes and carved away the piles of the bridge, rubbing mud over the new cuts to conceal their handiwork, and as she went under on next day's tide the owner was heard to utter the one satisfied comment "Exact!" The name stuck, as the barge nearly had; no one noticed the vessel's lop-sidedness till one day the Ipswich pilot, rowing past her bow, paused on his oars in astonishment to ask David Francis why there was more bloody barge on one side than on the other; and apparently no one ever did notice the nocturnal enlargement of Hythe bridge.

As well as being lop-sided, the only barge ever built at Colchester[1] was painfully slow and undeniably leaky. "She was built cod's head and mackerel tail, so she ought to have been fast, but she drove me to despair," was David Francis' summary. When I asked him if she was noticeably faster or stiffer on one tack than the other he said she moved so slowly at her best that she could not go any slower at her worst.

One time they were bound down to Mistley with grain when it came on to blow. The other barges slipped over the Ridge on the high water, but by the time the *Exact* arrived the tide was gone, and they had to go blundering down to the Spitway in the dark, both hands at the tiller. They found the then unlit Spitway, and the mate asked if he should sound. "No," said David; "for we can't turn back, so she's got to go through"—and through she went, and into Harwich. Their hands had been too full to pump, and when they brought up she lay listing from the water in her, part of her cargo wet. David Francis got on the train at Wrabness and came home to tell Beckwith, who merely observed that the barge of which he was so proud had done well to beat the other craft. "She wouldn't have done it but for being like a duck on the water," he declared, still glorying in his creation. So back to Groom's office at Harwich travelled David Francis to carry out the ritual of "lodging a protest," as the bargemen still picturesquely call claiming on the insurance club for damage by stress of weather.

Next came the *Arnold Hirst*, a cranky little 65-tonner. Beating up Swin one day she lay over with a deck-cargo of barrels so much that the spray was landing in her mainsail peak. That was a sign she had had enough, so they ran her on to the sand, let go, put a bass spring on her chain, and when she came adry hopped overboard to gather a bag of cockles. The Maplins were a favourite harbour in those days with the men who preferred cockling to swinging round the anchor, till the Harwich 'club' put a stop to the practice among their members' barges.

The *Pride of the Colne*, which came next, was altogether a better model, doing a good deal of passage work. Loading the town's groceries in London one morning, she was in Colchester delivering them at 5 P.M., and off went Beckwith to the newspaper office to insert a paragraph recording that he had beaten the Great Eastern

[1] This is according to local tradition. The 1885 Mercantile List also mentions *A.B.C.D.* (1865), *Ceres* (1807), and *Mary Ann* (1826).

Railway. At the end of the last century there were always two of Beckwith's hoys on this carrier service, aiming to arrive Tuesdays and Fridays. When it looked as if one would miss her freight, another took over. Thus one day the *Jessie*, already in London, reported doubt about loading an urgent lot of goods on the next day's tide. Away from Colchester went the *Pride of the Colne* with a freshening north-easterly breeze. As she passed the Regent's Canal David Francis saw the *Jessie* inside, her gear down, so he carried on to Black Eagle Wharf and was half-loaded when up came the *Jessie*, just saving her tide, but too late. She took the *Pride's* cargo of loam, and away went the *Pride of the Colne*. She was in Colne next day, but lost her tide in 'Roman's' (that awkward reach between Wivenhoe and Rowhedge which catches you with the wind westerly) and had to bring up. However, the huffler carried the news up to the Hythe, and at dawn horses and men came down the wall to help the crew poke and pull up: and doubtless the *Pride* stuck to passage work till she, in her turn, fell out in favour of another barge. Such was the strenuous hoy trade in the days of the last, hopeless struggle of the river against the rail.

Brightlingsea was the one considerable barge-building centre on the Colne; in fact, after the old *Rebecca* the only barges built elsewhere on the river were, I believe, the Government barge *Sir Stafford Northcote* (which I credit to Wivenhoe shipyard, since a half-model in my possession came from the loft there), and the *Atrato, Niagara,* and *Wyvenhoe,* built at Wivenhoe, 1896–98, and now working from Rochester as motor-barges.

Aldous', of Brightlingsea, who developed small fishing-craft to the peak of their perfection in their little twelve-ton Colchester oyster smacks, must also have been among the pioneers of the boomies, for the *James Bowles, Dovercourt, Harwich,* and *Antelope* were built there between 1865 and 1869. Captain Steggles, who had the *Harwich* for many years, tells me she had the Aldous characteristic of a rather narrow bottom and flaring sides, which detracted from her stiffness, but he counted her a fast and handy craft. The *Masonic* was another Aldous boomie; and at least four spritties were built in the town—*Peace, John and Ann, Energy,* and *Ada*—presumably at Aldous', though locally they are unrecorded. Thereafter the yard seems to have found yacht work, and even the little oyster smacks at £10 a ton, more profitable. Bob Eves recalls the smack-like qualities which made the *Peace* the best sea-barge he ever had. She carried a little lee helm—to steer her you stood to windward of the tiller and leaned on it—but as she hit each sea she rose and wriggled to windward. He has turned down Swin in his slippers when other craft had decks awash.

In 1924, however, Aldous Successors, Ltd, built the hulls of a pair of 200-ton giants for Paul's, of Ipswich: *Aidie* and *Barbara Jean*. With a registered tonnage of 119, against the *Redoubtable's* 99 and *Greenhithe's* 89, they were second in size only to the Everard quartet built at Yarmouth about the same time; but, alas, that was their only claim to distinction, barring their honourable end—for both were lost on the beaches of Dunkirk in 1940. I have been told their sterns were filled out after the original plans were passed; anyway, they had the hindquarters of mules, and were among the ungainliest things on the coast.

Stone Brothers, however, built four good spritties, *British Empire* and *Federation*[1] for Howe, of Colchester, and *Greta* and *Millie* for Jarvis and Hibbs, the Brightlingsea owners, who also had the *Centaur*, *Burnham*, and the little *Unity*, which was so small that her crew worked on a two-thirds share instead of the usual half.[2] The *Lancaster* they rebuilt on the bottom of another barge which had been burned out.

George Ventris, skipper and part-owner of the *Anglia*, was perhaps the greatest yarn-spinner among the barging fraternity. A very popular figure at Mark Lane, he often charmed a freight from the merchants there simply by reason of his delightful personality. He was part-owner with Hibbs, of Brightlingsea, and skipper of the *Anglia* from the time she was built until she was sold to Paul's on his retirement.

Hibbs and Jarvis also had the craft later associated with Owen Parry's, of Colchester, who sold them in 1932, on closing their oil-mills at the Hythe, to the London and Rochester Trading Company —*The Brownie* (never, for some reason, referred to even casually as *Brownie*), *Victor*, *Sirdar*, *King*, and *Queen*, of which the last three are mentioned among the racers in Chapter XVI.

The Brightlingsea Stones are unconnected with the Mistley family, but descend from the noted Erith barging family, of whom Robert Stone was owner of the famous racers *Anglo-Saxon*, *Anglo-Dane*,

---

[1] Now with London and Rochester Trading Company.   [2] See plate facing p. 32.

and *Anglo-Norman*, which last-named in 1873 sailed and won a
£100 challenge match with Wood's *Sappho*—"the race between
Wood and Stone." Nine years later the *Anglo-Norman* was fitted at
Brightlingsea with what is claimed to have been the first wheel ever
put in a spritsail barge. Robert Stone also designed the *Plantagenet*
—which was such a fast barge loaded that, in 1883, she earned her
skipper the princely sum of £5 a week—and owned the *Challenger*,
one of the few successful racers which were also among the fastest
craft loaded. His sons, Douglas, John, and Frank, established Stone
Brothers, which under the next generation, Robert and Douglas
Stone, made a great name for small one-designs before being incor-
porated with James and Company, Ltd, during the Second World
War. Stone's were among the few barge-builders to work from
lines, which were then interpreted in a half-model before building
began.

Sawyer's, of Brightlingsea, were latter-day boomie-owners,
round about the time of the First World War, with shares in the
Medina and the Littlehampton *Kindly Light*.[1] After that war they
had the *Sarah Colebrooke* and *Ethel Edith*, which Frank Ainger took
after his *Medina* was run down and sunk, keeping her running till
1927, when the game was up, and he turned to yachting, taking
charge of the *Tamesis*, the last of the old-time schooner yachts on
Colne. They also owned the sprittie *Delce*, which later was bought
by Francis and Gilders, and three others still with that firm, *Alaric* (a
Sandwich barge originally named *Shamrock*, mulie rigged under
Sawyer, and later the first Colchester auxiliary), *Lady Helen*,
and *Leslie West*, which both came from Samuel West, Ltd, of
London.

Thomas and Carolina and *Theodosia* were among the 'furriners'
regularly trading to Brightlingsea in the days when most of the coal
was unloaded on the hard, and when 'cotchelling' freights were a
commonplace. That was the name given, eighty-year-old Ben
Hibbs tells me, to freights which had to be picked up at several
places. Twenty thousand bricks and one hundred sacks of flour was
a common Brightlingsea job which he recalls the *Lucretia* (an Ipswich-
built barge owned by C. F. Frost, of St Osyth) and Murrell's *Colne
Valley* handling. The bricks came from a field at Thorrington, and
were loaded at the top of Alresford Creek; then you sailed round

---

[1] A painting of this ketch, by R. Chappell, who painted most of the boomie pictures in
this book, hangs in the bar of the Evening Star, at Brightlingsea.

and up Brightlingsea Creek to St Osyth for a half-cargo of flour,
and finally picked up the rest at Walton tide-mill—receiving seven-
pence a quarter for your pains!

Having surveyed the old days in Blackwater and Colne, the picture
may be brought up to date.

After Beckwith's days the Colchester 'seeking' fleet comprised
six barges owned by Henry Howe, and distinguished by their black
topsails. They were the *British Empire*, *Falconet*, *Keeble*, *Federation*,
Surprise, and *Peace*. In 1915 Joshua Francis, Howe's nephew,
nephew also of David Francis and son of the skipper of the old
Rebecca, returned to his native Colchester to manage these craft,
and, after Howe's death, in partnership with Cecil Gilders, to gather
round them into one fleet all the local craft, with the exception of
the mill barges—Green Brothers' *Ethel Maud* and *Mayflower* at
Maldon, and Marriage's *Fleur-de-Lis*, *Leofleda*, and *Violet* at Col-
chester. Sadd's came in with the *Oak* (now back at Maldon, timber-
lightering) and *Emma* (that beautiful Maldoner which was smashed
up by a mine at Rotherhithe). *Ready* (since renamed *Mirosa* when
Trinity House wanted her old name for a new tender) came from
Keeble's, of Maldon, the last of that old fleet. The Harwich-built
Centaur, perhaps the finest all-rounder of the fleet, came from John
Sawyer, of Brightlingsea, as did the *Alaric*, *Delce*, *Lady Helen*, and
Leslie West. *Varuna*, a Shrubsall racer, *Sea Spray*, *Clara*, and *Agnes
and Constance* came from Stanford-le-Hope; *George Smeed*, as her
name suggests, derives from the old Kentish Smeed Dean firm;
Saltcote Belle and *Beaumont Belle* were the beauties of the upper
Blackwater and Walter Backwaters, Colonel R. C. Bingham
brought in the auxiliaries *Castanet* and *Bankside*, while *Ethel Ada*
and *General Jackson* were the last of Eldred Watkins' Ipswich-men;
and the latest acquisition, *Colonia*, was previously one of Cranfield's
fine ladies.

War casualties were heavy in the Colchester fleet. Besides the
Emma, the *Gertrude May* was mined in the Wallet in 1942 and the
Norwegian mate lost, though Skipper Farrington was saved, and
to-day has the *Alaric*—which was herself machine-gunned, skipper
Harry Eves being killed. Both Colonel Bingham's craft were
victims of enemy action, *Bankside* being mined and lost with her
skipper off the Maplins, and *Castanet* ripping her bottom out on a
wreck in the Orwell. Many East Coast barges suffered less spectacu-

lar damage from neglect and worm as they lay flying barrage-balloons or acting as mine-spotting stations.

In addition to the craft flying the gold-and-purple bob, *Mayland*, now owned by Prior, of Burnham, and Shrubsall's *Gladys*, *Verona*, and *Veravia* also work with the Colchester fleet. *Alaric*, *Varuna*, and *Leslie West* have recently been provided with 66-horse-power Kelvin Diesel auxiliaries, and doubtless several others will enjoy the same mixed blessing. The smaller, less profitable craft are gradually being sold off, but Joshua Francis, who was himself sailorman and tug skipper before swallowing the anchor and resigning himself to the office, believes there will be some left working entirely under sail at least as long as crews can be found to man them.

In addition to local craft, Paul's have a depot here, and there is generally one of their big Ipswich mulies lying hard by the bridge. Everard's coasters continue to serve the gasworks, and their smaller sailormen join in the Colne trade, with Sully's and an occasional London and Rochester Trading Company craft or a Whitstable barge under Daniels' flag during the timber season or when the baled straw is going away to the paper-mills in Kent. Though the present-day activity is nothing to what went on thirty years ago, there is plenty of life and variety in the craft to be seen at Colchester. After the ten-day fog of December 1948 ten craft towed up on one busy Sunday.

Though most of the old practices are gone, Colchester is the last place on the coast where you may still see barges 'poked up,' as is yet done to reach Marriage's mills when the motor-boat is not available. These mills are among the most exacting destinations still in regular use, for barges must pass under two bridges so low that a few inches too much water means hitting the bridge, and a few inches too little means stopping. One of the best carriers to achieve this squeeze is Sully's *Valdora*. The London and Rochester Trading Company built the *East Anglia*[1] specially for this work in 1908, and she was chartered for it till 1926. At this time many Colchester craft were reputedly too big for it. Oddly enough, however, when the lean times of the thirties made 'lowering down and poking up' less unpopular several of these barges mysteriously shrank, and became capable of squeezing under the bridges which their skippers had vowed them incapable of negotiating as long as easier freights were available!

[1] Foundered 1949.

XIII

CROUCH AND ROACH

Shore Ends and Havengore—The Burnham Boomies and Wakering Brickies—Battlesbridge and Paglesham—Meeson and Rankin—Sailing for Turn—Toll of the Buxey—The 1914 Blow

TIME was when you might find fifty barges waiting a slant in Shore Ends, taking it in turns to sail to Burnham for bread, and if you sailed through that fleet up Crouch and Roach, in among that fascinating archipelago of creeks and islands that makes up the southernmost Essex pensinula, you would find sprits decorating the sea-walls of Foulness and Potton, Wallasea and Rushley, New England and Havengore, in 'the Parlour' at Millhead, at the mills of Rochford, Stambridge; and Battlesbridge; little brick barges slipping in and out through the back door of Havengore Creek; and sturdy boomies occupying the tideway at Burnham where now the flimsy masts of the yachts cluster like a thicket of saplings. But over the last forty years the barges have decreased as the yachts have multiplied, and to-day there are only two owned and working in these waters, the *Joy* and *Lord Roberts*, and probably few of the Burnham week-enders have even heard of the fleet of boomies formerly owned by Smith there.

They were comparatively rough craft employed in the coal-trade, and unequal to tackling dry cargoes, but they included an interesting vessel in the Kentish-built *Friendship*, which shares with the *Jubilee*, built by Vaux, of Harwich, and the *Expedience*, built at Yarmouth, the distinction of being the only schooner-rigged craft finding a place in these tales. The *Friendship*[1] was on one trip three weeks in the North Sea, during which time she was given up as lost. She worked chiefly with coal to Dover and Folkestone, where on one occasion she sat on a buoy which came right through her bottom into the hold. Finally she was sunk by a steam collier off Spurn Head in 1911. Other craft in Smith's fleet were the *Speedwell*,

[1] See plate facing p. 81.

Magnet, Vanguard, Thistle, and *Dauntless.* Another Burnham oyster-merchant, Peter Richmond, owned the boomie *Lucy Richmond,* built for him by Robertson at Ipswich, and named after his niece.

Prior, the local shipwright, had the *George and Annie* and *Jesse,* and later took over the *Mayland,* which his son, Reg. Prior, still owns, though she works with Francis and Gilders' fleet, for which Prior's carry out big jobs, such as the conversion of the *Alaric* and *Varuna* into auxiliaries. Other craft owned at Burnham included the *Crouch,* which was run down and sunk in the Swin, the 'little' *Energy* (so called to distinguish her from a ketch of the same name), and the *Crouch Belle,* built at Hullbridge and later with the London and Rochester Trading Company.

The great home of barging on Burnham river was, however, Battlesbridge, the limit of navigation. As lately as 1936 James Agate wrote[1] of "the lovely unexpected village of Battlesbridge, where, suddenly, in the middle of the inner landscape, arise masts and brown close-furled sails of some sea and river-going barge." To-day, though the village retains its unexpected and untidy loveliness, with its great mills dwarfing the weather-boarded bargemen's homes, though the Barge Inn sports a most spirited signboard showing a well-painted craft in full sail, and barge-paintings adorn the walls of the bar parlour, only a very occasional motor barge or auxiliary pays a visit. The last regular traders were Rankin's *Joy* and *Lord Roberts.* The latter, which was formerly one of Meeson's fleet, can claim the unique record of having had only two skippers in the forty-eight years of her life—W. Moss, who is in charge of her now, and T. White, who commanded her for over twenty years and then retired to take the Barge Inn, of which his widow is still landlady. During Moss's time the *Lord Roberts* was lying at the mills, when her stemband broke and all her gear crashed on deck. The topmast snapped short over the wheelgear, putting the steering out of action and carrying away the mizzen, while the sprit made matchwood of hatches, 'fore-and-afters,' and coamings. But those days are gone, and now only the old Ipswich *Haste Away* lies there, an unrigged house-boat, to recall faintly the days when Saunders, the huffler, can recall fourteen craft up, some with maize, some light to load wheat.

That was when the mills, which are now Matthews', belonged to Meeson's, of whom A. J. Meeson was the barge-owner. In addition

[1] In *Ego 2* (Gollancz).

to *Malvoisin* and *Paglesham*,[1] his craft were the *Sarah and Helen*, *Roach*, and *James*, all of which had the name for being well found. Anything those barges wanted they had; and those of over a hundred tons were all three-handed. He also had the noted little *Rainbow*, built away in the heart of the Hertfordshire countryside. A stumpie of only fifteen tons register (one ton less than the *Cygnet*), the *Rainbow* was about the smallest of all the miniatures, and spent her time scooting about the Crouch and Roach, though once Saunders took her as far as Harwich. She was later converted to a yacht barge, and was to be seen at Leigh complete with a new suit of sails just before the Second World War. In addition to the craft he owned, Meeson also hired to serve his farms and mill the *Thomas and Ann*, belonging to Daniels, of Hullbridge, the *Hope*, owned by Paine, of Battlesbridge, and the *Alfred and Clara* and *Landfield*.

In the Roach, as has been mentioned, only the *Joy* and *Lord Roberts* now survive. These two craft certainly know their way up Paglesham river. Cook's barges may not have the reputation of racers, but on one occasion the *Lord Roberts* was off the Mouse at low water and saved her tide to Stambridge Mill, carrying three headsails all the way, with a martingale rigged on the bowsprit to prevent that long-suffering spar from giving up the ghost.

Many yachtsmen at Burnham and Paglesham recall the 'brickies' which used to scrap about in these waters in such capable and handy fashion. The Wakering 'pitch-piners,' as Rutter's brick barges were known, came to an end when the last was sold in the Second World War. They were cheaply built at Crayford, in Kent, the headquarters of the firm, from the pitch-pine which gave them their name; they were flat as planks, narrow, wet, leaky, and ill-paid, but they were sailed like the devil. They had to be, for they raced for turn to load, the marks for Millhead being at Devil's House, in the Roach, and at Havengore, coming in across the sands. Many a skipper would stealthily turn out on a calm night, feeling a breath of wind, and lift the pawls of his windlass so as to get his anchor without the tell-tale *clinkety-clink* giving the game away to his rivals sleeping peacefully round him. (This game, much practised by the sturdy individualists of Whitstable, worked all right till the barge took a sheer and the handles took charge of the sweating crew. Then, as the chain ran out instead of in, despite all their struggles, the joke was on the crafty ones.)

[1] See Chapters IV and X.

It was said of the pitch-piners that they worked as they sailed, till you could hear the bricks chinking in their holds, and that they were so flat they disappeared under water at the Nore and only came to the surface at the South Whitaker buoy, because there wasn't enough water to submerge any longer. They had water all over them so constantly when on passage that the gear carried on the hatches of more seaworthy barges was regularly stowed in the fo'c'sle before getting under way.

The brickfields were situated just inside Havengore, and before the erection of the bridge, about 1920, this entrance was used by light craft on spring tides, fair wind and foul, both entering and leaving, but loaded craft only came through with fair winds. Shelford Creek, now blocked, also had nearly as much water, but was seldom used. Bound out, the barges were generally brick-laden; inward bound, they often brought sand or ashes for burning in the brickfields.

Before the building of the bridge, traffic to Havengore used the strange, romantic road across the Maplins known as the Broomway, five miles of track, marked by beacons, or brooms, which has for centuries been a thoroughfare when the tide is out, though buried under a fathom of sandy water at high tide. This give and take between the elements leads to some strange situations. Nowhere else probably has a sailing-ship ever collided with a coal-cart. It happened here when the carter, nervous about saving his tide on to Foulness, unhitched his horse and left the cart to its fate off the mouth of the creek, and a barge coming out on the next tide ran full tilt into it.

Millhead was the chief field of recent years, and the day is recalled when twenty 'millheaders' were beneaped together in the Parlour, as the little mud harbour containing several of the berths was pleasantly termed. When the brickyard wanted help from outside craft they flew a Norwegian ensign on a prominent staff, and any barge not fixed for a freight would answer the invitation, sail up, and load bricks. Fred Stow, for thirty-two years master of the K.C., whose rich memory furnishes much of this chapter, recalls the wreck of the Norwegian timber barque *Minnet* on the Maplins. He was mate then in Howard's *Charles and Esther*, and they took three freights from her to the Surrey Commercial, being paid £12 for the first and £20 each for the others. Did this flag come out of the same ship, I wonder?

Landwick has been disused since about 1914. The older men recall this berth and those at Millhead all being occupied together. The latter was worked by Mr Gregory, whose son, Dick, was skipper of the *Gascoigne*.

The original tiller-steered pitch-piners (as memory serves) were *Maplin*, *Dart* (lost in the 1914 gale), *Rushley*, and *Clyde*. Only about sixteen feet beam, they carried 35,000 bricks, and, as these were reckoned at two and a half tons per thousand, they were just under ninety tons burden. *Margaret* and *Landwick* were about five tons bigger. All had topsails and black mizzens, and flew a burgee-shaped bob with blue surround and white centre, with ensign in the fly. They were built at two-year intervals. Then after five years' interval another class, loading 40,000 bricks and flying a yellow cross on a square bob, was built, also at two-year intervals. This class comprised *Elizabeth*, *Nile*, *Wakering*, *Butterfly*, *Havengore*, and *Avon*, which was later cut down to a stumpie.

The *Anthony* (40,000), *Gascoigne*, and *Juniper* (45,000), all three still at work in 1946, were also built by Rutter's, but the *K.C.* (45,000), now a house-barge, was by White, of Conyer, Kent. She took her name from the initials of Katherine Craig, daughter of Eustace Craig, manager at Rutter's. These four were staysail craft without bowsprits, and had wheel-steering. They used Millhead only, though the others worked to Landwick also. The *Juniper* was owned by Mr Juniper, foreman at the brickyard, who also had the *Joseph*, which lay for years as an oyster store-vessel at Brightlingsea, and *Josephine*, and these three were not pitch-piners. In one blow the *Joseph*, after breaking her chain at the Swallowtail, drove ashore on the Buxey, where her master, E. Chapman, and his mate were rescued after many hours in the rigging. The *Juniper*, together with the *K.C.* and *Gascoigne*, were later sold to Tester's, of Greenhithe. The *Anthony* is now an unrigged timber lighter at Heybridge and the *Juniper* a mooring tender at Gravesend.

Most of the brick work was to London, paid at the princely rate of three shillings per thousand bricks, with sixpence a thousand extra for going above bridges. Forty years ago a mate might find himself with seven shillings for a voyage after expenses were paid. When the craft were on the ways the skippers were paid twenty-four shillings a week, and as the yard was at Crayford, to get home took three shillings out of this.

The four large craft, however, voyaged farther afield. Fred Stow took freights to Colchester when the Royal Eastern Counties Institution was building, and to Osea for use in the erection of the Inebriates' Home. (He called it Wood Island; whether because barges take timber from the Norwegian ships anchored there, or because, from a distance, it looks like a clump of trees afloat in the water, I do not know.) Once he went to Melton, up the Deben, leaving Millhead on the daylight high water and arriving in Woodbridge Haven the same evening.

The Howard family were among the earliest Wakering owners. George Howard was the local hoyman a century ago, till, in 1859, J. Wright took over, leaving Shoebury and Wakering for Hartley's Wharf, Horsleydown, on Mondays and returning on Wednesdays. The Howards' craft included the *George* and *Susannah* (run down off the Nore by the *Kathleen*, owned by Mason, of Shoebury), *Flower of Kent*, *Henry and Annie*, *Rawreth*, *Invicta* (now a house-boat at Benfleet), *Harriet Howard*, *Charles and Esther* (later sunk on the Yantlet when with Francis and Gilders), *John and Caroline*, and *Rachel and Julia*. About 1890 the three first named were taken over by Thomas Beaumont Hutson, of Barling, whose foreman, Daniel Watson, had the *Mildreda*, a Shrubsall racer, originally owned by Wakeley's, and run for Watson by Francis and Gilders as a 'ten per center.' Watson was also owner of Howard's *Henry and Annie* (which the *Mildreda* replaced), *R.O.W.*, *Duke of Kent*, and *Gazelle* (built at Milton, Kent). The two latter were mostly in the brickfield work from Wakering and Rochford, but the *Mildreda* did at least one coal freight from the North, and the others did a good deal with stacks. *Gazelle* and *Duke of Kent* were both broken up at Little Wakering.

The regular coal-traders were the boomies *Ladybird* and *Number One*, owned by Cockerton, of Barling; John Cowling, of Stambridge, had the *Royal William*, and bought the *Rawreth* from Howard; and another regular trader sixty years ago was the *John and Mary*, skippered by B. Belton, grandfather of Fred and George Cooper, skippers of the *Persevere* and Marriage's motor-barge *The Miller*; while Mattham's, of Foulness, had the *Louisa* before she went to Parker's. In 1857 Harry Matthams, bargemaster, sailed every other Saturday to Hartley's Wharf, Horsleydown, and "returns to Foulness every other Saturday."

These craft were refitted, doubled, and generally looked after by James Shuttlewood, whose picturesque yard at Paglesham is carried on to-day by his son, Frank. New building was also carried on spasmodically there. Up to about 1880 the place belonged to Kemp, who built the *Louisa* and *Ernest and Ada* in 1855 and 1865. Both these barges were London-registered, *Louisa* being owned first by Mattham's, of Foulness, and then by Theobald, of Leigh, and *Ernest and Ada* by Matthews, of Creeksea. In 1867 and 1868 came two Maldoners, *Crouch* for Hawkins and *Falcon* for Sadd's, and in 1875 *Trotter*, which was one of Eastwood's Kentish brickies after a spell with Jackson, of Shoebury. *Trotter* was the only barge no one ever saw launched. They got her to the top of the ways outside the shed at six o'clock one morning and went home for breakfast. When they came back she was in the river, afloat, and though the dredgermen were at work close by not one of them saw it happen!

James Shuttlewood was an apprentice at the yard two years later when the *Paglesham* was laid down as a wedding present for Mrs Meeson. That barge was to put in a full seventy years' hard work, for it was not till 1947 that she sank in Surrey Docks, bearing her last freight of timber. She is now, I believe, to serve as a Sea Scout guardship.

After a spell at Greenwich, where he helped build, among other craft, the *Orinoco*, for Mason's at Waldringfield, James Shuttlewood returned to Paglesham and took over from Halls, Kemp's successor, before the *Ethel Ada* was laid down in 1903. He and his brother built that big 140-tonner, starting on October 15 and launching the following July 30, with the help of only two boys. Perhaps it was as well they were short-handed, for Shuttlewood's shed measures 85 feet by 24 feet, and *Ethel Ada* was 84 feet by 19 feet 6 inches. She was single-skin oak, rabbeted, and to launch her they took the tie-beams out of the roof of the shed to jack up one end and get the ways under her on a slope. She was started as a speculation, but was bought by Underwood, of Southend, before she was finished.

The brothers also doubled many of the pitch-piners, which were better barges after this operation than when they were new; whether doubling or building, each took charge of one side—James, by right of seniority, taking the starboard, or 'leading,' side.

Those were the days when Paglesham boasted twenty-four oyster smacks (many of them built by Shuttlewood), and a hundred men went back and forth night and morning to work on the Roach. Indeed, it was said that only one man in Paglesham was employed otherwise than on the river or in Shuttlewood's. The firm's hard

has seen thirteen barges on it at once—there were five clustered round
the shed as lately as 1929—with fourteen shipwrights to minister to
them. One Christmas saw no less than four craft all being doubled
together. There was a blacksmith's shop over the wall, and where
the yachtsmen now park their cars was the saw-pit, where every
plank was cut by hand.

The skippers of the pitch-piners used to watch the tide creep up
to the step of the big black shed (built to replace one blown down in
the gale in 1881), knowing that when it reached that mark there was
water through the Havengore. That shed housed the *Joy* for
doubling just before the Second World War, but she is likely to be
the last barge in it; and there is but one oyster smack left working
part-time in Paglesham River, beside which the remains of Meeson's
old *Runwell*, built way back in 1834, moulder quietly in the mud.
Happily Frank is able to find a new outlet for the old tradition in the
construction of husky little yachts, but being a Shuttlewood his
heart is in barges, and when he was away from the Essex saltings
during the Second World War it was to the making of a model
sailorman that he turned his hand. *Reminder* he has named her, not
so much after the Mistley racer, as because she was a reminder of
happy days, familiar places, and old ways.

The Buxey, lying off the mouth of the Crouch, has claimed many
a barge. The *Eva Annie* sank there, and Joshua Francis, of Colchester,
was asked to go and have a look at her. On the way to Hythe
station he met an old crony, who said he would come too. So down
to Brightlingsea they went and boarded the tug, with only a packet
of sandwiches and the shore-going clothes they stood up in between
them. The tug steamed up the Whitaker, and there, sure enough,
lay the poor *Eva Annie*, showing the effects of several tides flooding
over her. They were about to return, when they had a fancy for a
closer look. So it was off shoes for a walk across the Buxey. One
man walked round her bows and saw the cause of the trouble: her
anchor had been let go in shallow water to check her from going
ashore and she had pricked herself on the fluke—a common mishap,
against which bargemen are (or should be) ever on their guard,
making a practice of lowering the stock well below the water in
dock in case of a collision. But what Mr Francis saw under the
quarter was of more immediate interest—to his sharp eyes. The
Eva Annie was sitting on the end of her vang fall tackle, which had

ABOVE: *Veronica* sports a suit of sails such as broke the heart of working barges among her rivals, including a racing foresail set from upper mast-cap to well out along the bowsprit

Racers (1)

ABOVE AND RIGHT: *Queen* and *Reminder*, clippers of the Colne and Stour. *Reminder* wears a leech-line to trim the head of her outsize topsail

(See Chapter XVI.)

Racers (11)

ABOVE: *Mermaid* wins at Maldon. BELOW: *Sara* on Cann's blocks. The rockered bottom, curved rudder foot, bold deadwoods, and racing leeboard mark her type. This shaped leeboard is efficient when only partly lowered. But when the pattern was fitted to the *Percy* at Mistley her handiness was destroyed. She preferred a narrow board, round which she could pivot
(See Chapter XVI.)

washed overboard. That meant only one thing. After the first tide had washed that rope off the deck she had been afloat and drifted over it. If she had floated once she might float again. It was worth trying.

They had not even a hammer and nails with them, but, finding the crowbar stowed in the traditional position across the fo'c'sle

BARGES BRINGING UP, SHORE ENDS

hatchway, they broke away some of the lining, and, with one man emptying the bags of linseed she was carrying and stuffing them in from outside, and the other ramming them down from within and jamming up with any bit of wood that would find a bearing, they stuffed the hole up after a fashion. But when the water came round her, up her sides, over the iron band, and began to run on deck, it all looked to be in vain. Then at the last moment she wriggled, lifted, swung. They set the topsail and, still with water on deck and wondering what was keeping them afloat, blew into Colne.

K

There was still a scare in store for them, for they gave her the anchor as she drove straight up on the flood-tide, and when the chain snubbed the water in her ran forward and she lay drunkenly dabbling her nose in the river for long minutes before finally swinging to her anchor. Wet through and chilled, with nothing to drink and their sandwiches gone, the salvagers found what shelter they could for the night in the foresail, but they had some reward in the Club's gratitude.

Indeed, Mr Francis was looked on as such a wizard for sailing home in a barge which had been sunk nearly a week that when the *Defence* met her end on the same sand his fellow Club members insisted on his going to see her, despite his protest that it was useless; for this time it had blown a gale, and the Buxey had been hungry. Sure enough, when they rowed the boat alongside on the first few inches of flood-tide they were level with the decks. The sand had swallowed the barge up to the iron band in a few wild days' devouring.

The most dramatic memory in these waters, however, ranking with 'Black Tuesday' in 1881 and the great gale of 1884, is of the terrible blow which came out of a clear sky one day just after Christmas in 1914, stripping roofs off the houses in Paglesham village and causing much loss of life on the water.

Harry ("Gallon") Manning, of Wakering, was running up Sea Reach that day in a light south-easterly breeze in company with a number of loaded Smeed Dean barges, when the wind suddenly shifted to south-west and almost at once blew a whole gale, overwhelming several craft. Theobald's *Rover* dragged from the Mid-Blyth to the back of the Chapman light; then the wind flew into the north-west and her chain parted. She drove twelve miles down to the Spile, where an M.L. took off the crew, and she beached herself in Herne Bay, practically unharmed.

Fred Stow, master of the *K.C.*, recalled that Dick Daniels, of the *Paglesham*, called his attention to the unusual behaviour of the barometer, so several barges brought up together in Shore Ends. There the *Dart* broke adrift, drove down the Whitaker, and sank with her crew. Her skipper was twenty-three-year-old Harry Shuttlewood, Frank's cousin, and the mate was a boy of seventeen. A diver declared that she could not be raised, but James Shuttlewood insisted that she could, and set off with Ernie Springett, skipper of the *Anthony*. Choosing a very low tide when the wreck could be reached, they got the *Anthony* over her, and passed rigging wires under the *Dart*. These, however, were not strong enough, and special wires had to be obtained from London. Three months after the disaster another attempt succeeded; the *Dart* was got up on the sand, where her bricks could be unloaded, and she was still at work for Benstead, of Northfleet, in 1940, being eventually broken up at Murston in 1948.

There had been speculation as to where the bodies of the crew would be found. James Shuttlewood declared his nephew was too active a sailor to be caught in the cabin, and he had at least the satisfaction of being proved right in this. The mate's body was below, but nothing was ever found of the skipper. The lead-line, however, was at the masthead, suggestive that he had tried to use it in a last desperate attempt to lash himself there after the foundering.

Eleven bargemen were drowned that night, but there were some miraculous escapes. The *Joy* was among the fleet, only half-loaded, which probably saved her, for she dragged over the Ridge on to the Mouse, and when her crew looked out in the morning they could see seven barges sunk round them, including the *Ethel* on the Whitaker. The skipper of the *Harriet Howard*, having lost both his anchors, found a kedge which had no stock. He drove a broom-handle into it and, bending on a rope, got it overboard, more or less as a despairing gesture. By a miracle it held, saving him and the barge.

Only one barge held fast through it all, the *Jessie*, and curiously enough she was stack-laden, and lay over with the lowest tier of trusses in the water. The stowboat smacks were in similar plight, and when one of them tried to get out of it under close-reefed mainsail her crew had to take a knife and rip her mainsail to enable her to pick up. She then dragged and ploughed her way right over the Buxey, knocking off her keel. Her skipper was found next day lying on the cabin floor, and he died soon afterwards, of exhaustion and exposure.

XIV

SOUTHEND AND SEA REACH

The Market-town of South End—Building the Pier, and Quarrelling over it—Vandervord's Veterans—Shoebury's Shipyard—'Overside' Work—'The Drudger'—Mucking Creek and Hole Haven—A Rough Harbour

As we pursue this voyage of exploration and research up to London from the north the coast keeps changing in character. At Harwich we left the bright, steep, clean shingle-banks and beaches of the Suffolk shore in favour of the shoals and shallows of the muddier Essex saltings. Orfordness, jutting boldly into the blue North Sea, is a very different headland to Walton Naze, where the water is thick with sand and only a few feet deep half a mile from the long pier's head. Alde, Deben, and Orwell are essentially Suffolk rivers, graced by gay shell-duck and elegant heron; Colne, Blackwater, Crouch, and Roach, home of the sombre cormorant and placid oyster, are of the duller but no less endearing Essex soil. Now, rounding Foulness and coasting along the wild and desolate Maplins, we sense for the first time the influence and atmosphere of London River.

This south Essex shore is dominated by Southend, of whose present style and character the less said the better. By a kind of social Gresham's Law much that was useful and wholesome has been steadily ousted over the last half-century by much that is vulgar, artificial, and meretricious, till only old Leigh still retains some trace of integrity—and that is steadily being overwhelmed. I am happy that for present purposes our chief concern is with old Southend: a homely country town, with some of the characteristics of Maldon and Burnham, a handy port for the farmers and brickmakers of the district, and home of hoys and hoymen—"goods barges" to the locals.

Even Southend pier could not originally have been intended as a trippers' paradise. The *Essex Chronicle* made this comment in March 1829:

It is remarkable that along the line of coast of the County of Essex, reckoning from Tilbury Fort to Harwich, an extent of nearly 100 miles, there does not exist a single harbour or landing place at which it is practicable to land passengers or goods with safety and convenience at low water.

The subject of the article was the Southend proposal:

To construct a pier and jetty or causeway from the shore to the deep water . . . so that passengers as well as goods may be landed and shipped at all times of the tide without the delay, inconvenience and risk of accidents which have been so long and justly complained of.

At a meeting at South End in 1829:

A drawing of the Pier and Jetty was produced from which it appeared the pier would give great protection and facility to the shipping and craft as well as to the farmers' wagons and horses which at present had to encounter the muddy shore and beach, and that at certain times of the day when the tide was out. The proposed Pier dues were gone through item by item which, after some discussion, principally between Alderman Mr Thorn and the Messrs Vandervord, who are the only hoymen at South End and who appear to have taken great interest in the concern for the farmers, were unanimously agreed to.

These dues were $1\frac{1}{2}d$. a quarter for corn, and "all else in proportion."

Vandervord is the great name in Southend barge history. This old Dutch family came to Essex to escape the Duke of Alva's persecution at the end of the sixteenth century. There were three brothers, of whom one returned, one settled at Horndon-on-the-Hill, and one at Benfleet. The Benfleet branch seem to have been hoymen from earliest days, and perhaps it is one of their skippers, a certain James Matthews, who is commemorated in this delightful if somewhat incomprehensible South Benfleet epitaph[1] of 1768:

> Sixty-four years our hoyman sailed merrily round
> Forty-four lived Parishioner where he's Aground
> Five wives bear him 33 children Enough
> Land another as honest before he gets off.

While the Vandervords supported the pier project, however, they came to loggerheads with its sponsors over its site and construction, neither of which they approved, and when the tolls began to be enforced, not only on the pier itself, but along the whole shore

[1] To make sense, the verse must be taken as written before honest James' death.

within three miles of the Pier Hotel, their resistance became violent. On August 9, 1834, John Patterson, the company's collector, accompanied by his assistant, John Ingram, boarded the *Minerva*, and in his report to the company he describes how Vandervord

> called for his gun and threatened to shoot me, refusing to pay the dues, prevented Ingram by force from getting aboard the barge and called upon his crew to throw me overboard. I, having laid hands on an anchor for the purpose of distraint . . . the three men prevented me from taking it away and George Vandervord (brother of James) threatened to knock me down with a hand spike.

This *Minerva* must have been a very ancient craft, for the Minerva Inn near the gasworks was named after her, and that was built in 1793.

Three days later the same thing occurred aboard the *Royal Oak*, and the watermen also broke down the pier toll gate, evidently led or incited by the Vandervords, since summonses were taken out against them in the matter. The Vandervords also tried to evade payment by landing goods at Shoebury, but this was still within the three-mile limit, and no less than four of the family were convicted by Wickford Magistrates in 1837 and 1838.

By 1878 the struggle was on more Parliamentary lines, for we find Vandervord then offering the Local Board (as the Council was at that time known) full dues for his ordinary working barges and £100 for his trade (hoy) barges—an offer which was accepted. Two years later it was proposed that hoy cargoes should remain at fifteen shillings a freight—empty barges to pay.

Best known of the Vandervord barges was the *West Kent*, which was built at Deptford in 1865 and later passed to a Wakering owner. Captain Joshua Brand, who died in 1926 at the age of 91, was her skipper for thirty-nine years, working in the limits of Burnham and Rochester to London.

Another of the Brand family had the *George and Alfred*, a Kentish-built barge named after the two senior members of the firm, and sold to Faversham in the early 1900's. *Essex Farmer* was one of the most interesting Vandervord craft, having an overhung spoon-head, transitional between swim-head and the fully developed round bow. She sank off the pier in a gale in 1896 or 1897, but washed up on the beach undamaged, and, after various Leigh and Southend ownerships, did not disappear from the Register till 1921. *John*

Evelyn was an iron 150-tonner, owned by Bowman in 1912, *Emily* dated from 1844, and *Landfield, Deerhound, George Canning,* and *Assistance* were others of the fleet, of which the smartest craft were busy in the hoy work, bringing small parcels for local shopkeepers on a weekly service from Pickled Herring Wharf, and the rest were rough, elderly craft engaged in the local stone, timber, and ballast trade. Last survivor was, I believe, *Jane,* sold about 1913 to F. T. Everard, and lost in 1947, crushed between a ship and the quay in the Royal Docks.

Southend owners seem to have specialized in ancient relics, often second-hand from Maldon. In 1893 Vandervord was still working one of the oldest barges in the Register, the Maldon *Royal Oak,* built at Limehouse in 1798 and cutter (boomsail) rigged.

The Brasiers were another interesting family, barge-owners as far back as 1845, with some incredibly antiquated craft. Their *Gregory,* of Maldon, was built back in 1797, and *Two Brothers* was even older (1795). *Gregory* was going till 1887, and *Two Brothers* finished about two years earlier. Brasier's *William and Mary* was also a veteran, being launched in 1812. On the death of Mr Edward Brasier four topsail barges were sold in 1888 at the following prices, which were regarded as satisfactory: *Lord Palmerston,* £295; *Factor,* £265; *Royal William,* £185; *Three Friends,* £115.

Potter's Southchurch brickfields kept a big fleet busy, and Howard's owned two old-timers in the *Catherine,* built at Bankside in 1826, and *Quartus,* which was twenty years younger. Underwood's, the coal- and corn-merchants, had a useful fleet, including the old Maldon *Maid of the Mill, Ethel Ada,* from Paglesham, and the boomie *Lily,* which ran to Hartlepool for coal; while Turner's, the Southend flour firm, had the *Hearts of Oak.*

Peters, a family firm founded in 1893 by S. J. Peters, worked several old craft, including the Ipswich *Haste Away* and Horlock's *Percy* (broken up at Erith in 1950). They had the *Evening, Twilight, Blanche, Shannon, Eureka,* and *Ashingdon,* now the last barge owned at Southend.[1] Theobald's is a Leigh firm, similarly founded on Billy Theobald's knack of shrewdly buying old craft. But Billy was a shrewd man: he always had a half-pint of beer served in a pint mug! He had the *Sophia* from Eastwood's, who in turn had her

[1] Craft owned in the late 1920's and early 1930's by S. J. Peters and his son A. J. Peters included *Glenrosa, Duplicate, Shannon, Ninety-nine, Twilight, Neepawa, The Portage* (later *Donald A*), *Winnipeg, Mary Jane, Gannet, Haste Away, Blanche, Percy, Eureka,* and *Evening.* All flew a bob having a white diamond on a red ground.

from Parker's, the *Louisa* (which had the distinction of being copper fastened), the *Eliza Mary*, *Waterloo*, *Alfred and Clara*, *Josephine*, and *William Sankey*. With their "L.B.S." bob (standing for Leigh Building Supplies) these craft were familiar as far round the coast as West Mersea, where they were the last regular traders on the hard with timber some years after West's auxiliary *Leonard Piper* brought the last freights of coal. Now Theobald's craft, including the well-known coaster *Persevere*, are all unrigged motor-barges.[1]

Shoebury was another barging centre in this district. The blacksmith's shop on the beach off Rampart Street (demolished in 1933) was put up by Mr George Cook to build barges for the brick trade. Here at the end of the last century a Brightlingsea shipwright named Rose employed six shipwrights, largely on work for Howard, of Wakering. Here were built Howard's *Shoebury* and Eastwood's *Scud*. This famous Kentish firm of barge-owners had a brickyard at Shoebury, and their craft, in which many Wakering men served, did a lot of work in the area right up to the Second World War. Barges owned at Shoebury included Josiah Jackson's *George Pearson* (built at Grays), *Hartley*, *Othello*, and *Shorne*, W. Bowman's *William and Ernest*, J. Gundy's *Ness*, and W. Stafford's *Rover* and *Six Sisters*.

Generally, as has been shown, owners in this district bought second (or third!) hand, and besides the Shoebury craft the only new building I can trace in the area was the Maldon *Betsey*, built at Leigh way back in 1819. Owned by Handley, of Maldon, in 1885, she was out of the Register about 1894.

Behind Canvey Island, up Hole Haven Creek, Curtis' brickfield at Vange (which, as long ago as 1848, had its Barge Inn beside the barge quay) owned the *Pitsea*, *Vange*, and *Fobbing* (35 to 40-thousand-brick craft), and the 44-thousand-brick *Bassildon*, later sold to Ellis, of Stanford-le-Hope. At Benfleet Wood's were barge-owners before the coming of the railway, with the *Hadleigh* and the *Canvey* engaged in 'seeking' work. Fred Cooper, who took the last freight of chalk up Benfleet Upper Way, recalled that the side of the creek was so steep that he had to breast in to the wall at high water and let

---

[1] The original Theobald bob was blue, red, and blue horizontal stripes, flown by *Shoebury*, *William and Arthur*, *Welsh Girl*, *West Kent*, *East Kent*, *Unique*, *Eva Annie*, *Faith*, *Albion*, *Coombedale*, *Paglesham*, *Herbert and Harold*, and *Bassildon*. The L.B.S. bob was adopted in 1934, when the ex-A.P.C.M. barges *Maid of Connaught* and *Persevere* were acquired. Other craft from the same source were *Maid of Munster*, *Florence Myall*, *Gordon*, *Spurgeon*, *Russell*, *Ada Mary*, *Burton*, *Mary Ann*, and the stumpies *Derby* and *Emma*.

the barge slide down into the bed of the creek while she was un-loading as the tide ebbed.

. At Thorpe Bay the Jubilee brickfield, under Cook and Potter, caused plenty of 'overside' work. When the tide uncovered Leigh sandhill two Leigh-men would come off and help load each barge, the crew also working. They were paid six shillings each per tide, and two tides sufficed to load a medium-sized barge. The difficulty for a newcomer to the job was to decide when enough had been thrown in, as the skipper, being paid by the amount carried, wanted to load a full cargo, and yet not too much in case the barge sank. Alf Eaglestone, of the *Venta*, has told me of anxious moments doing this in the *Levitt* as the water crept up to the iron band and he hoped desperately he had not been too greedy!

Fred Cooper once loaded his *Bassildon* single-handed, taking six tides to throw ninety tons of sand over her 5 feet 6 inches side into the hold. A steel-tipped wooden shovel was used, and the sand, spitted out as in digging an allotment, was thrown over the shoulder. If the barge had more than about five and a half feet of side, a hatch would be put down on a block of wood, and you had to run up this before each throw.

Another method of sand-loading, less heavy on the muscles, but even harder on the barges and the judgment of their crews, was from the P.L.A. dredger. This fearful juggernaut scrapes up ballast from the Blyth, or from various places in Sea Reach and the Lower Hope, working the ebb tide only, and at the height of the trade, when three dredgers were employed (*No. 10*, *No. 4*, and *India*), as many as forty-five craft were sometimes waiting on turn. Two rounds of 'the drudger's' belt of buckets would fill a barge in ten to twenty minutes, and smacking alongside in the strong tideway, with other barges milling round, receiving this crashing christening of sand, mud, and salt water, and getting smartly away again, loaded sometimes till the water was on deck up to the batten studs, remains an exacting though ill-rewarded performance. In 1935 Theobald's and Peters' crews were averaging £2 14s. to £2 16s. a week when they struck for better freight rates, and the owners conceded twopence a yard. The craft in the work look rough, and no wonder. But I fancy in the hands of more conventional seamen of naval or yachting experience they would very soon look a whole lot rougher.

Sometimes the waiting craft would be anchored in a cluster up-tide, and one more artful than the others would leave his chain a bit short. Then an invisible hand turning the wheel through the cabin-hatch would give the barge such a sheer that the anchor started, and she would drive down on to the dredger, jumping her turn in the queue. "They had to load you to get rid of you," recalled one skilled practitioner of this dodge with a grin.

In the real old days there were many 'sandies' in the upper reaches above Grays. The crews of these barges, which made a living dredging their own sand, were credited with a fondness for grabbing a sheep from over the sea-walls, and it was a dangerous luxury to make a sheep-noise in passing them. Joshua Francis recalls how, making a trip as a boy, he was egged on by the mate to bawl out a resounding *Baa-aa-aa* at the top of his young voice on such an occasion, and how the reply was a devastating cannonade of stones which the 'sandies' kept on deck for the purpose, bringing down the skipper's wrath on the head of the mischievous mate. Last of the 'sandies' was the piously named *Band of Hope*.

A little farther up the London River the salubriously named Mucking Creek was the home of the fleet of Ambrose Ellis, of Stanford-le-Hope, engaged in serving the explosive works on Curry Marsh as well as taking stacks out of the Creek and bringing 'London mixture' in. "Chick" Cripps, who had the Colchester *Centaur* for over thirty years, and retired from her to take charge of Francis' bargeyard, started with this fleet, his first command being the *Matilda and Amy*, in which he once actually made fifty-three freights in a year to Mucking Creek, as well as spending three weeks on the ways. Other Ellis craft were the *Caroline*, the only one in the dry trade, *Minnie*, *Sea Spray*, *Clara*, and *Alaska*. The *Rettendon*, *Mary Ann*, and *Maria* were working to Maidstone, and the *Frederick* and *Three Friends* to Vange. "Chick" Cripps later took the *Minnie*; her contemporaries included Shrubsall's *Varuna* and *Robert*.

Sea Reach has probably seen more sailing-barges in trouble than any other place, for here, in a dreadfully exposed anchorage, craft must trust to their ground-tackle when the weather is not fit to go farther seaward. Off Southend pier they lie rolling, and only when the seas begin to wash them will they make for the better shelter of Sheerness—if they have not by then left it too late.

The January gale of 1881 saw scenes of great havoc at Southend. Brasier's *Two Brothers* dragged from the gasworks nearly into the pier before she was secured. Potter's *Mary Ann* dragged, and her crew succeeded in jumping ashore. The Rochester *Higham*, lying in the harbour (as the area formed by the base of the pier is optimistically called), broke her rudder, damaged her bow, and sank close to the pier. The Rochester *Halstow*, unloading broken granite on the pier-end, was so battered that she sank, and the little *Good Intent*, owned by Landfield, of Grays, breaking adrift, was washed on to the harbour breakwater, ultimately crashing through and drifting alongside the unloading stage, which she considerably damaged before herself sinking.

But what was described in the local Press as the "crowning disaster" occurred at high water, when Vandervord's *West Kent*, which had been unloading timber in the harbour, was swept bodily under the pier, a large part of which was washed away, marooning the look-out till he was later relieved by boat. The *West Kent*, which must have been staunchly built to get the best of that encounter, was got out and repaired. In fact, she was trading till 1925.

The *Robert* also had the distinction of breaching this pier, and in March 1933 the ex-boomie *Matilda Upton* was involved in a hardly less spectacular incident. Bound from Plymouth to London light, she had been at anchor off the pier for three days, when she dragged and struck it about three-quarters of its length from the shore. The master and owner, William Last, of Ipswich, and the mate (W. Hartnell, of Harwich) jumped clear as she struck, but the barge remained fast in the pier four or five days.

In July 1924 Peters' *Mary* filled and capsized off the Hole Haven Lobster Smack. Her crew got aboard the *Susan*, and both craft dragged ashore. In December of the same year Theobald's *Welsh Girl* (which finished up as a house-boat in Leigh Creek) was wrecked off Leigh, ballast-loaded from Stanford-le-Hope, in very heavy weather. The crew were four hours in the rigging. It was nothing new to the skipper, Captain W. Smith, for he had been in the *Unity* when she was lost the previous year; but it was the mate's first experience, and he kept on saying, "It won't be long now, Captain —will it, Captain?" And it wasn't, for at low water they were able to climb down and walk ashore.

XV

GOLDSMITH'S OF GRAYS

*"Pickford's of the North Sea"—'Ready-made' Sail-tailoring
—The 'Ironpots'—A £1450 Round Trip—120 Barges
under one Bob*

You are still in Essex, according to the map, at Dagenham, where
Henry Ford makes his cars (and the barges bring him loam for his
foundries), or where the river Lea, down which so many little
barges have made their first trip from remote Hertfordshire build-
ing-yards, empties its waters among the dark satanic mills and yet
darker dumps of Bow Creek, but so far as sailormen and sailing-
barges are concerned I stop at Grays and Tilbury. The Cockneys
can have the rest; where the water thickens, wealth accumulates
and men decay. This is where

> The river sweats
> Oil and tar
> The barges drift
> With the turning tide
> Red sails
> Wide
> To leeward, swing on the heavy spar.
> The barges wash
> Drifting logs
> Down Greenwich reach
> Past the Isle of Dogs.[1]

It is a far cry from the clean and breezy saltings of Blackwater or
Deben, yet as far as Grays one may still find the authentic Essex-
man, dry, shrewd, tough, humorous, and here till lately one could
find also the biggest of all the Essex barge fleets. Indeed, it was the
biggest anywhere, for its only rival was the London and Rochester
Trading Company, in Kent, which in the early 1930's mustered 120[2]

[1] T. S. Eliot, *The Waste Land*.
[2] The A.P.C.M. fleet numbered 300 after the amalgamation of many cement firms into
the combine, but this was a collection of fleets rather than one working unit.

craft, against 147 owned by E. and J. W. Goldsmith twenty-five years before.

Just as Richard Horlock, of Mistley, founded his fortune on a quarter-share in the *Pride of the Stour*, so this great fleet, comprising every type, from the Vaux-built boomie *Esmeralda* through tops'l coaster to stumpie and lug-rigged craft, grew from the earnings of one old swimmie, the fifty-ton *Richard*, built at Chiswick in 1833. The great-grandfather of the present director of the firm sailed her, 'rose-on' her, doubled her till her sides were six inches thick. Finally, when she could work no longer, her swim fell off. But she had laid some foundations by then.

The fleet which was built on them was distinguished not only by its size but by its unique nature, for it represented the one large-scale achievement in planned barge-building and organization. Goldsmith's laid down their fleet in classes, and gave them interchangeable gear. Only at Grays did a barge wear a ready-made suit of clothes or borrow her sister's topsail or mainsail. Every other one of the hundreds of craft afloat had to be tailored to measure, or at least to have reach-me-downs altered to fit.

Biggest among these fleets within a fleet were the "-ic" class, built in Holland, some at Krimpen and some at Papendrecht, in 1903-4. These craft, of 120 tons register, only thirty tons less than the *Will Everard* and her sisters, could load 250 to 300 tons.[1] They were wonderful earners in the boom years of the First World War, when Captain Frank Buttershall (who started as mate in the original *Richard*, and went on to serve half a century in Goldsmith's craft) made a trip worth £1450 in the *Runic*,[2] out from London to Ostend with pitch and back to Sandwich with stone. I never heard of another job to match that one.

Norvic and *Cymric* made probably the longest voyages ever accomplished by flat bottoms when they sailed out to the river Plate, boomsail ketch-rigged for the purpose, with half-cargoes of coal for ballast, and carrying certificated master mariners as well as their regular crew. Some of the others were converted to motor-barges, and *Gothic* capsized off Dover when a power-craft.

The eight 180-tonners, built at Southampton in 1898, were big craft too. Some of them inherited their sisters' gear when the 250-

---

[1] In addition to those mentioned here, they included: *Cedric, Servic, Oceanic, Celtic, Britannic, Doric, Teutonic,* and *Germanic.* The last two had their names tactfully altered in 1914 to *Maymon* and *Lais.*

[2] *Runic* is still at work, converted into the M.B. *Gold Rune.*

tonners turned over to power, *Trojan* taking the *Britannic's* and
Briton the *Oceanic's*; but among these *Saxon* and *Spartan* have also
now become motor-barges, and only *Scot* and *Briton* survive under
sail.[1] *Gloria* was a barge of this size built specially for racing. She
competed only once, however, and that without success, for she
was designed to race with iron leeboards, and owing to a last-minute
change of rules had to fit wooden ones.

At the same time a big fleet of twenty-two 160-tonners was laid
down, some in their Deptford yard by Braby's and some at
Southampton by Fay and Co. Fay's craft all had round chines,
which made them travel well off the wind but crippled them to
windward, leaving them quite dependent on the leeboard, so much
so that *Briton* has rolling chocks fitted on which the leeboard can get
a bearing. The London-built vessels had square chines.[2]

These were the main Goldsmith 'ironpot' classes. There were,
however, many other wooden-built vessels in the fleet. *Vulture*,
Vampire, *Viper*, and *Thetis* (now a yacht) were 180-tonners, built at
Sittingbourne in 1898–99. *Cetus*, *Perseus*, and *Dominion*, of 150 tons,
were built on the firm's own yard at Grays in 1902, followed a year
later by *Atom*, which was the last swimmie working on London
River, a familiar and not unattractive-looking model, right up to
the outbreak of the Second World War. *Atom* and her swim-head
sisters were smart enough to earn the nickname of "the Southend
planes" when working to the gasworks in that town. *Henry*, referred
to later in this chapter, was another product of the yard in 1904.

Other Goldsmith swimmies, some of them built as lighters and
later rigged to sail, were *Snail*, *Tortoise*, *Mite*, *Midget*, *Romeo*, and
Juliet, the last of which was also working into the 1930's.

Then there were the stumpies,[3] among which *Bee* and *Fly* were
built at Appledore, Devon, and *Panama*, *Suez*, and *Kiel* were sixty-
tonners built at Grays for the canals—not the far-away waterways
whose names they bore, but the homely Regent's and Surrey canals.

There was even a class of lug-rigged swimmies[4] of 100 to 160
tons, Blackwall-built, just before the turn of the century. These
seldom ventured below Gravesend. They were rigged with brail-

[1] Others of the classes were *Grecian* (mentioned in Chapter XVII) and *Norman*.
[2] Square-chine craft included: *Ailsa*, *Asphodel*, *Audrey*, *Corsair*, *Eileen*, *Geisha*, and *Kismet*.
Round-chiners included: *Astrild*, *Calluna*, *Decima*, *Esterel*, *Lorna*, *Siesta*, and *Virocca*. Another
distinction was that Braby's craft had wooden rudders; the rest steel.
[3] Including also: *Adder*, *Cobra*, *Wasp*, *Scorpion*, *Hornet*, and *Ferret*.
[4] Including: *Success*, *Purfleet*, *Dartford*, *Grays*, *London*, *Brothers*, *Nansen*, and *Fram*.

ing lug, small mizzen, and foresail, and though some of them could not carry any headsail to windward, *Nansen* and *Fram* took some catching to windward loaded.

Many other craft also passed in and out of Goldsmith's fleet at different times, and in a special class were the racers, including the famous *Haughty Belle*, round-sterned, rocker-keeled, white painted,

UP-RIVER: A DEEP-LOADED 'IRONPOT'

E. J. Goldsmith's own design, and perhaps the handsomest sprittie ever built. Goldsmith's triumph in the Jubilee Races of 1897 with four specially built craft[1] is narrated in a later chapter.

The general run of Goldsmith's craft were, however, by no means racers. The firm may be called the "Pickford's of the North Sea," for they built up, on 'seeking,' all this fleet without work of their own, and their argosies were snug rigged for steady rather than

[1] *Castanet, Her Majesty, Giralda,* and *Satanita.*

spectacular progress. Even an amateur could generally spot an 'ironpot' afar off by her undersized topsail.

Nevertheless some smart runs were done. Frank Mummery, who did twenty-three years with Goldsmith's, as well as a spell in charge of the famous *Lady Daphne* before she came to Ipswich, left Southampton with seventy tons of brass eyes in the *Madcap* (a Kentish-built 120-tonner) at 6 o'clock one morning, and anchored at 10.15 that night in the Downs. In the course of the day he covered a hundred miles in ten hours. When he had the Ipswich-built *Ardwina*, which sailed for many years out of Grays and is still active on the coast, he ran from that town to Calais in $10\frac{1}{4}$ hours, and on another occasion went to Nieuport and returned with a cargo of bricks between Tuesday and Friday.

The 'ironpots' were by no means all alike, though they were all laid down to standard pattern—and all had the standard vice of 'sweating' in the cabin. To keep bedding and clothes aired, the cabin fire had to be constantly going, with doors and drawers open. On the other hand, they could be driven as hard as the crew could stand, and be made to carry full sail long after a wooden hull would have had to be eased. *Corsair*, Frank Mummery's favourite, was six inches wider on deck than her sisters, and this made her both dry and handy in a seaway.

Life in a firm of this sort was less carefree and casual than in running some farmer's stack barge with hardly a pretence at keeping accounts. In Goldsmith's if you wanted a new deck-scrubber you had to show the store-keeper the old one as evidence. Work was normally fixed by the office, but sometimes a skipper would do his own 'seeking' in slack times. In one slump Frank Mummery obtained permission to take *Corsair* off on his own to the Humber, and was rewarded with a freight to Maidstone at the then princely rate of 12s. 6d. a ton, plus two guineas gratuity. During the First World War he led a deputation to the office to protest at the rate of 3s. 6d. a ton to Lowestoft and Yarmouth, for which ports eight craft were loaded. The merchant, Mr Barber, offered another 6d. a ton and a gold sovereign to the first barge off Lowestoft. During that race Mummery had as passenger his Union lawyer, who wanted to learn more of the life of the men he had to represent. He was particularly intrigued about the meaning of a gybe. "Now, you see that bit of wood up there?" explained the skipper, indicating the sprit. "Well, in a moment it is going to be over *there*. Now

Scenes on Deck

ABOVE AND RIGHT:
Aboard West's *British
Oak*, one of the few
sailing coasters sport-
ing a wheel-house.
LEFT: The ballast-man
Squeak hard driven
BELOW: Aboard
Remercie

160

Sailormen

'Pincher' Bloyce (*Remercie*), Jerry Mann (*George Smeed*), and Bob Potton (*Arthur Relf*) in his winter rig. BELOW: Skipper Josh (*Ardwina*) and Peter get down to it

stand clear of the main horse!" Whether or not he was enlightened, the lawyer was sufficiently impressed to add another sovereign to the stakes, which the *Madcap* succeeded in collecting.

In more recent years the firm has been increasingly occupied in the Colne sand trade, having interests in the Fingringhoe workings, and the old iron hulls have come in for some rough treatment in this trade, handled often by skippers whose tactics would have brought tears to the eyes of their predecessors of coasting days.

Now, however, even this has come to an abrupt end. Goldsmith's to-day see their future in motor-coasters, and only *Briton* and *Scot* remained, in 1949, under their bob.[1] *Thetis, Virocca*, and *Viper* have been sold during the same year, *Asphodel, Siesta*, and *Esterel* sank during the winter of 1948—the two latter wheat-laden, *Siesta* run down off Grays, *Esterel* abandoned off Clacton. Raised five months later, she unloaded at Rowhedge, and her cargo, washed and dried, went for cattle-food—a queer example of Davy Jones' demurrage.[2]

The Grays chalk quarry, which had a fleet of seven or eight barges, has not had a craft for some years, and the other chief Grays owners, Cole and Lecquire, have sold their last, the well-kept little *Henry*, whose blue sprit made her easily recognized.[3] She will find a good owner in that well-known amateur sailorman Arthur Bennett, who is to make her his home and yacht, a successor to *June*, of Rochester.

Soon there will not be a barge out of Grays. Before the Ipswichmen had their motors they made it a regular port of call to lie in easterly winds, and often twenty craft rode off its happily higgledy-piggledy waterfront, their crews sailing like mad up and down Swin all over the bargemen's bar of the Theobald Arms, where on Saturday nights the barging songs were sung under the presidency of members of those great Grays barging families of Dines and Bannister. The memories of the days now ending will last a little longer, till the new Grays beyond the railway-crossing creeps down with its flash shopfronts and overwhelms even these, and then old Grays, whose very name seems to stir an echo out of the tideway, will itself be but a memory.

---

[1] *Scot* was sold to a Queenborough owner in 1950, and *Briton* turned into a lighter.

[2] *Astrild, Asphodel, Calluna, Carina, Geisha, Kismet, Lorna, Senta*, and *Yarana* were in 1949 sold to the London and Rochester Trading Company, and *Esterel* is also to join this fleet as a motor-barge.

[3] Other Lecquire craft were: *The Major, Emma, Gladiator, Rose, Valentine, Burnham*, and the round-bottomed lugger *James*.

XVI

THE RACES

*A Half-washed Champion—Goldsmith's Triumph—Horlocks
to the Fore—Parker's Fliers—Southend's Regattas—The
Maldon Races—Harwich and Colne—Some Private Chal-
lenges—Excelsior!*

WILLIAM HENRY DODD, the man who first thought of organized
barge races, must have been an interesting character. Born in 1801,
he started work as a ploughboy in fields now covered by London
city streets, made a fortune (and earned the title of "The Golden
Dustman") from refuse disposal, was owner of a big fleet of sailing-
barges, and died at the age of eighty, leaving £100,000. He also
left the design for his own vault, decorated with a team ploughing
and barges sailing, and bearing the epitaph "Originator of the Sailing Barge Matches. True School for the Navy. His motto was
Economy in Time, Labour and Expense."

After his death these races were—and will, I trust, continue to be
—endowed from a £5000 bequest to the Fishmongers' Company,
but they were started in his lifetime, in 1863, when, appropriately,
his own *W.H.D.* was the first winner. Their object was not merely
sport, for Mr Dodd rightly saw the need to raise the status of bargemen and to improve the design of barges. Nothing could have done
more to achieve these ends, and thus to enable sailing-barges to
survive in later days of competition, then unforeseen.

While Robert Stone, Erith father of the Brightlingsea builders,
was an early competitor with a barge bearing his own name, Essex
and Suffolk men seem to have been at first conspicuous by their
absence, till in 1867 a new class for tops'l barges of over fifty tons
registry was started. Only two entries were received, one from
Robert Horlock, grandfather of Alfred and great-grandfather of
Marcus, present managing director of F. W. Horlock and Co., Ltd.
Just before the race his two sons were unloading the *Excelsior*, built
by Bayley, of Ipswich, five years before, and had only time to tar
round one side. In that trim, with one side clean and one side dirty,

they sailed and won, and, though no one suspected it at the time, introduced to the races a name which was to dominate them sixty years later.

For the next twenty-six years the Essex coasters seem to have been little disposed to challenge; then, in 1894, Goldsmith's, of Grays, entered the lists with the Rochester-built *Majestic*, which won the championship. The firm also purchased Harry Munns' racer *Early Bird*, and that celebrated skipper later sailed their *Pastime*, winning several prizes. In the next two years the new Ipswich-built barges *Violet* and *Rowland* participated, and in 1896 the *Clara* (later at Colchester) won the Medway event (started in 1880) and was second in the Thames to Goldsmith's *Haughty Belle*.

The Jubilee Races of 1897 were all Goldsmith's. They built no less than four craft specially for them: *Her Majesty* and *Castanet* (which was ultimately a Colchester casualty) at Shrubsall's, Ipswich; *Satanita* at White's; and *Giralda* at Piper's. *Giralda*, which was as plain to the eye as *Haughty Belle* was striking, was the only one of these to make a lasting mark as a racer; but in her first year *Satanita* showed a form she never repeated, and by winning a first in the Medway and finishing second in the Thames to *Giralda*, with *Haughty Belle* third, gave the Grays owners a big haul of the valuable special prizes offered that year. Unhappily, owners and builder fell out over *Giralda*, which was alleged to leak, and after a lawsuit J. R. Piper was awarded £300 and took back the barge, which won for him year after year and did a lot of hard work as well.

The year 1899 saw *Sirdar* in fourth place, and in 1901 Alf Horlock entered the fray with the Ipswich-built *Teaser*. *Mildreda*, from Foulness, was third in 1901, taking second on the Medway the previous year. In 1903 the Mistley *Sara*, new from Conyer the year before, won one of the grandest races of them all, beating *Giralda* in half a gale of wind which started the throat of her mainsail. She also took second in the Medway. Nearly thirty years later *Sara*, by then a Londoner, was to return to racing and more than hold her own with her final successors at Mistley.

The other chief Essex racing enthusiast, Clem Parker, of Bradwell, made his debut in 1905. *Violet Sybil* carried off the coaster class (in which *Lady Helen* finished fifth), and *Verona*, new from Shrubsall, at Greenwich, was second to *Giralda* in the tops'l class, being revenged on her in the Medway—though unhappily on a foul, which caused some feeling, as *Verona* had also protested, unsuccessfully, in the Thames. But 1906 was Parker's great year, for *Violet Sybil* repeated her success both in the Thames and Medway, and the new *Veronica* and the *Verona* took first and second places among the tops'ls in both races, relegating *Giralda* to third in the Thames.

Records of 1907 are missing, but in 1908 *Giralda* was revenged on *Veronica*. Instead of a coaster class, a new class for working-barges was tried, and was won by Horlock's Harwich-built *Marjorie*, with *Creeksea* second. *Falconet* was sent from Colne to try her paces in this race, but was unplaced. She came to Colchester with a reputation for speed which she did not at first live up to. Some say a small tops'l took the pace out of her—or it may have been a question of jockeys.

There end the records of pre-war racing, but not before the Essex-men had fully established their ascendancy. The Ipswich owners never seem to have been tempted to participate, which is a pity, for it would have been interesting to see what some of Orvis' hollow-lined fliers and Cann's stout clippers would have done.

The races were not resumed till 1927, when *Castanet* took a third in the Medway, *Verona* snapping her bowsprit and finishing sixth, staysail rigged. In the Thames Francis, of Colchester, challenged with *Varuna*, in which Alf Keeble secured a third in the Thames River Bowsprit Class, *Portlight* taking second, to start the real Mistley onslaught, which increased in 1928 with the coasters *Vigilant*, sailed by Alf Horlock, and *Remercie*, sailed by Joe Gear, beating *Alf Everard* in half a gale, and *Portlight*, sailed by Jim Stone, beating *Queen*, the greyhound of the Colne, sailed by Fred Keeling, for first place in the river bowsprits. This was the occasion of a tremendous race between *Vigilant* and *Portlight*—though they were, of course, in different classes—which *Vigilant* just won.

It blew hard again next year when *Redoubtable* scored her first success with the coasters in the Thames, and *Reminder*, which had yet to carry a cargo, engaged in a tussle with her sister *Portlight*, culminating in the latter's mast going overboard. For all her load of canvas, *Reminder* was the only barge to gybe without rucking her tops'l that year. This left *Reminder* champion of Thames and Medway at the first attempt, with *Queen* second in both rivers. In the Medway *Varuna* tried again, but carried away her topsail; Groom's old *Alderman*, however (racing for her new owners, the

London and Rochester Trading Company), made her only appearance in the prize lists, finishing third to *Northdown* and *Redoubtable* in the coasters.

It was *Redoubtable* and *Reminder* again in their respective classes in the much lighter airs of 1930 (when *Fortis*, winning the new staysail class, made history by being first past the post), but in 1931, 1932, and 1933 *Sara* made her comeback and beat *Reminder* both in Thames and Medway. The coaster class in both rivers was a duel between *Phœnician* and *Redoubtable*, in which the Harwich barge scored two firsts to Horlock's Sittingbourne craft's four, *Phœnician* winning one encounter in the Medway despite the loss of her bowsprit. *Queen*[1] (now racing for the London and Rochester Trading Company) took yet another second in 1933, having the satisfaction of beating *Reminder*.

Now alterations to rules enabled barges to be transferred to other classes, and *Veronica* left her bowsprit behind to take first in the staysails, a feat she repeated in 1934, when *Reminder* moved into the coaster race, which she won on both rivers, leaving *Sara* to lord it among the river bowsprits. It is interesting to note, however, that the extra gear and hands allowed to *Reminder* as a coaster enabled her at last to show *Sara* the way home.

In 1935 (when Southend saw the town's only entry in the Maldonbuilt *Percy*), 1936, and 1937 *Veronica* was winner of the bowsprit, staysail, and (believe it or not!) coaster classes respectively on the Thames. *Queen* at last began to win on the Medway in 1935, and in Coronation year (1937) her new Rochester owners appropriately gave the old Colchester *King* a chance to show her paces as well. *Reminder* took one more second in the Thames, but was not a winner after Jim Stone left her in 1936.

The 1938 races, sailed in nearly a calm, saw *Sirdar* out again after nearly half a century, victorious in the staysail class on Thames and second in the Medway, with *Reminder* second in the bowsprits on the Thames and third in the Medway.

An attempt was made in 1949 to restart the Thames race, under conditions favouring genuine working craft, but it fell through. After that setback it seems doubtful if barges will ever race again.[2] But with so much keenness remaining among bargemen, and so much new enthusiasm guaranteed among the public, nothing is

[1] *Queen* became an unrigged motor-barge in 1949.
[2] The Medway revival of 1950 is referred to at p. 188.

impossible. Certainly the financial inducement is not lacking, for the endowments accumulate and can be used for nothing else.

If the day dawns when the red stocking-caps and white duck trousers are again donned by racing crews—even if it means taking the propellers off the auxiliaries for the day—there should be no attempt to return to the intensity of competition which caused barges to be specially built, and all sorts of extravagant and even fantastic sails to be used. *Veronica's* headsails[1] were enough to take the heart out of any honest working sailorman, and *Reminder*, in addition to rigging a special leach-line in the head of her tops'l, lugged a sixty-six-foot sprit about with her for a whole year (ten feet longer than the biggest spar in the Colchester fleet). She also had immensely heavy racing leeboards—though whether they did her any good is another matter, so thick and clumsy were they. This sort of nonsense would certainly not have appealed to the economically minded Mr Dodd.

In any future race there will be no Mistley cracks to re-establish the reputation of their town, no Bradwell-men to fly Clem Parker's hand and heart, but there are plenty of young skippers—some dreaming of the day in the wheel-boxes of their motor-barges—who will be in it by hook or by crook if the chance comes their way.

Certainly the barge races were a spectacle unequalled even by the J-class yachts. To have participated must have been a tremendous experience—and a tremendous ordeal. Jim Stone reckons 1929 was the hardest race he ever was in. *Reminder* was ready to capsize at any moment going up the Lower Hope. She began a sickening, unnatural, lurching roll, and he told a hand to stand by the tops'l halyard. Over she began to go, and only the order "Down tops'l!" saved her. Her crew, in addition to handling four thousand square feet of canvas, were trimming her by shifting thirty-five fathoms of anchor-chain about the deck, and when they finished they fell down on the hatches where they stood and lay there exhausted till some one said "Come on. Let's get ashore out of this."

Local barge-racing was a good deal less spectacular than the annual Thames and Medway events, but at least it never developed into a contest between rival bank-balances. The only races of any continuity seem to have been the Maldon and Southend events.

Southend's annual regatta, now grown into a yachting week, was

[1] See plate facing p. 144.

inaugurated in the 1860's by local tradesmen, farmers, and barge-owners. At that time yachting did not play an important part in Essex regattas, and most of the races were for trading craft such as the local bawleys and shrimpers, with rowing matches for the watermen and coastguards. At Southend it is clear that from early days the barge race was the main attraction of the day, and the first race sailed. Most of the local fleet made a showing, sailing as they were, with little in the way of special preparation, the hoy barges in the first class, and a battered assortment of elderly, rather slow old river craft enjoying a day off from ballast-lumping to make up class two.

Some weeks before the day chosen, usually in late August or early September, notices would appear in the local Press, and subscriptions from tradesmen and landowners were called for. When money was short in the town, as it sometimes was after a bad season, the whole affair had to be abandoned, though prizes and expenses were modest enough. In better years there would be more show, with silver cups for the winning owners, as well as champion flags and prize-money, and an imposing list of patrons to watch the events from the bunting-covered committee barge.

The first definite report is for 1876, and in that year the race, held on August 24, was open to all comers. There were two classes, with a first prize of £7 and a second prize of £5, and champion flags for the two winners. There were seven entries, and in the round-headed class the well-known Medway barge *Challenger*, third in the Thames topsail class that year, was second, the winner being *Conqueror*, new that year, and also winner of the Thames topsail class. Her ribs can still be seen buried in the mud of Leigh Marsh. In the swim-headed class *Catherine*, owned by Howard, finished first, with the London *Quartus* second.

Next year, with the same two classes, the race was again open to all. This time *Challenger* won in her class, while the old Maldon swimmie *Rogue in Grain* was the winner of the second-class barges. Prizes this year were £7 for a win and £2 for second place.

In 1878 there was no regatta, as the committee could not raise the £200 needed for prizes and other expenses; the local Leigh event was held as usual, but there seems never to have been a barge race in the port. But, if there were no races, *Rogue in Grain* still managed to get talked about, and lived up to her name. When the pier-master tried to arrest her for debt to the harbour-authority he and his men were repelled by the owner, skipper, and sixteen toughs, and, as the piermaster ruefully reported, it was almost impossible to find the names of all the offenders among the waterside population. This sort of thing was not uncommon at Southend at this time.[1]

The year 1879 was a better one for local tradesmen, and with two barge-owners on the regatta committee things went better than usual. The course in all matches was roughly the same. The start was from anchor off the esplanade, just east of the pier. The committee barge was moored off the Ship Hotel, and this was the winning-mark. The first stretch was along the coast eastward to a mark about two miles away, out to the Knock and Swatch buoys, with a return past the pierhead inshore to the winning-mark—in all about twelve miles.

This course was sailed in 1879 with a good west-sou'-west breeze. The swimmies got away first to a smart start. *Rogue in Grain* was first to get her anchor, but Brasier's *John and Jane* soon took the lead, and finished off the committee barge in just over two hours, with the same owner's *William and Mary* thirteen minutes later. The round-headers started fifteen minutes after the swimmies. Ellis' *Matilda and Amy* got off first, but was soon passed by Vandervord's *West Kent*; then Howard's *Henry and Annie* took the lead, winning by five minutes, her time being twenty-five minutes better than the winning swimmie's. The following year the committee was again short of funds, and prize-money had to be reduced. The race was held in September, in moderate weather, and the first-class barges had to make two circuits of the course. The four competitors in the first class got away well at the gun. Brasier's *Three Friends* had a slight advantage, and she increased her lead so much that when she passed the committee barge at the end of the first round none of the others had rounded the pier. She carried on, and was an easy winner from Absalom's *James*, Potter's *Mary Ann*, and Ellis' *Joseph and John*. The second-class barges were slower getting away and met a strong tide off the pierhead. Underwood's *Maid of the Mill* was winner, with Brasier's *Gregory* second, and their *Two Brothers* third.

The proceedings at a meeting to consider the 1881 race throw some light on the status of the local fleets. One committee-man, Mr Ivimey, thought it undesirable to have an open match, as they would "probably only receive subscriptions from Kent to the amount of £5, while £15 would be taken in prizes." Mr Storey

[1] Chapter XIV.

suggested it would be best to confine the barge matches to Essex. The Chairman (Mr Brasier) remarked that the Kentish barges were admitted last year in order to promote a good race. Mr Arnold said that "Southend barges were all of about a class, but they would be nowhere were the Colchester barges admitted." He thought it should be for Southend only. Mr Arnold proposed they should have two matches confined, and that Mr Knowles should be left to get up another open to the port of Maldon, if he could make the necessary arrangements. In the event, over a ten-mile course starting off the Hope Hotel, *Three Friends*, a fifty-year-old Ipswich barge owned by Moss at Vange, beat Vandervord's *Lord Palmerston* by thirty minutes. Cowling's *Royal William* was disqualified for passing on the wrong side of a mark. The second-class barges started at the same time, and the winner, home one minute fifty seconds after *Lord Palmerston*, was *Sarah and Elizabeth*, with *John and Jane* second, and *Gregory* third.

There may have been a race in 1882, but for some reason it was not included in the regatta. An open barge race was on the 1883 programme, but reports are missing, as are those of 1884.

In 1885, there was only one class, and all entries were locally owned. A new introduction was a third prize of £2. There was a good start, though *George and Alfred* was very slow getting her anchor. *West Kent* and *Lord Palmerston* were the first round the mark-boat at the end of the inshore lap, and they kept the same order round the Knock and past the pierhead. *Alfred and Elizabeth* had a disastrous day, for coming up the Reach she lost her topmast, and rounding the pier to come inshore broke her sprit.

Bad advertising, or lack of any at all, made the 1886 regatta something of a flop, when *Alfred and Elizabeth* beat *Alfred* and *Emily*. The race was resumed in 1888, but by this time the local fleet had passed its peak and hoy barges were losing their importance. As usual in the last years, there was only one class, with five entries: Gundy's *Ness*, *Factor* (yet another of Vandervord's Maldon antiques), *Essex Farmer*, Underwood's *Alma* and *Walter Hawthorn*.

Alma ran well before the wind [says a report], but the *Ness* overhauled her and was first to round the mark boat, from which point she seemed to go away from the other craft until getting into the river [deep channel] where she lost ground, and *Alma*, with Mr Underwood at the helm, took the lead; *Essex Farmer* took second place.

The next race year for local traders seems to have been 1900. By this time Peters' *Mary Jane*, with "Tubby" Blake aboard as third hand, was carrying off the champion flags in great style. Winner of the 1900 race (with *Luddesdown* and *Gannet* following up), she was a nice little 42-tonner, built at Milton in 1877. Tom White was her skipper in the 1890's. One year she was off the pier on the last lap when her topmast came down just as the mate was going to climb the weather vang with the champion flag wrapped round him to put at the peak. Tom White called to him to wait till she had won. Anyway, she *did* win. *Mary Jane* was like a yacht, black-leaded and polished up—even the anchor was blackened for the race. She was built to carry about forty thousand bricks; sold in the 1920's, she is now a house-boat at Benfleet.

The last Southend race seems to have been held in 1904. There had been some hard feelings among the watermen in the old town over the arrangements of the year before, and the Regatta Committee split up. The barge race was sailed by Old Towners. Underwood's fine new *Ethel Ada* was none too lucky in her first race, for, coming up to the winning-mark with a huge spinnaker set, her topmast snapped, but she won easily, and no one was hurt. Vandervord's *Jane* took second place, with Goldsmith's old ironpot *Bras de Fer* a poor third.

Bawleys raced at Southend up to 1920, but the Brasiers and Vandervords gave up their barge-owning interests before the First World War, and by 1910 there were not enough starters to make a race.

Records of the early Maldon races are lost, but George Hales can remember one of these events about sixty years ago when Gutteridge's little *Morning Star* beat the *Surprise*, *Sisters*, and *Minerva*. The start then was from the Promenade, and though she was far from the smartest of these craft, the *Morning Star's* small size enabled her to wriggle away to a good start in this narrow reach. These races were held from time to time, the *Keeble* being victorious at least once, and the *British Empire* and *Falcon* being among the remembered competitors. They then lapsed, being revived in 1921 when John Sadd and Sons, Ltd, gave a Challenge Cup, won in that year and in 1922 by Green's *Ethel Maud*, under George Hales. In 1923 Billy Austin in the *Mermaid* (then owned by James Last) was the winner, and in 1924 the *Dawn* (S. A. Keeble, master) scored a surprise win in light airs. Keeble and Company's *Saltcote Belle* was successful in the next three years, winning the cup outright. Her skipper, E. J. Keeble, then gave a new cup in memory of his father, Ebenezer Richard Keeble, and four races were sailed for this. In 1929 and 1931 the *Mermaid* was successful, in 1934 the *Ethel Maud* staged a come-back under R. Hedgecock, and the last winner, in 1936, was the *Emma*, owned by Francis and Gilders (R. Dent, master).

The later events were started from Hilly Pool, off Mill Beach, the course being round a mark off Goldhanger Creek to finish at the Promenade. There were generally about four barges sailing. Once they put the round-sterned *Oak* in, and her skipper, grumbling that it was no good challenging Derby winners with a carthorse, let go his anchor in the Ballast Hole and finished on the next day's tide, when some sarcastic individual raised a cheer.

Better sport would have been enjoyed by the barges had they started on the ebb and sailed down to round the Bench Head, but the cramped course was chosen to give the regatta crowd a spectacle. Plenty of keenness was shown by skippers and crews, for on one occasion the *Ethel Maud* was put on Cook's blocks and a crew of fishermen who liked to join in the sport black-leaded her bottom and polished it with a hand-brush. Then they took her down to Heybridge and laid her across the gut of the channel leading into the Basin for the night ebb, piling all her gear in the middle of the hold. She dropped her belly, and, in George Hales' words, went like a mad thing, continuing to do so after the race till she sat in a berth which pushed her back into normal shape.

The *Ethel Maud* is a fast barge loaded as well as light. Once she came out of Oare Creek, stone-loaded, and was off the Maplin lighthouse at low water when it came on to blow hard north-easterly. In the thrash down to the Spitway over the tide she passed several Tollesbury smacks, and when George Hales retired from the water to keep the Tollesbury Queen's Head those smackmen often used to speak of that day, saying no loaded barge had ever done that to them before or since. Hales, a rare goer at work as well as on race day, was taken to sea by his father when the Maldon Club decreed that all stack barges going to London must be three-handed. At the age of ten he became third hand, and later was master of the *Ann Elizabeth*, *James and Harriet*, and *Albion* before taking the *Ethel Maud*. On his last freight he tried to cut across the top of the Buxey with an hour's flood by the tide-table, touched—and the tide left him. It came on to blow hard easterly, and, though the *Ethel Maud* floated unscathed, he was struck by a flying windlass-handle in the struggle to get the anchor, and was thrown against the rail, cutting his head open so badly that he was not allowed to return to sea.

A Harwich race was sailed in 1897 or 1898, and was won by the *Centaur*, sailed by Jim Stone. I heard the tale of it from that fine old Ipswich sailorman Robert Ruffles, for fifteen years skipper of the *Thalatta*, and before that of the *Blanche* (1901–6) and *Justice* (1906–15) At the time of the race he was mate in Mason's *Orinoco*, which finished third, Groom's *Consul* being second. Others sailing were *Primrose*, Paul's *Ida* (which broke her bowsprit), *Petrel*, and *Iverna*, a Sandwich-built barge (1892) which was registered at Harwich and later became the headquarters of the Greenwich Y.C. The day before the race they were unloading the *Orinoco* at Waldringfield, and tried to get her ends emptied first so as to flatten her out into racing trim, but the owners declined. As it was, they only got to Harwich at 6 A.M., and the race started at eleven. Each barge was allowed five hands, and the course was round the Cork lightship and the Stone Banks buoy and finish round a steamer in Harwich. They carried their boats in the hold, and the *Centaur*, which had been a week on the ways black-leading and generally tuning up, had hers slung from the beams so that as she hit the seas the impetus of its swing should help to keep her moving. There was a fresh breeze, and the *Orinoco* was handicapped to windward by too big a jib. A 'tempest' (thunderstorm) knocked the heart out of the wind and headed them as they came into the harbour, *Centaur* a few minutes ahead, and as the ebb was just starting down she scraped round the mark, leaving the *Orinoco* to turn back and forth for three-quarters of an hour. "In fact," said Bob Ruffles, "I don't think we ever should have got round, only I was forward tending the jib-sheet, and as we kept making boards up to the steam-boat I whispered to them I'd heard my skipper say 'if we don't get round the next time I'm going to sail into him.' That made them give her some chain, and we got round at last."

A private challenge match was also sailed between Bentall's *Hyacinth* (H. West, master) and the *Mermaid*, then owned by Gutteridge (Sim Staines, master). The course was from Maldon round the Cork and back, and *Mermaid* was the winner.

A race was arranged in connexion with one Harwich Regatta, but only the Ipswich and Mistley *Excelsiors* turned out. Jim Stone, skipper of the latter, declared it was a waste of time to sail against the Bayley racer, and, despite the Ipswich-men's proposal for a handicap event, they both went home! Excelsior, indeed!

Races in the Colne were occasional, irregular, and unrecorded. They were generally challenge matches between two craft, and were probably timed to coincide with one of the regattas. George Hales recalls Marriage's Colchester *Fleur-de-lis* competing against the Maldon *Violet* (later also owned by Marriage's), but has forgotten the result. He also remembers the *Fleur-de-lis* being beaten by the *Ready* on another occasion. Tom Howard, son of the Maldon builder, was aboard the *D'Arcy* as a boy when she was beaten by the *Ready*, which still had a championship flag aboard up to a few years ago. The *D'Arcy* made the better time, but fouled a yacht at the start, all of which provoked some argument when the crews met ashore at the fair that night. I suspect that the impetuous individualism of those days was not ideally suited to the niceties of racing to rules, as could be illustrated by many a story of the old-time Essex smack races—but that is another story.

"SARAH," WITH WHITE TOPSAIL, OVERTAKING
"GIRALDA" IN THE 1903 RACE

XVII

BARGING TO-DAY

*Brisk Business for the Lifeboats in 1938—Last of the Colliers
—A Week-end up Swin—The Leeboard leaning on the Tide*

WHAT remains at the present day of the great and glorious game of barging?

Most of the surviving boomies gave it up in the 1920's, but a good deal of long-distance work continued to be done by spritties right up to the Second World War, though the trade slump in the 1930's dealt a blow from which there was no full recovery. Even so, barges were going down Channel half a dozen together up to 1936, and there were usually three or four in Dover until 1939. Similarly, on the East Coast freights to and from Hull were not uncommon up to the 1939 War, though the number of craft tackling them was steadily decreasing.

Each year the November gales took their toll. On November 1, '1937, the *Audrey* was escorted into Yarmouth harbour, and the *Mary Graham* was driven ashore there with a broken sprit through a faulty tow-rope parting just as the tug reached the pierheads. Ten days later Everard's *Hibernia* broke in two on the beach at Runton, Norfolk. The mast stood on the forward part with the foresail set, and even the bob still flying on the topmast-head. The skipper, Harry Couchman, was rescued before she struck, and the deserted barge was described as "sweeping past Cromer in the north-easterly gale like a phantom ship, one light still showing." A week later, on November 19, the *Greenhithe*, owned by the same firm, was driven ashore at Yarmouth, and the *Lord Rosebery* foundered near by. The *Britannic*, bound from Hull to Wells with meal, got ashore in the Wash, and, having damaged her rudder, was abandoned lying at anchor there.

More spectacular still were the rescues in the sudden 70-mile-an-hour gale of November 23, 1938, when seven barges were assisted by tugs and lifeboats off Yarmouth and two more to the southward off the Suffolk coast. The fleet (mostly Goldsmith's) had left

Yarmouth deceived as to the weather prospects. The *Ailsa*, Everard's
Britisher and *Royalty*, and Sully's *Raybel* were being towed in—the
Royalty with sails and sprit gone, and the *Raybel* having dragged
her anchors for three miles—when three more craft were seen
driving down from the southward. The lifeboat succeeded in
getting the crew out of the *Una* just as she grounded on Yarmouth
south beach, herself hitting the bottom in doing so. She then turned
her attention to the *Cetus* and got alongside her—suffering further
superficial damage—taking out the crew off Winterton. The barge
had been in trouble in the same place only two years previously,
having been towed in with broken sprit in November 1936. Returning from this second rescue, the lifeboat, by the greatest good
fortune, happened on the *Decima* driving before the gale pursued
by the Lowestoft lifeboat, and saved her crew just five minutes
before she hit the Scroby Sand.

Meanwhile the *Grecian* and *Astrild*, both bound for Colne to load
sand, had anchored, the former at Thorpness and the latter near the
Sizewell Bank buoy. There the Aldeburgh lifeboat rescued the
crews, after which both barges parted their cables and disappeared.
Lowestoft and Southwold lifeboats were called to barges driving
past out of control, but could find only one, abandoned high and dry
on the Scroby—presumably the *Decima*.

This was one of the most arduous days in recent lifeboat history,
and the worst in modern sailing-barge annals. A number of the
abandoned barges were later salvaged, one of them having driven
nearly across to the coast of Germany.[1]

Many of these ships and men were no longer available to resume
the work after the long, grim interlude of the War, but the last of the
sailing-colliers, Everard's great 280-ton *Will Everard* and the 180-
ton *Greenhithe*, work still from the Humber to Colchester and
Harwich gasworks. On one trip Captain Uglow of the *Will* was
caught out in a south-westerly gale and had to bring up, when his
tops'l carried away just before he could bear up for Harwich. The
lifeboat went out to him where he lay to two anchors, and his own
characteristic comment was, "We didn't seem to be doing much
good where we were, so we came ashore in her." The barge
dragged foul of the moorings of the Cork lightship, but there was no
damage, and she was later towed in to Harwich, discharging

---

[1] A full account will be found in *Coasting Bargemaster*, by A. W. Roberts, skipper of the
Greenhithe, who was out that day in the *Northdown* and just made Harwich.

her cargo there. She was soon off to fetch another lot for Colchester.

One Sunday evening in August 1948 the *Greenhithe* had got as far as Southwold when it came on to blow with sudden violence. The old coaster *British Oak*, reduced to sand work, had left Colne that morning and lay off the Knoll. She began to leak at 4 P.M. and sank at midnight. The crew, lying astern in their boat, were not picked up by the Clacton lifeboat till Monday midday. That breeze, in skipper Roberts' words, turned the *Greenhithe* round for him, and, under nothing but the foresail, he had to go running back whence he had come, hoping to bring up in Yarmouth Roads. But he ran through that anchorage "like a dose of salts," and was off Happisborough before he could heave-to under the lee of Caister —which was nothing unusual for a barge which sometimes has to run for the Humber for shelter and work back to the Wash from there.

But those two, with their handsome sister, *Cambria*, are really about all that is left of the East Coast sailormen now. Just an occasional Yarmouth freight makes a change for a skipper venturous enough to welcome it—and too many of these, alas, are now in motor-craft, for it is a sad feature of the end of sail that the best sailormen are the first to be offered the more profitable auxiliary and motor-barges. Yet there is still pride of craft among the Swin rangers left to sail the old, old road round Blacktail Spit and Sheers, Whitaker and Spitway from London to the Essex ports.

A few weeks after the loss of the *British Oak* I fell in with Jerry Mann, skipper of the *George Smeed*, and, as he was sailing for London on the Saturday tide, the temptation to make a week-end of it was too great to resist. It turned out a typical summer sail up London River; nothing to write home about, but for that reason perhaps the more worth chronicling in detail, for it will not be long before such uneventful, commonplace, everyday affairs are no longer to be experienced.

Jerry Mann is, in his own words, "an incurable romantic." At the age of twenty-four he had had a dozen jobs ashore and was supposed to be looking for the next when he fell in with a Colchester skipper at his native Erith and begged a trip. It was so obviously his *métier* that he was taken on as mate before they reached Harwich. Within a few years he was given charge of the *Falconet*, and after a spell in

Sully's *Convoy* and Shrubsall's *Gladys* returned to the purple and orange bob to take the *George Smeed*, an eighty-ton Smeed Dean Sittingbourne barge, rebuilt in 1922 when forty years old to load 150 tons, and soon afterwards sold to Colchester.

"You're promoted," were his first words as I dumped my bag on deck. "The mate hasn't shown up, and I'm not waiting for him." It was a glorious September afternoon, when a record crowd of fourteen thousand citizens with nothing better to do had gone to see Colchester play Chelmsford at the local football-ground, and we guessed the missing mate was among them. Anyway, we got Vince's motor-boat lashed under the lee, and, with Ernie Vince to steer, had the hatches on before reaching Rowhedge, which distracted attention from the sickening sight of the *Reminder*, daubed all over with red oxide, lying on the slip for conversion to a motor-barge. The topsail went up, and the boat was hauled to the davits by Wivenhoe, and below Alresford woods the mainsail was dropped down and foresail set. Then off went Vince's rope, and as he sheered away to tow the *Violet Sybil* into Alresford Creek the *George Smeed* filled on the starboard tack and the multitudinous murmur of a barge under way delighted my ears again for the first time in eight years.

After a yacht, a barge sailing is a noisy thing. The water, thrust apart by her bows, rushes past the thick leeboards, rustles along her sides, and foams past her rudder, the chains of the mizzen sheet and leeboard pennants each making their own addition to the chorus. In fact, you can only really hear the wind in the gear standing by the mast-case away from the sound of the water.

Down went the bowsprit, and after a couple of tacks the jib was set to the south-west breeze, and at 4 P.M., as the anchored craft swung to the high water, the *George Smeed* slipped close under the lee of East Mersea point and out for the Bench Head buoy.

The *George Smeed*'s bowsprit is no mere ornament. It suits the barge—which, having the original gear she carried before being enlarged, is under-canvassed—and it delighted the heart of her skipper, who was never quite happy in his "incurably romantic" disposition with the *Falconet*, because she was only a staysail barge without even boat-davits to make a coaster of her. The jib is permanently hanked to the stay, which serves to top the spar up in docks and rivers. It drops down easily enough, and the running bobstay is smartened up with a turn of the tackle fall round the windlass,

M

smack fashion. This also sets up the topmast stay, and a turn of the
jib stay on the mast-case winch completes the trimming of the standing rigging. Then the stemhead topmast stay carrying the staysail
(spinnaker to the old-timers) can be cast off. Correctly, this staysail,
which now becomes the jib topsail, should be rehanked to the bowsprit-end topmast stay, but this bowsprit-end job is saved on the
George Smeed by resetting the whole stay to the bowsprit-end.
Lengthened by a wire led through a bowsprit-end sheave and taken
to the dolly winch, it can then be sweated up tight and the staysail
reset above the jib. Some barges, including the *Centaur* and *Colonia*,
set a jib flying on a traveller, smack style, and each method, of
course, has its own advantages.

So, under the old coaster rig, all too seldom seen south of Harwich
nowadays, we slipped away from Colne, all hands in high content:
I at the prospect of a better week-end's yachting than any of the
small craft even then emerging from Mersea Quarters would enjoy;
Jerry Mann because he had a chance of seeing his wife and children
at Erith next day, and had a freight of potash for Ipswich all fixed
after that, to be loaded from a steamer at Tilbury without even going
into dock after it. The Bradwell shore lay smoky blue to windward,
and the Blackwater glared orange-red beyond it. Behind the Bar
buoy the poor torn canvas of the sunken *British Oak* streamed and
flapped disconsolately. The water lapped her cross-trees and had
burst the brailed peak of her mainsail. As we bore away close to her
for a look and a snapshot the empty foresail halyard block showed
that the old traditions of the Brightlingsea 'salvagers' were not yet
dead. We both felt chilled and saddened at the sight of another old
craft which would not fight again, and which would never be replaced. To windward of the Knoll we came on the wind again and
stood southward for the Whitaker beacon. Had the wind been
more westerly we should have fetched away through the Rays'n to
bring up in Shore Ends. As it was, in using this unmarked cut
between Knoll and Whitaker we were rediscovering the "new or
west spitway" marked in a chart of 1808, and since reinstated as the
buoyed Spitway, though at the time of our trip the Spitway buoys
were still in the position off Clacton which they had occupied for
the past century.

Jerry Mann, coming up on deck from his tea, sniffed the air,
sensing fog. The Bradwell shore was a faint blur as the light began
to fail. A cast of the lead gave a fathom and a half, and the leeboard

was carefully adjusted to act as watchdog, but we came to the darker-hued, deeper water of the Whitaker Channel without the tell-tale kick of the chain and the tapping of the iron block on the deck which signals that the board is bumping the sand. Down came the jib, and a tier secured it on the bowsprit; the mainsail was gathered easily by the brail winch; the heavy foresail slid down the massive stay to the deck; and as the *George Smeed* rounded into the wind and tide the topsail head rattled down on to the mainmast cap, and the windlass barrel grunted, shuddered, and grumbled as the heavy chain was thrown over it till the fifteen-fathom shackle appeared. And there, hard by the old tide-mark which has served so many generations of coaster-men, the *George Smeed's* anchor bit into the sand, and the tide kicked up a chuckle all about her as the lights of Clacton began to twinkle away to the north behind the flash of the Knoll. The port lights of the traffic dropping down Swin and Barrow Deep gleamed red to the southward, away behind the near-by flash of the Whitaker buoy. Watching the light fade and the night transform the scene, we spared a thought for the poor *J.B.W.*, *Ailsa*, and *Blue Mermaid*, which finished their days within a few miles of this place in wartime years. You could no longer slip over shallows with impunity then and anchor where you chose, with no worse enemy than a possible change of weather to be afraid of.

It would have been a bad anchorage for a yacht under twenty tons, and was not ideal for a barge, but if it really came on to blow Harwich lay to leeward. The topsail sheet was let go, clew-lines secured, and vang falls hardened on the quarter crab-winches in recognition of the exposed nature of the berth, but in the event we lay as quiet as if in dock. On a straight working-trip we should have been out on the low water at 10 P.M., but the skipper gladly produced the excuse that I wanted a daylight sail, and when the rain began to come down as the ebb finished that settled it. The warm light from the brass lamp gleamed on varnished panels and polished latches and handles as we pored over barging papers and photos—this book in embryo, to be exact—and I sought again the secret of the peculiar spell of a barge's cabin which makes it the snuggest place in the whole wide world, whether the ship is moored with a dozen others on the buoys and the smoke grows thick as the company vies with tales of the good old days, or whether, as now, two men share one little oasis of warmth and comfort in the dark waste of sand and water reaching out on every hand.

The ladder from the hatch originally led straight into the *George Smeed*'s roomy cabin, a regular Smeed Dean practice, but when she came to Colchester a half bulkhead and door were built round the foot of it to form a lobby for oilskins and for the general comfort and cleanliness of the ship. All the shallower barges, such as the Maldon stackie type, have cabin-tops, and so have a few of the coasters with long runs in the quarters, such as the *Venta*; but *George Smeed*, a full-sterned barge, is flush-decked, with a big square sky-light in which hangs the compass—visible on deck and also in the cabin, as it has a glass bottom and double-faced card.

In days when she was three-handed the cooking-stove was for'ard, and an open fireplace occupied the traditional position in the cabin against the bulkhead. "Those were the days," said Jerry Mann, "when I had two keen lads aboard." He showed me the tiny cabin he had built in the fo'c'sle to be the cook-boy's own domain. "Up came the grub regular every day. Breakfast at seven, dinner at twelve, tea at six, and a cup of coffee before turning in. I wouldn't have changed places with the King of England." But he was nearly willing to swop with the cook one night when he came down in a hurry to get some gear from the fo'c'sle about two o'clock of a wet, blowy morning as the barge raced for the Spitway, and there was that young gentleman enjoying his right to sleep the sleep of the just in his bunk. In addition to serving the meals, it was the cook's job to fill and polish the lamps in the *George Smeed*. Since the disappearance of the third hand, however, the cooking-stove has come aft, and the fo'c'sle is chiefly a gear-store.

The morning saw a light air sou'westerly right in our teeth, so we made no great haste over putting straight rigging displaced for stowing the previous timber freight. Chains spanning the hold had to be shackled up and pulled tight with a rigging screw (revealing that the timber had spread her open a full inch); leeboard chains, temporarily led outside the rails clear of the deck-cargo, needed to be reshackled along the now unencumbered decks.

It was a blunder to be so leisurely over this, for by the time we got the anchor it was low water, and the first of the flood sets strongly on to the sands. Had we been wise, we should have used the last of the ebb, draining southward off the Ridge, to give us a good start to windward, even if it allowed us to make good no westerly distance. A loaded barge which dropped down from Shore Ends and crossed well above the tide-mark—Billy Austin's

Mirosa, which had left Colne the day before, grit loaded, we suspected—had such advantage from this that we never got near her again all day.

However, who cared? Already the decks were warm in the sun, and, as we stood away on the starboard tack to get clear of the tide on to the Maplins, a pair of loaded craft bound the other way were a feast to the eye, just stemming the flood in the light air. The burgee-shaped bob of one proclaimed her a Mistley-man, the other was a Colchester barge; but Jerry Mann frankly confessed he laid no claim to the old skippers' knack of barge recognition, apparently by instinct, actually by an amazingly intimate experience of every peculiarity of rigging detail, plus a memory trained to carry the likely whereabouts of scores of craft at any given moment.

Over the Middle we went, standing away to windward on a south-easterly course till there was only a cable or two between us and the Barrow—this morning an innocent-looking stretch of yellow sand bordered by a white wisp of mildly breaking water, as if it could never boil up into the raging cauldron of death and destruction which has claimed so many good ships and brave lives. Then round she came as the jib topsail (sheeted through a bull's-eye up the rigging to a cleat on the rail) and the jib (taken to the bitts by a fair-lead through the bowboards) were let fly. The foresail slapped across its wooden horse; I caught a turn on the jib, and the skipper darted forward to seize the vital moment to get the last inch on the jib topsail sheet; then sou'westerly she went for the Sheers, as they still call that Maplin corner where the old Sheers lighthouse once stood, and the Horns before it. Were we going to fetch our course or have a long day turning? Sou'-sou'-west she stood, and as the breeze gained heart with the brilliant morning we promised ourselves a south-easterly. Before long a look ahead told another tale. The *Mirosa* was making a leg off many miles ahead. We settled down to it. It was a good long leg, anyway.

The *George Smeed* is a light-headed barge—"light-headed as a cuckoo" in Billy Austin's phrase—and with three headsails needs watching on the helm. Twice I let her come up so that the foresail sheet kicked on its horse. "You're always interested in what went on fifty years ago," observed Jerry Mann dryly. "Well, if you did that the old man's hard hat would have jumped off his head overboard. You want to try her loaded," he added. "When we get a hundred and fifty tons of potash in her it will be hard up and hard down, rudder right across her stern; and whether she luffs up or bears away is all a matter of chance. The way she goes tearing along puts you in mind of a ruptured duck!" And then, with the apologetic afterthought of the sailor who feels an instinct of shame at mocking a ship which has seen him through a tight corner or two, he added, "But there, she's not a bad old thing. You sort of get fond of them."

The M.B. *Convoy* came by to leeward, prompting him to recall the time he had in her in her last sailing-days. She was towing a sailorman, and we pondered on the 'cauliflower' of bow-wave which appears round the bows of a barge dragged through the water by power, whether her own screw or another's, though she would sail at the same speed without causing it.

The next tack took us close inside the Blacktail, and we could have crossed a corner of the sand without going about again, but we were already out of the best of the tide, and a low-way on to the sand ahead would, in the skipper's graphic phrase, give us a further "lee lope," so we made a final hitch.

Soon the conical buoys were astern, and we were well in the tide again. "Lee-oh," sang out Jerry Mann. "Now I'll promote you again. Keep her on the wind, and I'll put the potatoes on"—the joint had been in the oven all morning. I wish I could record the making and consumption of the traditional Sunday duff, but to our grief and horror the pot was revealed to have a hole in it. Past the broken defence boom and the forts which now unromantically replace the historic Nore light-vessel we went—recalling a destroyer's infuriating signal to the fed-up wartime garrison: "And how are the little Princes in the Tower this morning?"—past the grey, grim grandeur of the Medway mouth to windward and the long inane straggle of Southend to leeward; past the Yantlet beacon, marking yet another little corner once frequented by barges where probably a barge will never go again; past a pleasure launch which circled us, her passengers' cameras clicking busily; past week-end yachts and a fleet of one-designs running into Leigh Ray.

The south-west breeze was fresh by now, and the jib tops'l was beginning to make the topmast look whippy. Jerry Mann cast off halyard and sheet, and nipped out to the bowsprit-end to stow it. The sheet fouled, and I darted forward to clear it, locking the wheel clumsily so she shook again—earning me a further rebuke. Now the *George Smeed* was marching. "There's a ruddy steamer trying to go through our lee," Jerry called through the skylight in pained indignation as I was finishing my dinner. And then, in the burlesque Essex accent to which I am generally treated when sailing with a Kentish man: "Don't you moind about them owd steamers, booy. They own't larst. Tellyerfwy. They're agin nature, thasswhy."

Then, just when we wanted all the help we could to make Tilbury on the tide, the wind eased. "Shan't do it now," ruled Jerry Mann ruefully. "We ought to have started an hour earlier. Just to think, if this ruddy river was any other shape I'd see my wife and kids to-night." Indeed, it was clear by the time we turned to windward into Gravesend Reach the ebb would be starting down. So, as the evening sun did its best to glorify the ugliness of Thames Haven by painting the oil-tanks glittering silver, we sailed slowly the last mile of Sea Reach, stowing away the jib and topping up the bowsprit for the river, till, under the lee of the point, the anchor rumbled down once more. In the last of the daylight the boat was dropped into the water astern, sidelight boards were rigged, anchor and stern lights set up fore and aft, and, over a cup of coffee and a final pipe, the decision was reached that a 5 A.M. start would suffice, to allow some daylight for coming alongside our tier. A last look round on deck revealed that night had done the job the sunset could hardly achieve. The flat commercialism of the banks of Sea Reach was transformed into long necklaces of sparkling lights gleaming like diamonds against the black velvet of the river, a setting in which the coloured flashes of the channel buoys stabbed the night. Wink, wink, wink went a green wreck-mark ahead; a Scandinavian steamer, masts right in the ends of her, slid by to leeward; a 'flat-iron' bound up showed both lights before closing out the green as she thrashed over the tide. Our own sails, spars, rigging, hatches, and decks gleamed in the beams of our anchor light; the taut kicking-chain, keeping the rudder quiet, glistened in the beams from the stanchion on the stern.

So it was when the alarm whirred us out to it again six hours later. Grinding up the anchor is no sane man's idea of pleasure, least of all at four o'clock in the morning. Three times the chain was 'fleeted,' and then at last the stock broke surface, chain foul round it, giving us a job with which to pass the time while the *George Smeed* slowly answered her lee helm, coming into the wind's eye and backing the fores'l on its bowline just as the heavy links were straightened out again over the windlass. Clumsily she crept up on the sluggish neap-tide in the feeble dawn breeze. A dredger took shape on the weather-bow and was soon a triangle of lights again on the quarter. A wrecked steamer's upper-works sticking out of the water looked grim for a moment to leeward. An unlit powder hulk under the south shore gave us the pleasure of swearing at it. Dawn revealed the shape of old Gravesend, and the lights were restored to their place on the fo'c'sle shelf again. The clock ashore showed nearly seven, and the skipper gave her the staysail—yesterday's jib tops'l, but now set from the stemhead. Under the Gravesend shore we were becalmed, but a Swedish steamer, berthing on Tilbury pier, spoiled a fetch along the lee side. "There ought to be a tug-boat kept here for every sailing-barge," grumbled Jerry Mann. Soon, however, our tier was visible, and we were glad to see two sailormen on the buoys. "What's the drill?" I asked apprehensively, always nervous of letting the ship down in close quarters under the critical scrutiny of professional eyes; "anchor to windward and drop in?"—for the tier lay right to leeward, wind-rode. "No, no, Mate, that's old boomie-barge tactics," was the horrified reply. "We'll edge her right in alongside somehow."

Up went the mainsail, and, as far to leeward as we could, we crept up to the tier. "Down foresail," came the order as the helm went down. "Down tops'l." Stupidly I jumped for the sheet. "Halyard-halyard-halyard," came the frantic correction from the wheel, and, just escaping the disgrace of trying to stow her topsail without lowering it, the *George Smeed* rounded to. "Drop your anchor down," came a reminder from the skipper of the moored craft. I had forgotten the universal precaution of getting the anchor out of harm's way when coming in alongside or in dock. It took only a moment, and, with a squeeze and grunt from a fender on the lee bow, the *George Smeed* rubbed noses with the old Sandwich hoy barge *Trilby*. Beyond her lay Cremer's *Edith*, whose skipper, Charlie Ward, came aboard to enliven our breakfast with tales of days long ago in Faversham Creek. He was puzzled at having a cold, which was something he wasn't used to. And he was only seventy-four, he protested.

The voyage was done, and with its accomplishment came that sense of satisfaction and relaxation which crowns every voyage under sail, no matter how commonplace. A motor-barge would have been there in half the time—but with less than half the delight, as every skipper of an auxiliary sadly confesses.

The bus back to Colchester seemed particularly bumpy, crowded, noisy and smelly; the streets of Grays meaner than ever; and as I caught my last glimpse of the river I wished I were back aboard that little cluster of barges waiting for their ship to come and fill them with the potash they were to distribute all about Kent and Suffolk, parting to go their various ways, to meet again perhaps next month, perhaps not for a couple of years.

Going their various ways. . . . A fair wind for one, a head wind for another. Patches of luck, patches of disappointment. Cargoes slipped through in record time, cargoes windbound, cargoes wet. The slam of the foresail across the horse as the bowline is let go; the lift and fall of the topmast staysail as it alone responds to the light air. The mainsheet and vang fall running through the blocks as the buoy is weathered after the long plug to windward. The stiff, sudden, silent drop of the mainsail as the brail is let go, and the last heave on the mainsheet to get the final wrinkle out of it. The clatter of topmast hoops and headstick on the masthead as the voyage ends. The cold gleam of the anchor light on the dewy foredeck; the warm glow of the cabin lamp on the varnished panel. The great sprit straining; the leeboard leaning on the tide. . . .

GLOSSARY

Batten studs. The iron clips on the sides of the hatch coamings in which are wedged the battens securing the hatch cloths.

Bob. Flag mounted on the topmast truck, bearing owner's colour scheme or other device. Sometimes termed bob-fly, or in Kent vane-fly.

Boomie. Ketch-rigged barge. (The variation 'booms'l rig' was also applied to the early cutter-rigged barges.)

Brails. Ropes or wires with which main and mizzen sails are stowed. Hence to brail up, to stow up sails in brails.

Chamfers. Carved decorative flutings.

Chine. Angle between side and bottom.

Cockbill. Of spars to stow by swinging askew. Also, to carry the anchor across the stem. **Tripcock** Point is said to take its name from the fact that ships cleared anchors acockbill ready to let go above this point.

Cotchel. A part freight.

Crab. Winch used for raising leeboards, etc.

Dandy. Rig with very small mizzen abaft the steerage.

Dart. To run dart is to sail dead before the wind.

Dolly winch. Small winch over anchor windlass used for handling a long, light line in warping, and for the mainbrails in a stackie when the brail winch is covered by the stack.

Fearnaughts. Garments made of thick woollen cloth.

Flushing board. Board inserted vertically in cabin entrance under slide.

Fore and afters. Removable wooden beams running along the centre of the hold openings beneath the hatches, which they support.

Gear. The barge's sails and rigging.

Gripie. Cockney name for a barge.

Gutway. The deep rill or channel of a creek.

Gybe. Bring the sails from one side to the other as course is altered to bring the wind from one quarter to the other. In strong winds a difficult and dangerous manœuvre with too much sail set.

Horse. A sand lying in mid-channel. Also a wooden or iron beam across the deck carrying the fore or main sheet.

Hoy barge. Craft making regular passages with mixed cargoes. Sometimes called goods barge or passage barge.

Huffler. A combination of pilot and extra hand shipped to assist in difficult corners.

KEELSON. Stout longitudinal member, sometimes wood and sometimes steel, running from stem to stern inside the barge's bottom. The barge's 'backbone.'

KICKING CHAIN, or KICKING STRAP. Chain rigged from rudder to quarter. When it is pulled tight lying at anchor the rudder is prevented from kicking on its gudgeons.

LOWERS. The lower brails of the mainsail.

MAINS. The main brails of the mainsail.

MAST CASE. Iron deck-fitting in which the heel of the mast is mounted (the yachtsman's tabernacle).

MIDDLES. The brails below the mains and above the lowers.

MULIE. Barge with sprittie's mainsail and standing gaff mizzen.

NEAP TIDES. The weak tides occurring around nine o'clock at London Bridge, when sun and moon are in opposition.

PASSAGE BARGE. See HOY.

PEAKS. The uppermost brails above the mains. Upper and lower peaks are standard, and a third set is sometimes rigged on sails with long head-ropes.

'RIB-TICKLER.' Barge's tiller.

SAILORMAN. London River term for either a sailing-barge or a sailing-bargeman.

SEALING. The caulked floor of the hold.

SEEKERS. Craft which rely on fixing freight for merchants instead of carrying the owner's own goods.

SLIDE. The sliding cabin hatch.

SNUG LOADED. Having all cargo below hatches without deck cargo.

SPINNAKER. A headsail spread out on the opposite side of the mast to the mainsail when running before the wind. The bargeman's spinnaker is his topmast staysail tacked at the mast case, and sheeted round the weather cross-tree.

SPRINGS (tide). The big tides occurring around three o' clock at London Bridge, when sun and moon are in unison.

SPRITTIE. A spritsail rigged barge.

STACKIE. Barge loaded with stack of hay or straw. Hence sometimes barge designed for such purpose.

STANLIFF (literally, 'standing lift'). Wire rigged from main mast head to heel of sprit, taking downward thrust of the latter.

STAYFALL. Wire rove through stem blocks connecting fore stays and stem head, forming purchase used for lowering down gear.

STUMPIE. Barge without top mast. A tops'l barge under way without tops'l set is spoken of as stumpy-rigged.

SWIMMIE. Barge with square overhung bow like that of London lighter (known as swimhead).

SWATCH. A creek or low way through a sand or mudbank having access to deep water at each end.

UPPERS. The brails above the mains. (*See also* PEAKS.)

VANG. Wire rigged from the sprit end to the deck, controlling the sprit. The vang fall is the tackle rigged on the lower end of the vang. Rolling vangs are preventers led forward to complete the control of the sprit. (Pronounced 'wang.')

POSTSCRIPT

It is a sad reflection of our time that books tarry longer and longer in the press while sailing-barges hasten faster and faster into oblivion. During the production of this book Goldsmith's, of Grays, have parted with their last sailorman. Francis and Gilders have sold *Colonia* to Whitstable (where happily she will continue working for Daniels Brothers); *Saltcote Belle* has gone for a yacht; and *Ethel Ada* is for sale. At Ipswich less than a dozen craft remain under sail, including *Felix*, *May*, *Kimberley*, *Venture*, *Beric*, *Anglia*, and *Marjorie*. The mulie *Wolsey* has lain in forlorn and tragic majesty all summer beside the sea wall at Burnham, and is now being converted to a yacht; *Will Everard* is having an auxiliary installed, though she will retain her sails; and *Greenhithe* (at present laid up for extensive repairs) and *Cambria* thus become the last survivors of the East Coast sailing colliers.

The Medway barge race has, however, been revived, albeit chiefly for yacht barges, the competitors this year including *Henry* (winner), *Petrel*, and *Venta*, among craft mentioned in these pages. *Sirdar* was winner in the class for working barges.

It is no use any longer blinking the hard fact that the end is in sight, and as owners have generally given up hope of replacing existing crews the surviving sailing-craft are fated to drop out one by one. One motor-barge can do the work of two sailormen, and under the circumstances one can hardly blame a young man for seeking a change, especially as economic circumstances which previously bound him to a not always over-sympathetic owner have now been so drastically reversed. Happily, however, a small band of skippers remain faithful, immune from the temptations of easier or more lucrative occupations, determined to keep under sail as long as there is a living left in it. Good luck to them.

H. B.

August 1950

INDEX OF VESSELS NAMED

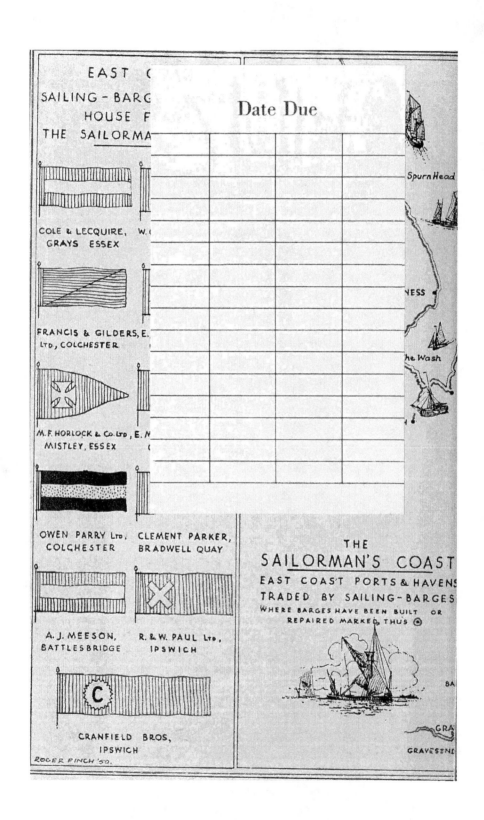

EAST C...
SAILING - BARG...
HOUSE F...
THE SAILORMA...

Date Due

COLE & LECQUIRE, W. ...
GRAYS ESSEX

FRANCIS & GILDERS, E. ...
LTD, COLCHESTER

M. F. HORLOCK & Co. LTD, E. ...
MISTLEY, ESSEX

OWEN PARRY LTD,   CLEMENT PARKER,
COLCHESTER   BRADWELL QUAY

A. J. MEESON,   R. & W. PAUL LTD,
BATTLESBRIDGE   IPSWICH

CRANFIELD BROS,
IPSWICH

ROGER FINCH '50.

Spurn Head

...NESS

...he Wash

THE
SAILORMAN'S COAST
EAST COAST PORTS & HAVENS
TRADED BY SAILING-BARGES
WHERE BARGES HAVE BEEN BUILT OR
REPAIRED MARKED, THUS ⊚

BA...

GRA...
GRAVESEN...

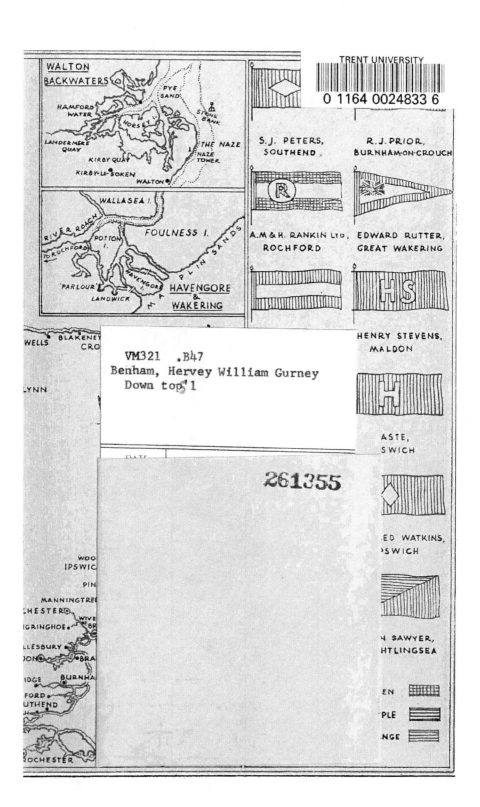

WALTON
BACKWATERS

PYE
SAND

HAMFORD
WATER

STONE
BANK

HORSEY I.

LANDERMERE
QUAY

THE NAZE
NAZE
TOWER

KIRBY QUAY

KIRBY-LE-SOKEN

WALTON

WALLASEA I.

RIVER ROACH

POTTON
I.

TO ROCHFORD

FOULNESS I.

P L IN SANDS

HAVENGORE

'PARLOUR'

LANDWICK

HAVENGORE
&
WAKERING

S.J. PETERS,
SOUTHEND

R.J. PRIOR,
BURNHAM-ON-CROUCH

A.M & H. RANKIN Ltd,
ROCHFORD

EDWARD RUTTER,
GREAT WAKERING

HENRY STEVENS,
MALDON

WELLS   BLAKENEY
CRO

LYNN

ASTE,
SWICH

ED WATKINS,
PSWICH

WOO
IPSWIC

PIN

MANNINGTREE

CHESTER

IGRINGHOE

WIVE
BR

LLESBURY

ON   BRA

IDGE   BURNHA

FORD

UTHEND

N SAWYER,
HTLINGSEA

EN

PLE

NGE

OCHESTER